The Theory of
The Growth of the Firm

EDITH T. PENROSE

with a new Foreword by
MARTIN SLATER

M. E. SHARPE, INC.
WHITE PLAINS, NEW YORK

First published in the United States by M. E. Sharpe, Inc.,
901 North Broadway, White Plains, New York 10603 in 1980.
No part of this book may be reproduced in any form without
written permission from the publisher.

Library of Congress Catalog Card Number: 79-91109
International Standard Book Number: 0-87332-166-9

Printed in Great Britain

TABLE OF CONTENTS

FOREWORD

BY MARTIN SLATER

This book—which, if the evidence of last year's students' essays is any guide, is likely to prove one of the most influential of the decade—does not purport to provide an integrated analytical model of the growth of the firm. Rather it describes the why and the way, the controlling boundaries of a historical process. It is far more than an institutional description; new concepts are introduced and defined, and to some extent interactions analysed: we could say that the author is concerned with the theoretical internal biology of growth, but not, at this stage, with the logical interdependence of the whole picture which emerges. The book is indeed so packed with ideas that it would be impossible for all of them to be consistent.

The above paragraph, taken from Robin Marris's review [35][2] of *The Theory of the Growth of the Firm* when it was first published in 1959, was a shrewd piece of perception. The influence of the book has been profound, not least upon the significant work of Marris himself. Even two decades after its publication it has not lost vitality. Scarcely any economist now writing on the growth of firms can afford to ignore Edith Penrose's contribution. If you look in the index of any subsequent book on the theory of the firm or industrial organisation, you cannot fail to come across her name.

Marris refers above also to the evidence of students' essays—in my experience his point still holds true today. That other stern measure of students' revealed preference, the number of date-stamps in the front of university library books, bears this out. ' The Theory of the Growth of the Firm ' has attained that rare distinction of being a classic that is actually read.

Yet perhaps it is not read carefully enough these days. All classics face the danger of being reduced to a standard, rather super-

---

[1] Many people have helped me with their comments on an earlier draft and I hope they will forgive me for thanking them collectively here. Of course I owe a special debt of gratitude to Edith Penrose for her help and encouragement.

[2] Numbers in square brackets refer to the bibliography.

ficial interpretation which picks out the major points and ignores much of the subtle detail. Something of this sort has been happening to Mrs. Penrose's work, in that although the broad outlines of her theory have become an integral part of economists' thinking about firms, much of the detail seems to have gone unheeded.

What is the secret of the book's success, and the reason for its importance? I would say that it combines a rigorous economic theoretical outlook with immediate intelligibility and an obvious foundation in reality. It is a very clear description of what business-men actually do, but it goes far beyond that. We have innumerable studies from organisation theorists and management scientists on what businessmen actually do: the economic theorist has no end of people telling him that economic theory has a totally unrealistic view of the business firm. The trouble with many of these studies, though, is that one is often left at the end without any very clear idea of what difference this particular alternative view of the world makes for the allocation of resources. Take for instance, the contribution of Cyert & March [11] on the 'behavioural' theory of the firm. No-one reading their book could fail to be impressed by its obvious real-world flavour: no-one even could level the charge that theirs is a purely institutional study, because they clearly do have a *theory* of how firms work. But the problem for many economists is simply that their theory does not have very obvious and clear implications to modify the traditional economic theory of how firms' behaviour affects the allocation of resources.[1]

Therefore the great achievement of Edith Penrose is that she draws out the theoretical implications for economists of a more realistic view of the business world. The book is primarily theo-retical, not institutional, and it is an example of theory at its best— picking out the important principles from a complicated real-world picture.

I think it also fair to mention at the outset what might be con-sidered the main weakness of the book, particularly from the point of view of today's students of economics. Again Marris puts his finger on it—the book ' does not purport to provide an integrated analytical model '. What Mrs. Penrose provides is a framework, a pattern of thought, within which such a model could be constructed, but she does not attempt the construction herself—it is clearly not

---

[1] Much the same could be said of many other works which stress the importance of the modern corporate environment, e.g. Galbraith [18].

her style. However, present-day students are schooled to think in terms of models, and they feel left somewhat in the air, missing the slick presentation of results and proof of theorems to which they are accustomed.[1] The import of Mrs. Penrose's work is therefore not quite as clear as it might be made, given modern techniques. But there are also advantages in not attempting a complete model. Modelling necessarily involves simplification, and undoubtedly the breadth of the work would have suffered. A model *is* needed, but we cannot really complain that Mrs. Penrose left it to others.

EDITH PENROSE'S CONTRIBUTION TO ECONOMIC THEORY

The contributions of the book to economic theory can be divided into the two categories mentioned in the first section. Firstly there is the broad overall outline of the Penrose schema which has been well accepted; secondly there is the detailed treatment of the various aspects of the growth process, which deserves more careful attention than it currently receives.

Looking first at the broad outline, the most important initial point is to get clear exactly what we mean by a ' firm '. Chapter 2 is entirely devoted to this question. The ' firm ' in the traditional neo-classical theory of the firm is simply a theoretical construct—the ' firm ' is effectively defined as a cost curve and a demand curve, and the theory is simply the logic of optimal pricing and input combination. But Mrs. Penrose is not concerned with such a disembodied ' firm '; her concern is with flesh-and-blood firms, organisations of people which have administrative control over productive assets, and whose fields of operations are not limited to particular markets.[2] The growth of this sort of organisation is a qualitatively different phenomenon from the simple increase of output of a neo-classical ' firm '.

The general rules governing the growth of such organisations may be thought of as having three components:
(1) Constant Returns to Scale in the Long Run,
(2) The Possibility of Diversification,
(3) Increasing Costs of Growth.
Mrs. Penrose was not herself the originator of the first two of

[1] I cannot offhand think of another book which economics students might read these days, which contains in 265 pages not a single diagram, equation or table. Even Keynes had one diagram (and many equations).
[2] The question of why firms should exist at all is one that periodically excites interest among economists, cf. Coase [10], Alchian & Demsetz [1].

these concepts,[1] but her achievement was to bring them all together
to form a sustained criticism of the static theory of the firm while at
the same time constructing an elegant and serviceable framework for
an alternative dynamic analysis of a firm which can grow continuously at a finite rate.

The importance of the first component was to overthrow the
notion that the firm's long-run average cost curve was U-shaped, a
notion that implied an ' optimum size ' of the firm at the level of
output corresponding to the lowest point of the U. This had long
been a rather uncomfortable proposition for economists. Sraffa [59]
had pointed out that for a firm to have a determinate equilibrium in
perfect competition, its long-run average cost curve must rise, at
least after some level of output; however, such empirical evidence
as there was did not confirm the existence of such diseconomies of
scale. On theoretical grounds it did not seem likely that there could
be *technological* diseconomies of scale at the plant level because of the
possibility of expansion by multi-plant operation. Therefore it was
felt that the solution must lie in ' managerial ' diseconomies of scale,
the greater difficulty of administering a large organisation. There
was certainly evidence that managerial problems did exist, and in
some large firms these were very serious indeed. Unfortunately
however, other large firms, including the very largest, were looked
upon as models of efficiency, were highly profitable and showed no
signs of ceasing their growth.

Several alternative theories had been developed in an attempt to
overcome Sraffa's problem, including the imperfect competition
theories of Chamberlin and Joan Robinson. In their work, the down-
ward-sloping demand curve did the job of restricting the size of the
firm that had been done in perfect competition by the upward-
sloping LRAC. The second component of the Penrose innovation
was therefore to release the size of the firm from this constraint as
well: by diversifying into other products, the firm need not be
limited by the extent of its original market, and it may expand faster
than this original market can grow, without having to accept lower
marginal revenues.

These two assumptions together then produce constant returns
to the firm both on the supply side and on the demand side. In the

---

[1] I think it would be fair to say that Mrs. Penrose was the first to make any significant
use of the concept of increasing costs of growth, although doubtless some earlier
writers may have given it a passing mention e.g. Robinson [52], p. 104.

long run therefore there is no single optimum size that the firm will
tend to, since any size is as profitable as any other. What then does
determine the actual size of the firm at any point in time? Is this also
indeterminate?

The answer to this question is given by our third component,
increasing costs of growth. This is perhaps the innovation most
characteristic of Mrs. Penrose, so much so that it has come to be
known by her name as the Penrose Effect.[1] Although there are
constant returns in the long run, this constancy will be achieved only
when perfect adaptation of all inputs to a particular scale has been
made. This will not be possible in the short run if certain inputs are
difficult to vary, and the faster the firm attempts to grow, the less
well adapted will the input structure tend to be. Thus a firm is
prevented from growing as fast as it may like because there is a very
distinct cost of rapid growth.

Particular emphasis is placed on the difficulty of increasing the
input of managerial services. Mrs. Penrose insists that management
in large corporations must operate as a team and not as individuals.
The decisions that any individual manager makes will normally be
influenced by past decisions of other managers, by decisions being
taken elsewhere in the organisation at the same time, and by assumptions about decisions that will have to be taken in the future. Since
many different but related projects are usually under way simultaneously, there is a problem of maintaining consistency throughout
the organisation. The complexity of business decisions therefore
means that the management must function harmoniously as a team if
it is to operate efficiently at all. Now a team can only learn to work
together by actual experience, and this can take considerable time.
Thus one cannot immediately increase the effective management team
simply by hiring more managers from outside the firm—the newcomers may be very well qualified in their particular specialisations,
and with a great deal of experience in other firms, but they will still
need to gain the experience of working in this particular team before
they can contribute effectively to decision-making in this firm. This
settling-in process takes time, and it also absorbs some of the energy
of the existing management, so it entails a cost to the firm. The
greater the rate at which newcomers are bought in, the greater are
the problems. Thus for Mrs. Penrose, managerial diseconomies are

[1] As far as I can discover, this attribution was first made by Marris [36], p. 202, and
[37], p. 114.

not a static phenomenon, related to scale, but a dynamic, transient problem which is more related to the rate of growth and would disappear eventually if the firm ceased growing.

Although management is reckoned to be the principal limitation on the firm's growth there are others. The diversification process is not costless: movement into a new market entails a considerable expense in research and initial marketing efforts. Also if the firm has to break new ground in production or selling, its costs may well initially be higher than its competitors' until it gains experience of the new field. Large requirements for finance may only be met at more than usually disadvantageous terms to cover the lenders' perceived increasing risk. These and other factors may help to limit the firm's growth, but Mrs. Penrose clearly believes that the managerial problem will predominate. She also suggests that some of these apparently separate constraining factors could equally be seen as failures of management.

So in the end one has a picture of a firm which may be of any size in the long run. It will probably be capable of continuous growth, but its rate of growth will be restricted by the factors just mentioned. From the point of view of economic theory we may bemoan the fact that the size of the firm is no longer fully determinate, but we are not left entirely adrift here: given the initial size of a firm, we have the basis for predicting its size at any future time. The convenient economic analysis of the optimum size of the firm must unfortunately be abandoned, in favour of the analysis of the firm's optimum rate of growth, but we can still talk of the optimum size of a plant or perhaps of a particular product line within the firm. So the traditional static analysis has not been destroyed, but rather displaced from its central position to play a supporting role as part of a more general theory.

So much for the overall outline of the book. However, as Marris says, there is more here than the bare bones of growth theory; it is indeed ' packed with ideas ' about the details of the growth process, and these ideas have yet to be fully utilised. Chapters 4–8 are to my mind the most interesting in the book, and they repay very careful reading.

There are important details concerning the exact nature of the increasing costs of growth and the managerial limit. Great emphasis is placed on the ' unbalanced ' nature of the firms' growth, with unused resources appearing from time to time, creating an incentive for the firm to find some way of using them. New resources and capabilities are being continually thrown up by the firm's experience in its current operations, as are new opportunities for expansion. This may be linked to the important concept of 'economies of growth', which are set against the better-known economies of scale. Here Mrs. Penrose indicates that one firm may be better placed (because of its particular unused resources) to build up a certain new activity than another firm, although on static considerations there might be no reason why this activity should be carried on by either, or indeed any existing firms.

The chapters on diversification and merger consistently stress that these business policies must be seen and analysed as constituent parts of the growth process. Unfortunately this message has not always been taken to heart in subsequent work. Also, consistent reference is made to the importance of opportunity costs in such policies. Because of the managerial constraints, the firm is not always able to pursue all of its opportunities that appear profitable. It must then concentrate on the most profitable opportunities and might be willing to give up apparently profitable operations if it needs to release resources in order to seize better opportunities. Thus some business policies make sense in a context of constrained growth which cannot be rationalised in terms of equilibrium analysis.

However, it would be otiose to enlarge further on these details within the covers of the book itself. Suffice it to say that I think they indicate that the growth of firms is a subject we should take very seriously indeed, for it has important ramifications for resource allocation. It was perhaps inevitable that the early formalisations of growth models should fail to capture this wealth of detail, but it is still waiting to be fully exploited.

A SHORT REVIEW OF SUBSEQUENT WORK ON THE GROWTH OF FIRMS[1]

(a) Economic Theory

The immediate most important implication of Mrs. Penrose's book therefore was that it laid the way open for other economists to

---

[1] This brief survey is in no way meant to be a comprehensive account of all subsequent work in the theory of the firm and industrial economics. I have confined attention to major contributions particularly concerned with the growth of firms and other related subjects covered by Mrs. Penrose in her book.

construct models of the firm in which continuous growth was possible, a growth which need not come to an end when an 'optimum' size was reached. As we have seen, it was perhaps an important failure of Mrs. Penrose not to construct such a model herself.

Baumol [5] [6] was the first to construct a mathematical model of a firm growing continuously at a steady rate, and use this model to analyse the implications of such a process. He was only able to analyse the case of steady-state growth, which is obviously a simpler task than a growth process where the rate of growth changes over time—other subsequent writers have also by and large confined their attention to steady-state growth. His model showed that the costs associated with growth had to increase at an increasing rate to ensure a finite rate of growth for a profit-maximising firm. He also assumed on the demand side that the firm could expand its output at a constant price, but did not use the possibility of diversification to explain this—his justification was that either the firm must be very small relative to its potential market, or that the market is itself expanding fast enough to accommodate the firm's growth.

Undoubtedly the most significant follower was Marris. In his book [37] Marris tackled the whole problem of the aims of firms in the modern age of separation of ownership from control. This was an area that Mrs. Penrose had not been very precise about. She refers to it on pp. 25–30, and it is clear that her basic view is that firms are attempting some form of long-run profit-maximisation. But 'long-run profit' can be a terribly vague concept if not carefully defined, and on p. 30 she suggests that profits and growth might be effectively identical as objectives of the firm. This rather vague equation is certainly not precisely true, and indeed much of the subsequent literature has been devoted to investigating this problem more closely. Again, one might ascribe this vagueness over motivation to the lack of a mathematical analytical model in the book. The construction of a maximising model obviously requires explicit thought about what is to be maximised, and it is for this reason that later writers have placed much more emphasis on this question.

Marris's view was that the salaried managers of a firm would be more likely to want high rates of growth than high profits, since they themselves did not receive the profits. Since the firm would almost certainly not be able to expand in its original market indefinitely without encountering increasing opposition from its competitors or attention from government anti-monopoly policy, it would need to diversify into new markets. Marris gave much attention to this diversification process, using modern marketing theory to analyse what sort of new products a firm would want to introduce, and the rate at which to introduce them. However, introduction of these new products was a costly business, and these costs obviously increased as the rate of diversification went up.

Marris's other major contribution was to formulate the mechanism by which the managers were constrained from pushing the growth rate to its limits. Although the managers themselves derive no direct satisfaction from the profits earned by the firm, unless sufficient profits are earned by the managers to satisfy the shareholders, the shareholders will be willing to sell their shares relatively cheaply to any potential take-over bidder. Since some-one who takes over the firm is unlikely to leave the present management undisturbed, this is something that the managers must guard against. Since the shareholders are typically too numerous and too diffuse to impose their will on their managers directly, in Marris's view the threat of takeover appeared as the main constraint on managerial freedom. To analyse the implications of this take-over constraint, he was led to develop a theory of how the stock market would value firms' shares, and how this valuation would vary with firms' performance as to profits and growth.

Marris also paid great attention to the financial aspects of growth. In order to aquire new assets, a firm must either retain some of its current profits, issue new shares, or borrow from outside the firm, usually at fixed interest. Thus a firm's growth policy comprises not only an investment policy, but also a policy for the financing of that investment. Different methods of financing may have slightly different implications for the dividend stream through time, and for the current market valuation of the firm. Risk and uncertainty also play an important part here because the firm may take on certain future commitments in the form of interest payments, which must be covered by uncertain future profits. The structure of personal and corporate taxation may also have a significant influence on firm's policies, because profits may be taken either as dividends or as capital gains on share values, and these may be taxed at different rates.

Thus a whole new area of theory, which might be loosely described as ' optimal financial policy ' has been opened up. It was of course not new to accountants and other specialists in business finance, but Marris's work undoubtedly gave it a boost and added importance in the eyes of economists. Important contributions have been made by Modigliani & Miller [41], Gordon [20], Lintner [32] [33], and by King [30].

In some ways there is a danger that the obvious success of the financial aspects of Marris's work might be crowding out in the popular imagination that other part of his work to do with the problems of diversification. Although it may be convenient to abstract from these latter problems in steady-state growth models specially designed to investigate the financial side, we should remember that finance is only one part of the growth problem—the possibility of diversification is not in practice a panacea which removes all necessity of considering individual markets. Unfortunately Marris's work in this area has not been built on so extensively by others as his financial work has been.

Other writers followed Baumol and Marris in analysing the implications of different aims of the firm on steady-state growth behaviour. An important contribution was made by John Williamson [64], who investigated pricing behaviour as well as investment and finance. He concluded that growth-maximisers and profit-maximisers would both in fact set prices on profit-maximising principles,[1] since high profits are a requisite for high growth. Where they would differ is only in their policies on investment and retention of profits, the growth-maximiser investing and retaining more than its shareholders would ideally like. Other important contributions in this area have been made by Solow [58] and by Heal and Silberston [28].[2]

Outside the realm of mathematical steady-state growth models, there are some other writers who have analysed the receding managerial limit in some detail. Chandler's book [8], written almost at the same time as Edith Penrose's, is a fascinating account of the development of the decentralised form of management which is now commonplace in large corporations. As the growth of the earliest large corporations in the USA led them to diversify their activities, their centralised management structures which had previously served them very well became increasingly unable to cope. The system of

[1] I have recently come to believe that this conclusion of Williamson needs slight modification since it depends on implicit assumptions about the cost of growth. The full details are in Slater [57].
[2] The Penrose Effect has also appeared in the literature on optimal growth of whole economies. cf. Uzawa [63].

decentralisation of control was evolved in its place and proved its superiority. Oliver Williamson's work [65] [66] [67] on U-Form and M-Form corporations is also very much concerned with the firm as an administrative organisation. Starbuck [60], in a survey of writings on organisational growth, produces an interesting formalisation of the process of management learning by experience. (Also possibly relevant here would be Arrow's work on ' Learning by Doing ' [2], although it was not actually directed at Penrose.)

Lesourne [31] has applied the mathematical technique of optimal control theory to the growth of firms, and although much of his work is directed at the financial aspects of growth, he does at one stage produce a formalisation of the way in which the need to recruit and assimilate new management places a limit to the firm's rate of growth. One advantage of optimal control theory, despite its level of mathematical difficulty, is that it is capable of analysing non-steady-state growth, and since Solow's paper suggests steady-state growth analysis has distinct limitations, this capability is likely to prove important. Other techniques of dynamic optimisation such as dynamic programming and the classical calculus of variations may also have a part to play here.

Finally, I have myself recently argued [57] that many of the steady-state growth models, although they apparently incorporate the Penrose Effect in the form of increasing costs of growth, are not able to specify it correctly in detail, because most economic models do not recognise explicitly the existence of managerial inputs to the production process. This is unfortunate because Mrs. Penrose's description of the increasing costs of growth is clearly in terms of the receding managerial limit—the costs arise because of partial failure of the managerial input. My own belief is that the whole process cannot be adequately modelled without explicit recognition of the managerial input, and that therefore a fruitful path for future progress seems to me to be the analysis of such explicit managerial growth models using techniques like optimal control. By carefully introducing extra complexities into the model, many of the important problems of industrial economics may be analysed in a truly dynamic context. This analysis need not be confined as before to steady-state growth paths. Most important, the traditional theory of price, output and resource allocation can be united with growth theory, whereas they now tend to lead a separate existence. Of the models mentioned above, only John Williamson's produces any real implications about pricing and output,[1] and my own paper argues that even these are only strictly true in a special case. Consequently, despite all the work put in over the last twenty years, the full realisation of Edith Penrose's work still awaits the construction of a more general model.

(b) Applied Studies of Growth

Alongside the theoretical development, there have been many empirical studies related to the growth of firms. They fall largely into two groups. The first is the case study, or business history, of an individual firm's growth experience. It is a notable feature of Mrs. Penrose's book itself that she draws heavily on such material to illustrate the theoretical points. There are clearly many such studies and I will not attempt a long list of them here. Of particular interest, though, is Mrs. Penrose's own study [45] of the Hercules Powder Company, which was apparently originally intended as a chapter of ' The Theory of the Growth of the Firm ', but was finally excluded on the grounds of space. It really is an admirable illustration of the Penrose view of the firm.

Another of the author's subsequent works which deserves more attention is her book on the international oil industry [46]. This also draws on, illustrates and further extends the concepts introduced in the earlier book. It too is a path-breaking book, for, in introducing the extra dimension of international operations, it was one of the earliest studies of the economic implications of transnational corporations, a subject which has now spawned an immense literature. It exhibits many of the same virtues as the earlier book, avoiding sensationalism and extravagant claims, but analysing with great care the economic problems arising from the institutional constraints of the real world. Two particular features are its demonstration of the extraordinarily complex blend of competition and cooperation which characterises the relationships between oligopolistic firms, and its analysis of the pressures for, problems of, and alternatives to, vertical integration. These are important topics that have not received that much attention from economists—however there is a very interesting later article by Richardson [50].

However, unfortunately for the present purpose, the book marks something of a watershed in Mrs. Penrose's career. Afterwards her

---

[1] A very interesting recent attempt to link pricing to firm's growth policies, though not in the context of a complete growth model, has been made by Eichner [17.]

interests have focussed more on the problems of the developing countries themselves, and she has written little subsequently on the growth of firms. Her articles on the subject have been collected in a volume of essays published in 1971 [47].

Turning to other writers, two early studies which analysed the growth performance of a sample of individual firms were performed by Barna [4] and Mackintosh [34]. Richardson's report and analysis [49] of an Oxford Economists' Research Group survey provides considerable verification of Mrs. Penrose's views. Hannah's account [22] of the development of the large corporation in the United Kingdom is also of considerable interest, as is Chandler's recent study [9] in a similar vein, of a slightly earlier period in the United States. Finally, one can easily find familiar themes running through many of the case studies collected by Edwards and Townsend [14] [15] [16].

The second type of study is the statistical analysis of firms' growth rates and their determinants, both cross-sectional and time-series. Again, the number of studies is enormous—there is a whole industry devoted to the attempt to find correlations between the size, profits, growth and many other characteristics of firms. A particular example of this type of study is the work by Singh and Whittington [55], using data from the public accounts of United Kingdom companies. A good survey of many of these studies is provided in the Appendix by Eatwell [13] in the Marris and Wood volume.

The conclusions of individual studies do vary somewhat, but some ' stylised facts ' seem to emerge:

(a) The *average* profitability of firms does not seem to vary significantly with their size (although the *variability* of profits declines with firm size). This would seem to be consistent with constant returns to scale in the long run over a wide range of output. However, it could also be interpreted as evidence of a very efficient capital market.

(b) The *average* growth rates of firms do not seem to vary significantly with their size (although again the variability of growth rates does). This therefore does not seem to confirm Mrs. Penrose's hypothesis in Ch. 9, that medium-sized firms might be expected to grow faster than very small and very large firms.

(c) There is a clear positive correlation between growth rates and profit rates. It might be thought that this indicates that the Penrose Effect is not operative, but in fact a simple correlation like this is not sophisticated enough to isolate and identify the Penrose Effect. Actually there are two relationships between profitability and growth: one is the Penrose Effect, while the second arises from the need to finance growth at least to some extent out of retained profits. Since most firms will be unwilling to increase indefinitely their proportion of external to internal finance, in the long run higher growth rates require higher levels of retained profits. Since there are these two relationships, profitability and growth are simultaneously determined and this gives rise to a classic econometric identification problem—in other words, it is impossible to say whether a simple correlation picks up one relationship or the other (or some meaningless combination of the two). There are some reasons for thinking that in this instance the correlation reflects the second relationship rather than the Penrose Effect. The ultimate solution to this identification problem undoubtedly lies in more sophisticated theory and econometric techniques.[1]

(c) Diversification

Mrs. Penrose devotes considerable time to the analysis of diversification. Here there have been relatively few subsequent empirical studies, mainly because of the difficulty of obtaining reliable data. The first study of note was performed by Gort [19], in the U.S.A. This has been followed by Narver [42] and by Berry [7]. Recently Utton [62], Gorecki [21] and Hassid [26] [27] have produced evidence on the extent of diversification in the U.K.

The studies seem to confirm the view that most firms tend to diversify into areas that have technological or marketing factors in common with their original production. However, one must take very seriously Mrs. Penrose's strictures (pp. 107–9) about the use of census data classified according to the Standard Classification or its equivalent in other countries. Such data perhaps tell us more about the principles of classification and the age in which they are laid down than they do about current economic reality.

(d) Merger

In the late 1960s the United Kingdom experienced a merger boom of vast proportions. Subject to the usual lags, this produced a corresponding boom in studies of merger activity. Interestingly, there has not been a great deal of literature on mergers in the U.S.A. Perhaps

---

[1] This problem is explored in greater detail in Singh & Whittington [55], pp. 148–50 and the notes on pp. 308–9; and Meeks [40], pp. 25–30.

this reflects a lower incidence of merger in that country, or the fact
that the more rigid antitrust laws there focus more on the level of
concentration than on the process by which it arises.

One broad conclusion is that there seems a disappointing lack of
economic rationale behind decisions to merge. According to Newbould's questionnaire survey [43], such decisions seemed to be taken
with very little forethought and analysis, and in quite a hurry. Singh
[56] analysed statistically the characteristics of acquiring and acquired
firms, but could find no significant difference between the two pop-
ulations except that the acquiring firms tend to be bigger.

More recent studies have had the advantage of being able to
observe the merged firms for a number of years after the merger
boom. The alarming conclusion, particularly in Meeks [40], seems
to be that there are few, if any, criteria by which most mergers could
be adjudged a sucess—for instance the profits of merged firms tend
to have been lower than might have been expected from the pre-
merger profits of the constituent firms. One explanation that stands
up at least initially to the facts, and conforms well with the Penrose
vision, is that firms simply underestimate the administrative, organisational and personnel difficulties of fusing different enterprises together. But one is still left with the interesting problem of why
managers should systematically underestimate this. Perhaps it is
evidence of the growth motive against the profit motive.

(e) Concentration

In Ch. 11 Mrs. Penrose expresses a cautious view that industrial
concentration might level off at some point. In terms of the data
available at that time, the most recent of which referred to the immediate post-war period, this was an understandable conjecture.
After a period of rapidly increasing concentration from the end of
the nineteenth century, industrial concentration declined slightly in
both the U.S.A. and the U.K. in the late nineteen-thirties and the
war years that followed. However, concentration resumed its upward
path shortly after, particularly in the U.K. where the whole post-war
period has been one in fact of very rapidly rising concentration (cf.
Prais [48]). General opinion now is inclined to put down the temporary reversal in the trend of concentration to the unusual conditions
of the thirties slump and the suppression of the normal competitive
processes by government controls during the war. When normal
business conditions returned and government controls were relaxed

in the fifties, concentration was able to resume its seemingly inex-
orable path.

There seems little disagreement among writers that concentration
is increasing; but there is considerable controversy about the part
played by mergers in this process. Some (e.g. Hannah & Kay [23])
argue that mergers have been responsible for all (if not more than
all) of the increase in concentration; others (e.g. Hart, Utton &
Walshe [25]) argue that internal growth is a substantial factor.

There is a considerable body of literature which looks at the
growth of firms purely as a stochastic process. This view is obviously
not in the Penrose tradition, and is considered in this section because
the concern of these writers is not with the growth of individual
firms as such, but with how the overall distribution of firms' sizes
in the economy has arisen, and the implications for future levels of
concentration. Certain stochastic processes are known to produce
distributions very similar to the observed distribution of firms' sizes
in many different economies. One popular explanation is the Gibrat
process (e.g. Hart & Prais [24], Prais [48]) whereby if there is a
random element in firms' growth, but all firms (regardless of size)
have the same probability of growth, the distribution of firms' sizes
will approach the log-normal distribution. We have already seen that
average growth rates do not seem to vary with size, and the observed
distribution of firms' size is indeed approximately log-normal, so
this hypothesis has attracted much attention. One interesting implication of the Gibrat hypothesis is that concentration will continue to
increase, even if there is no systematic difference in the growth
prospects of individual firms.

Other writers have favoured slightly different distributions.
Steindl [61] feels that the Pareto distribution fits the evidence better,
particularly at the top end, and has analysed the stochastic processes
that might produce this distribution. Simon (Simon & Bonini [54],
Ijiri & Simon [29]), making particular assumptions about the birth
and death of firms, arrives at a slightly different distribution called
the Yule distribution. Obviously the assumptions about birth,
death and merger of firms can be quite critical, and different assumptions produce different distributions.

CONCLUSION

At various points in this essay I have emphasised my view that
although the broad outlines of this book have found their way into

the corpus of economists' thinking about the firm, something still remains to be done. I would like to conclude by taking this a little further. A full realisation of the possibilities implicit in Mrs. Penrose's work would I think result in a considerable change in our analysis of industrial problems.

Even today, the major part of the theory of the firm that we teach to students of economics is primarily a static analysis. This is not without good reason: the questions of pricing and resource allocation which are central to the economist's concern, have been found easiest to deal with in a static theoretical framework. There is too much of genuine importance here to give up simply because of the easy observation that the world is not entirely static itself. Consequently we retain the well-worked-out static analyses and refer to the growth of firms as a somewhat separate topic which should be borne in mind and might modify the basic results. As we have seen, theoretical research has also tended to treat these areas separately.

When we turn to practical work in industrial economics, the dominance of the static framework is again apparent. Arguments for and against monopoly power, vertical integration, diversification, and merger are primarily framed in terms of comparisons of long-run equilibrium positions, as it is only in such terms that welfare implications can be agreed upon. Dynamic arguments are employed secondarily, but in most cases one can frame dynamic theoretical arguments in both directions. Empirical work tends to be based on the static theoretical foundations (if on any theoretical foundations at all) and is often inconclusive since most people agree that the dynamic effects are potentially just as important.

However, alongside the development of the more static theories of the firm there has always existed an undercurrent of dissenting voices whose writings were either difficult to fit into the standard schema, or indeed directly opposed to it. There is a view which discerns in Adam Smith's writings far more of a dynamic element in the competitive process than is evident in the current theories of the firm.[1] This change of emphasis seems to have occurred gradually over the years, and the more static conception really takes its origin from Cournot and develops through Edgeworth, with the help of increasingly precise mathematical arguments, into the theory of perfect competition we have today. The theories of monopoly, im-

[1] e.g. Allyn Young [68], Richardson [51].

perfect competition and most theories of oligopoly pricing also develop from the same static source.

One of the clearest exponents of the dynamic view was Schumpeter [53], and his work is still widely read and quoted today, although economists find it difficult to reconcile with the main body of teaching. For Schumpeter, competition was in its very essence a dynamic process where the winners would be growing and the losers declining; the restless nature of the capitalist system would not allow static equilibria to last. Furthermore he argued that the benefits that accrue from the unceasing search for new products and new techniques, in fact for new monopoly positions, would far outweigh any advantages to be gained from any improvement in the allocation of resources in the static sense. These new monopoly positions would anyway in their turn be overthrown by even newer innovations.

Alfred Marshall [39] on the other hand attempted a compromise. His view of the economy was clearly not a static one, and he was always at pains to emphasise the continuous nature of economic development, from primitive beginnings, through agriculture, to advanced industrial societies. This development was due to steady improvement in the methods of production, through increasing technical knowledge, expanding markets which facilitated economies of scale, the acquiring of new skills by the labour force and the seizing of new opportunities by bold entrepreneurship. New techniques and new forms of organisation took over from out-dated ones and overturned the values of the previous age.

However, in the analysis of individual industries, he took the view that the rise and fall of individual firms did not matter. Although he recognised the constantly changing population of firms, he thought nothing of importance would be lost by analysing the market in terms of a ' representative firm '. He felt that the rise of individual firms would be checked by the ageing and death of their owners and the subsequent transfer of control to less talented and less interested descendants. He likened this process, in a celebrated phrase, to the rise and fall of ' the trees in the forest '[1] with the implication that one did not need to know the individual histories of

---

[1] Joan Robinson, disagreeing, once suggested that ' the pike in the pond ' would have been a better analogy. This would be a good description of Marx's view that the combined action of competition and unlimited increasing returns would inevitably lead to monopoly and increasing concentration of capital generally. Marxian economists have also attempted to come to terms with the corporate economy, cf. Baran & Sweezy [3].

the trees in order to analyse the forest as a whole. But Marshall himself was having second thoughts about this towards the end of his life: the successful advent of the limited-liability joint-stock company was beginning to undermine the assumptions of his homely biological analogy, and he could clearly foresee that the continuous growth of very large corporations would produce a situation where the individual firm would not be simply an insignificant atom in the structure of economic matter.

This contrast between Schumpeter and the early Marshall is a most important one, perhaps the most important thing for readers of this introduction to consider. On the one hand Schumpeter insists that change is the *essential* feature of competition—in his view one cannot hope to understand the behaviour of firms and industries except in a dynamic context. On the other hand Marshall did not deny that change *is* a feature of competition—but for certain analytical purposes, particularly the analysis of prices and outputs, he felt one might ignore it without too much error.

Until now, it has been difficult to resolve this conflict between the static and the dynamic approaches.[1] One recognises the ring of truth in Schumpeter, but economists have been understandably reluctant to throw over their considerable body of static analysis. The solution obviously lies in the construction of a more general model of the firm which can comprehend both the dynamic and the static areas of interest, and here we see again the importance of Edith Penrose's contribution. Many other writers have pointed out the gap between the traditional theory of the firm and the current realities of the modern economy, but too often their criticisms have left little to build upon. This is not the case here—she has provided a framework which is capable of incorporating much of the older analysis into a more general and more realistic theory. But it is just a framework, and the actual construction of that theory has yet to be carried out. *August 1979*

[1] One might interpret the interesting work by Downie [12] as an attempt at a general synthesis. His view of the competitive process was that it comprised two opposing tendencies. The 'transfer mechanism' gradually reallocated the market shares of the less efficient firms to the more efficient and so tended to increase the concentration within the market, with the logical outcome being monopolisation by the most efficient. This was opposed by the 'innovation mechanism' whereby those firms currently losing out would have an incentive to hit back in some non-marginal fashion, by searching for an improved product or a different method of production, which would dramatically upset the current efficiency rankings and set the transfer mechanism working in a different direction. The continuation of competition is therefore dependent on a delicate and fragile balance between these two opposing forces, a balance which is by no means assured.

BIBLIOGRAPHY

[1] Alchian, A.A. & Demsetz, H. (1972), ' Production, Information Costs and Economic Organisation ', *American Economic Review*, LXII, pp. 777–795.

[2] Arrow, K.J. (1962), ' The Economic Implications of Learning by Doing ', *Review of Economic Studies*, XXIX, pp. 155–173.

[3] Baran, P.A. & Sweezy, P.M. (1966), *Monopoly Capital*. New York: Monthly Review Press.

[4] Barna, T. (1962), *Investment and Growth Policies in British Industrial Firms*. Cambridge: Cambridge University Press.

[5] Baumol, W.J. (1962), ' On the Theory of Expansion of the Firm ', *American Economic Review*, LII, pp. 1078–1087.

[6] Baumol, W.J. (1967), *Business Behaviour, Value and Growth* (Revised Edition). New York: Harcourt, Brace & World.

[7] Berry, C.H. (1975), *Corporate Growth and Diversification*. Princeton, N.J.; Princeton University Press.

[8] Chandler, A.D. (1963), *Strategy and Structure: Chapters in the History of the Industrial Enterprise*. Cambridge, Mass.: M.I.T. Press.

[9] Chandler, A.D. (1977), *The Visible Hand: The Managerial Revolution in American Business*. Cambridge, Mass.: Harvard University Press.

[10] Coase, R.H. (1937), ' The Nature of the Firm ', *Economica*, N.S. IV, pp. 386–405.

[11] Cyert, R.M. & March, J.G. (1963), *A Behavioral Theory of the Firm*, Englewood Cliffs, N.J.: Prentice-Hall.

[12] Downie, J. (1958), *The Competitive Process*. London: Duckworth.

[13] Eatwell, J. (1971), ' Growth, Profitability and Size: The Empirical Evidence ', in Marris and Wood (eds.), *The Corporate Economy*, op. cit., pp. 389–421.

[14] Edwards, R.S. & Townsend, H. (1961), *Business Enterprise: Its Growth and Organisation*. London: Macmillan.

[15] Edwards, R.S. & Townsend, H. (eds.) (1961), *Studies in Business Organisation*. London: Macmillan.

[16] Edwards, R.S. & Townsend, H. (eds.) (1966), *Business Growth*. London: Macmillan.

[17] Eichner, A.S. (1976), *The Megacorp and Oligopoly: Micro Foundations of Macro Dynamics*. Cambridge: Cambridge University Press.

[18] Galbraith, J.K. (1967), *The New Industrial State*. London: Hamish Hamilton.

[19] Gort, M. (1962), *Diversification and Integration in American Industry*. Princeton, N.J.: Princeton University Press.

[20] Gordon, M. (1962), *The Investment, Financing and Valuation of the Corporation*. Homewood, Ill.: Irwin.

[21] Gorecki, P.K. (1975), ' An Inter-Industry Analysis of Diversification in the U.K. Manufacturing Sector ', *Journal of Industrial Economics*, XXIV, pp. 131–146.

[22] Hannah, L. (1976), *The Rise of the Corporate Economy*. London: Methuen.

[23] Hannah, L. & Kay, J.A. (1977), *Concentration in Modern Industry: Theory, Measurement and the U.K. Experience*. London: Macmillan.

[24] Hart, P.E. & Prais, S.J. (1956), ' The Analysis of Business Concentration: A Statistical Approach ', *Journal of the Royal Statistical Society*, Series A, 119, pp. 150–181.

[25] Hart, P.E., Utton, M.A. & Walshe, G. (1973), *Mergers and Concentration in British Industry*. Cambridge: Cambridge University Press.

[26] Hassid, J. (1975), ' Recent Evidence on Conglomerate Diversification in U.K. Manufacturing Industry ', *Manchester School of Economic and Social Studies*, XLIII, pp. 372–395.

[27] Hassid, J. (1977), ' Diversification and the Firm's Rate of Growth ', *Manchester School of Economic and Social Studies*, XLV, pp. 16–28.

[28] Heal, G.M. & Silberston, A. (1972), ' Alternative Managerial Objectives: An Exploratory Note ', *Oxford Economic Papers*, XXIV, pp. 137–150.

[29] Ijiri, Y. & Simon, H.A. (1964), ' Business Firm Growth and Size ', *American Economic Review*, LIV, pp. 77–89.

[30] King, M.A. (1977), *Public Policy and the Corporation*. London: Chapman & Hall.

[31] Lesourne, J. (1973), *Modèles de Croissance des Entreprises*. Paris: Dunod.

[32] Lintner, J. (1964), ' Optimal Dividends and Growth under Uncertainty ', *Quarterly Journal of Economics*, LXXVIII, pp. 49–95.

[33] Lintner, J. (1971), ' Optimum or Maximum Corporate Growth

under Uncertainty ', in Marris & Wood (eds.), *The Corporate Economy*, op. cit., pp. 172–241.

[34] Mackintosh, A.S. (1963), *The Development of Firms*, Cambridge: Cambridge University Press.

[35] Marris, R.L. (1961), Review of ' The Theory of the Growth of the Firm ', *Economic Journal*, LXXI, pp. 144–148.

[36] Marris, R.L. (1963), ' A Model of the "Managerial" Enterprise ', *Quarterly Journal of Economics*, LXXVII, pp. 185–209.

[37] Marris, R.L. (1964), *The Economic Theory of Managerial Capitalism*. London: Macmillan.

[38] Marris, R.L. & Wood, A. (eds.) (1971), *The Corporate Economy*, London, Macmillan.

[39] Marshall, A. (1961), *Principles of Economics* (9th (Variorum) Edition, edited by C.W. Guillebaud). London: Macmillan.

[40] Meeks, G. (1977), *Disappointing Marriage: A Study of the Gains from Merger*. Cambridge: Cambridge University Press.

[41] Modigliani, F. & Miller, M. (1961), ' Dividend Policy, Growth and the Valuation of Shares ', *Journal of Business*, XXXIV, pp. 411–433.

[42] Narver, J.C. (1967), *Conglomerate Mergers and Market Competition*. Berkeley & Los Angeles: University of California Press.

[43] Newbould, G.D. (1970), *Management and Merger Activity*. Liverpool: Guthstead.

[44] Penrose, E.T. (1959), *The Theory of the Growth of the Firm*. Oxford, Basil Blackwell.

[45] Penrose, E.T. (1960), ' The Growth of the Firm. A Case Study: The Hercules Powder Company ', *Business History Review*, XXXIV, pp. 1–23.

[46] Penrose, E.T. (1968), *The Large International Firm in Developing Countries: The International Petroleum Industry*. London: Allen & Unwin.

[47] Penrose, E.T. (1971), *The Growth of Firms, Oil and the Middle East*. London: Cass.

[48] Prais, S.J. (1976), *The Evolution of Giant Firms in Great Britain: A Study of the Growth of Concentration in Manufacturing Industry in Britain, 1909–70*. Cambridge: Cambridge University Press.

[49] Richardson, G.B. (1964), ' The Limits to a Firm's Rate of Growth ', *Oxford Economic Papers*, XVI, pp. 9–23.

[50] Richardson, G.B. (1972), ' The Organisation of Industry ', *Economic Journal*, LXXXI, pp. 883–896.

[51] Richardson, G.B. (1975), 'Adam Smith on Competition and Increasing Returns', in *Essays on Adam Smith*, edited by A.S. Skinner & T. Wilson, Oxford: Oxford University Press, pp. 350–360.

[52] Robinson, E.A.G. (1958), *The Structure of Competitive Industry* (revised edition). Cambridge: Cambridge University Press.

[53] Schumpeter, J.A. (1976), *Capitalism, Socialism and Democracy* (5th ed.). London: Allen & Unwin.

[54] Simon, H.A. & Bonini, C.P. (1958), 'The Size Distribution of Business Firms', *American Economic Review*, XLVIII, pp. 607–617.

[55] Singh, A. & Whittington, G. (1968), *Growth, Profitability and Valuation*. Cambridge: Cambridge University Press.

[56] Singh, A. (1971), *Take-overs: Their Relevance to the Stock Market and the Theory of the Firm*. Cambridge: Cambridge University Press.

[57] Slater, M.D.E. (1979), 'The Managerial Limitation to the Growth of Firms'. Univ. of Bristol, mimeo.

[58] Solow, R.M. (1971), 'Some Implications of Alternative Criteria for the Firm', in Marris & Wood (ed.) *The Corporate Economy*, op. cit., pp. 318–342.

[59] Sraffa, P. (1926), 'The Laws of Returns under Competitive Conditions', *Economic Journal*, XXXVI, pp. 535–550.

[60] Starbuck, W.H. (1971), 'Organisational Growth and Development' in *Handbook of Organisations*, Chicago: Rand McNally (1965), pp. 451–522. Reprinted in *Organisational Growth and Development* ed. W.H. Starbuck, London: Penguin (1971). pp. 11–141.

[61] Steindl, J. (1965), *Random Processes and the Growth of Firms*. New York: Hafner.

[62] Utton, M.A. (1977), 'Large Firm Diversification in British Industry', *Economic Journal*, 87, pp. 96–113.

[63] Uzawa, H. (1969), 'Time Preference and the Penrose Effect in a Two-Class Model of Economic Growth', *Journal of Political Economy*, 77, pp. 628–652.

[64] Williamson, J. (1966), 'Profits, Growth and Sales Maximisation', *Economica*, N.S. XXXIII, pp. 1–17.

[65] Williamson, O.E. (1970), *Corporate Control and Business Behavior: An Enquiry into the Effects of Organisation Form on Enterprise Behavior*. Englewood Cliffs, N.J.: Prentice-Hall.

[66] Williamson, O.E. (1971), ' Managerial Discretion, Organisation Form and the Multi-Division Hypothesis ', in Marris & Wood (eds.), *The Corporate Economy,* op. cit., pp. 343–386.

[67] Williamson, O.E. (1975), *Markets and Hierarchies: Analysis and Anti-trust Implications, a Study in the Economics of Internal Organisation.* New York: Free Press.

[68] Young, A.A. (1928), ' Increasing Returns and Economic Progress ', *Economic Journal,* XXXVIII, pp. 527–542.

PREFACE

Just one warning: this book deals with familiar concepts, but in an unfamiliar way and the reader is cautioned not to treat the introductory chapters lightly; they are essential for the analysis to follow. The entire study is essentially a single argument no step of which can be omitted without the risk of misunderstanding later conclusions. Hence, readers interested in particular questions—say diversification, merger, or concentration—cannot safely turn to the chapters dealing with these subjects and ignore the foundations on which they rest. Those who do will find isolated discussions not only unconvincing but perhaps even unintelligible.

A book, like an invention, embodies the work of many people without whom it could not have been produced. I owe much to the contributions of the students, staff and visitors at The Johns Hopkins University, both in the seminar room and outside it, to discussions with numerous economists in various parts of the world, and to criticism of papers delivered at various meetings. Of the visitors, Mr. Donald Whitehead of University of Adelaide, Australia, and Dr. Jacob Schmookler of the University of Minnesota were especially helpful to me. Professor Schmookler read and severely criticised several chapters, which gained greatly in clarity of exposition as a result of my efforts to meet his objections. Mr. Whitehead read the entire manuscript and in several places was responsible for extensive revision. Of the staff, my greatest debt is to Fritz Machlup, who went patiently through several drafts, served as a sounding board for the testing of ideas, and again and again forced me to more rigorous thinking and clearer expression. Without his constant encouragement, acute perception of logical weakness, and willingness to discuss difficulties, I doubt whether this book would have appeared at all; certainly it would not have appeared in the present form.

Last, but by no means least, I must acknowledge not only the general support and encouragement of my husband, Professor E. F. Penrose, and his uncomplaining acceptance of the hardships a husband must bear when his wife is involved in the painful process of finishing a book, but also his active contribution to the study itself, in particular to its English style. I, of course, am responsible for all defects that remain, some of which are undoubtedly due to my own stubbornness.

I have received financial assistance from various research funds, for which I am grateful. The study was originally undertaken as part of a broader investigation of the growth of firms, directed by Fritz Machlup and G. H. Evans, Jr., and financed by the Merrill Foundation for Financial Research. The first year of work on this study was financed under that project. In addition, I am especially grateful to the John Simon Guggenheim Memorial Foundation for a Fellowship which permitted me to carry on research on the subject in Australia at the Australian National University. Expenses of typing and otherwise preparing the drafts and the final manuscript were defrayed from research funds of the Department of Political Economy at The Johns Hopkins University received from the Lessing Rosenthal Fund and the Ford Foundation.

EDITH T. PENROSE.

The Johns Hopkins University.
June 1958.

CHAPTER I

INTRODUCTION

The purpose of the study. The nature of the argument.

So far as I know, no economist has as yet attempted a general theory of the growth of firms. This seems to me so very strange that I am sure anyone attempting it should indeed watch his (or her) step, for naturally there is always a good reason for what economists do or do not do. Perhaps such a theory is impossible to construct, unnecessary, trivial, or outside the pale of economics proper. I do not know, but I offer this study in the hope that all four possibilities will be rejected.

We shall be concerned with the growth of firms, and only incidentally with their size. The term ' growth ' is used in ordinary discourse with two different connotations. It sometimes denotes merely increase in amount; for example, when one speaks of ' growth ' in output, exports, sales. At other times, however, it is used in its primary meaning implying an increase in size or an improvement in quality as a result of a *process* of development, akin to natural biological processes in which an interacting series of internal changes leads to increases in size accompanied by changes in the characteristics of the growing object. Thus the terms ' economic growth ' and ' economic development ' are often used interchangeably where ' growth ' implies not only an increase in the national product but also a progressive changing of the economy. ' Growth ' in this second sense often also has the connotation of ' natural ' or ' normal '—a process that will occur whenever conditions are favourable because of the nature of the ' organism '; size becomes a more or less incidental result of a continuous on-going or ' unfolding ' process.

But this is not the way the size of firms is looked at in traditional economic analysis, which examines the advantages and disadvantages of *being* a particular size and explains movement from one size to another in terms of the net advantages of different sizes. Growth becomes merely an adjustment to the size appropriate to given conditions; there is no notion of an *internal* process of *development* leading to cumulative movements in any one direction. Still less is there any suggestion that there may be advantages in *moving* from one position to another quite apart from the advantages of *being* in a different position. It is often presumed that there is a ' most profitable ' size of firm and that no further explanation than the search for profit is needed of how and why firms reach that size. Such an approach to the explanation of the size of firms will be rejected in this study; it will be argued that size is but a by-product of the process of growth, that there is no ' optimum ', or even most profitable, size of firm. As we shall see, traditional theory has always had trouble with the limits to the size of firms, and I think we shall find the source of the trouble.

In addition to the traditional approaches, there have been sporadic attempts to develop theories of the growth of firms using biological analogies and treating firms as organisms whose processes of growth are essentially the same as those of the living organisms of the natural world. There are many difficulties with this type of analysis, one of the most serious being the fact that human motivation and conscious human decision have no place in the process of growth. This alone, I believe, is sufficient ground for rejecting such theories of the growth of firms. All the evidence we have indicates that the growth of a firm is connected with attempts of a particular group of human beings to do something; nothing is gained and much is lost if this fact is not explicitly recognized.[1]

In spite of the fact that I depart from the traditional methods of analyzing the behaviour of firms, many of the ideas—indeed some of the basic ones—providing the bricks and mortar with which the analytical structure of this study is built are to be encountered in the literature of both theoretical and applied economics, and many parts of the structure will be easily recognized.[2] What I have done is to attempt to build a consistent, self-contained theory of the growth of firms, synthesizing my own ideas and those of others, moulding both into a reasonably formal whole which I hope provides a way of looking at the growth of firms that will be useful for both theoretical and ' practical ' purposes. Much more can be done than I do here by way of refinement of analytical constructions, exploration of

[1] See my ' Biological Analogies in the Theory of the Firm ', *American Economic Review*, Vol. XLII, No. 5 (Dec. 1952), pp. 804–819.

[2] Indeed, after having laboriously worked out for myself what I took to be an important and ' original ' idea, I have often had the disconcerting experience of subsequently finding the same idea better expressed by some other writer. I try always to mention such earlier expositions; I am sure that there are many I have overlooked, for which I offer advance apology.

ramifications, and development of the theoretical and political significance of the analysis. Some of the concepts used are not defined with great precision, largely because no highly refined definition is required for my purposes; a more detailed or more precise application of the analysis may well justify further effort in this direction.[1]

Although I am primarily concerned with a theoretical analysis of a process, I have tried to modify the impact of the unavoidable abstraction in two ways, for I would like to appeal to a wider audience than that of professional economists only. In the first place, the fundamental assumptions on which the analysis rests are chosen with a view to their applicability in the ' real world ', and I shall make some effort to justify them, although strictly speaking I suppose no justification of this sort is necessary provided useful results are obtained. Of course, in the process of developing an argument it is often necessary to make patently ' unrealistic ' assumptions in order to isolate particular problems with which we may be concerned. For the most part such assumptions are, or can easily be, dropped at later stages.

Secondly, I shall frequently illustrate the argument with concrete examples. Consistent examples are, of course, no more a proof than are inconsistent examples a disproof of a general argument unless the examples are presented in sufficiently large numbers and selected in such a way that they constitute a representative sample. The theory of the *process* of growth is, on the whole, susceptible to empirical testing against the experience of individual firms, although the examples presented in the following chapters are illustrative only. There is not sufficient systematic information available as yet to enable any comprehensive testing of the generality of the theory. Although there are many business histories and biographies of individual businessmen, only a handful are really good from this point of view;[2] annual reports of corporations, journal and newspaper reports, and interviews with businessmen are useful if carefully appraised, but do not yet provide a systematic and compre-

---

[1] I am much impressed by Mrs. Joan Robinson's insistence that ' There is no advantage (and much error) in making definitions of words more precise than the subject matter they refer to '. ' The Industry and The Market ', *Economic Journal*, Vol. LXVI, No. 262 (June 1956), p. 361.

[2] Charles H. Wilson's *History of Unilever* (London: Cassell, 1954) is a model of what good firm histories can be. I have leaned heavily on this type of work (and there are some others), as well as on direct discussions with businessmen, for insight into the processes of firm growth.

hensive body of information.[1] It is not possible in the framework of this study both to develop a theoretical analysis and to carry out an extensive testing of it in the light of available information, although I have tried at every point to satisfy myself that there is sufficient evidence to justify at least a *prima facie* case for the hypotheses advanced respecting the processes of growth.

The analysis of the *limits* to growth—the factors determining the maximum rate of growth of firms—on the other hand, cannot, in its present formulation at any rate, be tested against the facts of the external world, partly because of the difficulties in expressing some of the concepts in quantitative terms and partly because of the impossibility of ever knowing for any given firm what is, or would have been, its maximum rate of growth. Perhaps some of these difficulties will be overcome in different formulations constructed by others. At present the validity of the theory of the limits to the rate of growth of firms lies entirely in the extent to which it is consistent with the theory of the process of growth, in its logic, and in its intuitive acceptability.

The Nature of the Argument

A comprehensive theory of the growth of the firm must explain several qualitatively different kinds of growth and must take account not only of the sequence of changes created by a firm's own activities but also of the effect of changes that are external to the firm and lie beyond its control. Not all of these things can be discussed at the same time, however, without creating such a serious confusion between very different types of causal relationships that the discussion degenerates into a generalized description of a sequence of events that appears largely fortuitous and to have been introduced for the convenience of a pre-determined conclusion, like the coincidences of a poorly constructed detective story. Hence the development of the theory must proceed in stages.

After a discussion of the characteristics of the business firm, its functions, and the factors influencing its behaviour, we shall turn to an examination of the forces inherent in the nature of firms which at the same time create the possibilities for, provide the inducements

---

[1] There is, incidentally, a great deal of useful information available in the ' managerial ' literature which has, I think, been sadly neglected by economists who, however, are gradually beginning to take more seriously the literature of ' management ', and of the businessman generally, largely owing, I suppose, to the insistent hammering of those empirically-minded economists who have a foot in each discipline.

to, and limit the amount of the expansion they can undertake or even plan to undertake in any given period of time. It will then be shown that this limit is by its nature temporary, that in the very process of expansion the limit recedes, and that after the completion of an optimum plan for expansion a new ' disequilibrium ' has been created in which a firm has new inducements to expand further even if all external conditions (including the conditions of demand and supply) have remained unchanged.

In all of the discussion the emphasis is on the internal resources of a firm—on the productive services available to a firm from its own resources, particularly the productive services available from management with experience within the firm. It is shown not only that the resources with which a particular firm is accustomed to working will shape the productive services its management is capable of rendering (where management is defined in the broadest sense), but also that the experience of management will affect the productive services that all its other resources are capable of rendering. As management tries to make the best use of the resources available, a truly ' dynamic ' interacting process occurs which encourages continuous growth but limits the rate of growth. In order to focus attention on the crucial role of a firm's ' inherited ' resources, the environment is treated, in the first instance, as an ' image ' in the entrepreneur's mind of the possibilities and restrictions with which he is confronted, for it is, after all, such an 'image' which in fact determines a man's behaviour; whether experience confirms expectations is another story.[1] Even ' demand ' as seen by a firm is largely conditioned by the productive services available to it, and hence the ' direction of expansion '—the products a firm becomes interested in producing—can be analyzed with reference to the relationship between its resources and its own view of its competitive position. This will be discussed in an extensive analysis of the economics of diversification.

The theory of growth is developed first as a theory of internal growth, that is, of growth without merger and acquisition. The significance of merger can best be appraised in the light of its effect on the process of and limits to internal growth. Some attention to merger is given in the discussion of diversification, but not until

---

[1] These lines were written in a slightly different form before Kenneth Boulding's imaginative little book appeared. ' Image ' is so apt a word for my purposes that I promptly appropriated it. See Kenneth E. Boulding, *The Image* (Ann Arbor: Univ. of Michigan Press, 1956).

Chapter VIII does the full analysis of growth through merger appear, and with this the development of the theory of growth is completed. The emphasis of the analysis is then shifted from the internal resources of the firm to the impact of particular types of external conditions as firms grow larger and to the particular situation of small as compared with large firms in the economy. This permits the development of an analysis of changes in the rate of growth of firms as they grow, and finally leads to a discussion of the process of industrial concentration, which is, after all, primarily a question of the relative rates of growth of large and small firms in a changing economy.

Economists are sometimes criticized for not making clear the historical or institutional environment to which their theories are supposed to be applicable. The present analysis is concerned only with the incorporated industrial firm operated for private profit and unregulated by the state (hence not to regulated public utilities, financial organizations, or even ' trading ' firms) and is applicable only to an economy where the corporation is the dominant form of industrial organization; historically, therefore, only to the period since the last quarter of the 19th century. To be sure, the corporation was widely used in certain areas much earlier, but it did not dominate the field of manufacturing as it has since, at least in the western world.

The adaptation of the corporation, or limited liability company, to private manufacturing business removed the most important limitation on the growth and ultimate size of the business firm when it destroyed the connection between the extent and nature of a firm's operations and the personal financial position of the owners. So long as owners were personally liable for the actions of their agents as well as for the finance of their firms, there was in general a sharp limit to the risk attendant upon extensive financial commitments, in particular in illiquid industrial assets, that owners would be willing to assume, as well as a close limit on the delegation of authority in management that could safely be permitted. The business organization or bureaucracy could never become an entity in its own right, independent of the personal position of the firm's owners, as it has increasingly tended to become to-day.

The continued growth of a modern business firm can, I think, be most usefully viewed as the continual extension of the range and nature of the activities of an organization in which the role of the owners may or may not be relevant, and of which even 'central management' (or entrepreneur) is only a part, though a very important part. It is at the organization as a whole that we must look to discover the reasons for its growth. This stands in sharp contrast to the traditional economic analysis of the 'firm' in the economist's 'theory of the firm', and much confusion has arisen because of a failure to distinguish the different meanings in economic analysis of the term 'firm'; the economist's firm in the 'theory of the firm' is not at all the economic institution that ordinary people would think of as a firm. It will be necessary to make the distinction clear at the very beginning in order to avoid compounding the confusion.

Finally, a comment on an alleged 'tautological problem' which some have feared is inherent in a theory of the growth of firms concerned only with firms that can successfully grow. Many firms do not grow, and for a variety of reasons: unenterprising direction, inefficient management, insufficient capital-raising ability, lack of adaptability to changing circumstances, poor judgment leading to frequent and costly mistakes, or simply bad luck due to circumstances beyond their control. I am not concerned with such firms, for I am only concerned with the process of growth, and with the limits to the rate of growth, and therefore only with those firms that do grow. I am not attempting to present a theory which will enable an analyst to examine a particular firm and state in advance whether it will or will not successfully grow. One can easily state the necessary and sufficient conditions for successful growth, but how can one determine whether a given firm meets these conditions? In practice one cannot determine it in advance; one must wait to see whether or not the firm grows. Hence little is gained by posing the problem in this way—but one need not so pose it. I am not asking what determines whether a particular firm can grow, but rather the very different question: assuming that some firms can grow, what principles will then govern their growth, and how fast and how long can they grow? Or alternatively, assuming that there are opportunities for expansion in an economy, what determines the kind of firm that will take advantage of them and to what extent? For so long as there exist opportunities for profitable investment there are opportunities for the growth of firms.

The problem is not unlike the problem of diagnosing the prospects for the growth of, say, a tree. Upon examination, one can say, for example, that the tree will not grow unless certain identifiable conditions are corrected and certain environmental conditions satisfied—but one can never certify in advance whether the tree will or will not survive all possible vicissitudes and how they will affect its growth—the next winter may be severe, the spring rains may fail, or blight may set in. For a firm, enterprising management is the one identifiable condition without which continued growth is precluded—this is one necessary (though not sufficient) condition for continued growth, as will be demonstrated. Although our analysis is concerned only with growing enterprising firms, it is not on that account circular.

CHAPTER II

THE FIRM IN THEORY

Different ways of looking at firms—The firm in the theory of price and production. *Limits to size. The 'firm' is not a firm*—The firm as an administrative organization. *The function and nature of an industrial firm. Size and administrative co-ordination. Industrial firms and investment trusts. Continuity in the 'history' of a firm*—The firm as a collection of physical and human resources—The motivation of the firm. *The profit motive. Long-run profits and growth.*

In a private enterprise industrial economy the business firm is the basic unit for the organization of production. The greater part of economic activity is channelled through firms. The patterns of economic life, including the patterns of consumption as well as of production, are largely shaped by the multitude of individual decisions made by the businessmen who guide the actions of the business units we call firms. The very nature of the economy is to some extent defined in terms of the kind of firms that compose it, their size, the way in which they are established and grow, their methods of doing business, and the relationships between them. In consequence, the firm has always occupied a prominent place in economic analysis. It is a complex institution, impinging on economic and social life in many directions, comprising numerous and diverse activities, making a large variety of significant decisions, influenced by miscellaneous and unpredictable human whims, yet generally directed in the light of human reason.[1]

In the literature of economics, the firm of the ' real world ' has long lived in that uncomfortable no-man's-land between the high and dry plateaus of ' pure theory' and the tangled forests of 'empiric-realistic ' research. Border skirmishes between the natives of the two areas have been common, supplemented by formal jousts in the medieval manner between noble knights of the opposing allegiances, each warmly defending his faith. These encounters have one remark-

---

[1] I hope I shall be forgiven if, on occasion, I endow the firm itself with human attributes, considering it, not as a ' legal person ', but, by analogy, as an ' economic person ' (although not necessarily as the ' economic man '). This fiction permits me to speak of the ' firm ', rather than its managers or executives, acting in this way or that, and facilitates exposition in those cases where no distinction is required between the firm and the men who run it.

able characteristic—it seems strangely difficult for any participant ever to discover precisely where his antagonist stands, with the result that an uncommon number of thrusts seem to be made in one direction but countered from an entirely different direction, broad swords and rapiers forcefully cutting the air, without really clashing. When such difficulties occur in the world of thought one is likely to find the source of them in the meaning of words, and indeed so it is with the present problem of the ' firm '. A ' firm ' is by no means an unambiguous clear-cut entity; it is not an observable object physically separable from other objects, and it is difficult to define except with reference to what it does or what is done within it. Hence each analyst is free to choose any characteristics of firms that he is interested in, to define firms in terms of those characteristics, and to proceed thereafter to call the construction so defined a ' firm '. Herein lies a potential source of confusion that it is essential to deal with at the very outset of this study.

Because of its complexity and diversity, a firm can be approached with many different types of analysis—sociological, organizational, engineering, or economic—and from whatever point of view within each type of analysis seems appropriate to the problem in hand. Within economics itself there are several different approaches to the study of the firm, and one type—the so-called ' theory of the firm ' —continues to hold the field in spite of vigorous attacks; of all the approaches it is probably the most often misunderstood and mis-applied by both its defenders and its attackers.

Educated laymen as well as economists studying the vagaries of actual business behaviour often show an understandable impa-tience with the ' theory of the firm ', for they see in it little that reflects the facts of life as they understand them. It is therefore worth a little trouble, perhaps, to discuss at the very beginning the nature of the ' firm ' in the ' theory of the firm ', to indicate why it provides an unsuitable framework for a theory of the growth of firms, but at the same time to make clear that we shall not be involved in any quarrel with the theory of the 'firm' as part of the theory of price and production, so long as it cultivates its own garden and we cultivate ours. Much confusion can arise from the careless assump-tion that when the term ' firm ' is used in different contexts it always means the same thing.

The 'Firm' in the Theory of Price and Production

The 'theory of the firm'—as it is called in the literature—was constructed for the purpose of assisting in the theoretical investigation of one of the central problems of economic analysis—the way in which prices and the allocation of resources among different uses are determined. It is but part of the wider theory of value, indeed one of its supporting pillars, and its vitality is derived almost exclusively from its connection with this highly developed, and still basically unchallenged general system for the economic analysis of the problem of price determination and resource allocation.[1] In this context only those aspects of the behaviour of firms are considered that are relevant to the problems that the wider theory is designed to solve.

Since the theory of value is concerned with the factors determining the prices of particular products or productive services, the appropriate model of the 'firm' is a model representing the forces determining the prices and quantities produced of particular products in the individual firm; the 'equilibrium' of the 'firm' is, in essence, the 'equilibrium output' for a given product (or given group of products) from the viewpoint of the firm. It does not pretend to be an 'equilibrium' of the firm if the firm is represented in any other way, or if any other considerations affect it than those permitted in the theory of price and output.[2] Hence if we become interested in other aspects of the firm we ask questions that the 'theory of the firm' is not designed to answer. In that theory the 'growth' of a firm is nothing more than an increase in the output of given products, and the 'optimum size' of the firm is the lowest point on the average cost curve for its given product; the question what limits the size of a firm is the question what limits the amount it will produce of the given product or products with respect to which the cost and revenue schedules apply that are used to represent

[1] Consequently the various attacks on the theory of the firm, whether they come from theorists emphasizing the effect of uncertainty or from investigators of the actual behaviour of firms, have failed to dislodge it from its key position in economic theory. To do so, even for the competitive case, would, as Hicks has pointed out, involve the 'wreckage' of 'the greater part of general equilibrium theory', which can hardly be accepted until something better has been evolved to take its place. J. R. Hicks, *Value and Capital* (Oxford: Clarendon Press, 2nd ed., 1946), p. 84.

[2] It is not surprising, therefore, that this firm is '. . . a strange bloodless creature without a balance sheet, without any visible capital structure, without debts, and engaged apparently in the simultaneous purchase of inputs and sale of outputs at constant rates'. Kenneth Boulding, *Reconstruction in Economics* (New York: Wiley, 1950), p. 34.

the ' firm '. The model is not designed for the analysis of a ' firm '
free to vary the kind of products it produces as it grows.

The Limits to ' Size '

The conditions of equilibrium analysis require that there be
something to prevent the indefinite expansion of output of the
individual ' firm ' defined in the above manner. In the model of
the firm in ' pure ' competition, the limit to output is found only
in the assumption that the cost of producing the individual product
must rise after a point as additional quantities of it are produced; in
the model of the firm in ' monopolistic ' competition, the limit is
partly found in falling revenue as additional quantities of the product are sold. Without some such limit to the output of a given
product—which, in this context, means to the size of the firm—no
determinate ' equilibrium position ' can be posited in static theory.

Thus, regardless of the specific framework of their particular
theories, economists have looked to the limitations of management
(causing increasing long-run costs of production) or of the market
(causing decreasing revenue from sales), or to uncertainty about
future prospects (causing both increasing cost of larger outputs and
decreasing revenue from larger sales because of the necessity of
making allowance for risk) to provide a limit to the size of firm.[1]

The whole problem has been the source of much controversy,
especially the question whether managerial diseconomies will cause
long-run increasing costs; to establish such a result management
must be treated as a ' fixed factor ' and the nature of the ' fixity '
must be identified with respect to the nature of the managerial
task of ' co-ordination '. This identification has never been satisfactorily accomplished and many theorists have given up the task,
preferring to rely on other limits to size.[2]

The notion that the market limits the size of firms follows from
the assumption that a firm is tied to given products, that a specific

---

[1] The effect of uncertainty is not always put in these terms—see, for example, M.
Kalecki, ' The Principle of Increasing Risk,' Economica Vol. IV (New Series) Nov. 1937,
pp. 440–447—but most formulations can usually be expressed in terms of ' corrected '
cost and revenue estimates. See Chapter IV for further discussion of this point.

[2] Chamberlin attempted to meet the problem by abandoning entirely the principle
of a fixed factor and argued that mere increased complexity of organization would lead
to the requisite rise in costs as the firm expanded. E. H. Chamberlin, ' Proportionality,
Divisibility and Economies of Scale ', Quarterly Journal of Economics, Vol. LXII, No. 2
(Feb. 1948), pp. 229–262—This does not get to the root of the matter, however, since
complexity is a problem only if the capacity of men to deal with complexity is limited.
Hence we are again back to the same point.

group of markets governs its possibilities of expansion. If this assumption is dropped, however, one is dealing with a different concept of the ' firm ' and a different type of analysis becomes more appropriate. With a different concept of the firm one can recognize that a ' firm ', when appropriate resources are available, can produce anything for which a demand can be found or created, and it becomes a matter of taste or convenience whether one speaks of the ' market ' or of the resources of the firm itself as the consideration limiting its expansion. The fact that demand curves for given *products* can be assumed to be tilted downward does not mean that the expected net revenue from additional units of *investment* need ever become negative. Net revenue may well be rising as investment—and therefore total production—increases. To say that the expansion of a firm which can produce unspecified new products is limited by ' demand ', is to say that there are no products that the firm could produce profitably. This, of course, is not what is meant in the theory of the firm, simply because its ' firm ' is not a firm.

The introduction of ' uncertainty ' or ' risk ' as a limit to size merely underlines the fact that the expected cost and revenue calculations of firms reflect their expectations about the future course of events; these expectations are held with varying degrees of uncertainty which increase as output increases (thus increasing the risk of loss) and allowances must be made in a firm's calculations for the possibilities of disappointment. It in no way alters the nature of the analysis.

The ' Firm ' is not a Firm

When the ' theory of the firm ' is kept in its proper habitat there is not much difficulty with any of the explanations of the ' size ' of firms. Difficulties arise when an attempt is made to acclimatize the theory to an alien environment and, in particular, to adapt it to the analysis of the expansion of the innovating, multi-product, ' flesh-and-blood ' organizations that businessmen call firms. It makes little difference in the theory of the firm whether changes in the characteristics of the individual firm, for example its managerial ability, or changes in the expectations of the entrepreneur about the future course of events, are treated as causing changes in the size of a single firm or as causing the creation of a series of ' new firms '.[1] The theorist is free to adopt the technique most

---

[1] Kaldor, for example, has defined the firm as a ' productive combination possessing

suited to his problem. But how such changes are treated makes a great deal of difference to the theorist concerned with the growth of the firm defined, say, as an administrative organization in the real world. For the latter purpose it becomes necessary to use a very different concept of the firm and little is gained by tortuously trying to force an adaptation of the theory of the firm merely because it has proved to be a valuable concept for a different purpose. To some extent the adaptation can be forced, as we shall see, but we shall be dealing with the firm as a growing organization, not as a ' price-and-output decision maker ' for given products; for this purpose the ' firm ' must be endowed with many more attributes than are possessed by the ' firm ' in the theory of the firm, and the significance of these attributes is not conveniently represented by cost and revenue curves. Furthermore, not only is it inconvenient so to represent them, but it is also misleading, for it only compounds the confusion involved in a failure clearly to distinguish the ' firm ' in price theory from the ' firm ' as it is looked on by businessmen as well as by many economists dealing with the behaviour of firms— a confusion which has unnecessarily marred the reputation of the ' theory of the firm ' and done its credit in this world much wrong.[1]

a given unit of co-ordinating ability', and holds that ' all the theoretically relevant characteristics of a firm change with changes in coordinating ability. It might as well be treated, therefore, as a different firm '. N. Kaldor, ' The Equilibrium of the Firm ', *Economic Journal*, Vol. XLIV, No. 173 (March 1934), pp. 69–70. And Triffin explicitly states that for (his) theoretical purposes it is ' better to say that a new firm has been created ' when the producer's appraisal of cost and revenue conditions changes. Furthermore ' each innovation modifies the level of profit opportunities attached to a firm or rather creates a new firm, provided with profit opportunities of its own . . .'. Robert Triffin, *Monopolistic Competition and General Equilibrium Theory* (Cambridge: Harvard Univ. Press, 1940), pp. 169–171.

[1] It is for this reason that I would reject the attempt of Andreas G. Papandreou to construct a concept of the firm which takes into account the firm as an organization without ' doing violence to [the economist's] main conceptual schema '. He holds that ' organization theory and the economist's theory of the firm are seen to converge, in fact, as soon as we introduce organizational techniques as data into the latter, side by side with the technological data '. Andreas G. Papandreou, ' Some Basic Problems in the Theory of the Firm ', in *Survey of Contemporary Economics*, Vol. II, B. F. Haley, Editor (Homewood: Irwin, 1952), pp. 187–188.

The economist's ' main conceptual schema ' is designed for the theory of price determination and resource allocation, and it is unnecessary and inappropriate to try to reconcile this theory with ' organization theory '. E. S. Mason in his *Comment* (Ibid., pp. 221–222) is justified in confessing a ' lack of confidence in the marked superiority, *for purposes of economic analysis*, of this newer concept of the firm, over the older conception of the entrepreneur '. If the study of the process of growth of firms is a legitimate purpose of economic analysis, however, then I think it can be shown that the ' newer concept of the firm ' is of importance, but it should be clearly defined as a concept to be used for a different purpose from that of the traditional one.

The Firm as an Administrative Organization

It is not the *degree* of abstraction involved in the ' theory of the firm ' that makes it inappropriate as a starting point for an analysis of the growth of the firm, but rather the *kind* of abstraction. That is to say, the purpose of any study, ' theoretical ' or ' empirical ', must be defined, and only those aspects of ' reality ' selected which are relevant. Irrelevant matters are rightly ignored, or ' abstracted ' from. The object of the present study is to investigate the growth of the industrial (non-financial) firm as an economic entity in the broadest sense. But an economic analysis of the growth of firms has meaning only if there is some economic function or economic effect with respect to which the size and growth of firms is relevant. Consequently the definition of what constitutes a ' whole firm ' for our purposes depends upon its essential function as an economic entity in the economy.

The Function and Nature of the Industrial Firm

Probably it would be generally agreed that the primary economic function of an industrial firm is to make use of productive resources for the purpose of supplying goods and services to the economy in accordance with plans developed and put into effect within the firm. The essential difference between economic activity inside the firm and economic activity in the ' market ' is that the former is carried on within an administrative organization, while the latter is not. The growth in the ' size ', however defined, of the industrial administrative unit is of importance because the larger this unit is, the smaller is the extent to which the allocation of productive resources to different uses and overtime is directly governed by market forces and the greater is the scope for conscious planning of economic activity. The chief controversies over the social desirability of large firms come either from disagreement over the question whether the increase in the scope for conscious planning in the organization of production and distribution has ' good ' or ' bad ' results, or from disagreement over the question whether extensive administrative organization of productive resources, if ' good ', should be in private hands and conducted in response to opportunities for private profit.

One important aspect of the definition of the firm for our purposes, then, involves its role as an autonomous administrative planning unit, the activities of which are interrelated and are co-ordinated by policies which are framed in the light of their effect on the enterprise as a whole.[1]

All such units have some form of central managerial direction responsible for the general policies under which the firm's administrative hierarchy operates. Let us call this 'court of last resort' in the firm 'central management'. In practice it is made up of some combination of the board of directors or committees thereof, the president, and general managers of the firm. Just who is included in central management varies from firm to firm. Whatever the effective group, it must be accepted in practice as the highest authority within the administrative framework of the firm, and must be small enough to make more or less agreed decisions. In general, central management is responsible for establishing or altering the administrative structure of the firm, laying down general policies, and making decisions on those matters where no subordinate executive has been authorized to act or where no clear-cut principles have been set out in advance. In the last category are usually included at least the major financial and investment decisions of the firm, and the filling of the top managerial posts.

In the ideal case, once an administrative framework has been created within which the 'bureaucracy' of the firm functions smoothly, and once policies are laid down which are accepted as guides for decisions by the administrative personnel of the firm, no further intervention by the central management is required so long as each decision that has to be made is of a type and scope envisaged in established policies. This does not mean that all decisions must be rigidly circumscribed in advance and no exercise of judgment allowed, but merely that there must be no confusion as to who makes any given decision, the principles that shall be considered in making it, and the scope of its effects.[2]

---

[1] The concept of autonomy must not be taken too rigidly. It certainly can never mean complete independence of any external forces nor that there are not areas in which a firm is forced to adopt certain policies against its will. Furthermore, a firm can voluntarily give up its autonomy in certain respects, for example when it joins a price cartel, without becoming any the less a firm thereby.

[2] The brief discussion here of the nature of the firm's administrative organization is not intended to contribute anything to the extensive literature on business organization nor to discuss the important issues in organizational theory or the significant problems connected with determining the functions of different groups within the firm. I am concerned only with those aspects of these large and complex subjects which will be of use in the theory of the growth of the firm to be developed later. However, the general view of the administrative functioning of a firm set forth here does not differ fundamentally from the concepts underlying the analyses of Simon, Barnard, Papandreou, and similar 'organization theorists', nor is it at variance with the findings of

It is evident that there will be great variations in the number, range, and nature of the tasks of the central management of different firms, depending on the structure of the firm, the preferences and ambitions of the top management group, and the extent to which the firm is faced with external changes which require action not provided for under existing arrangements. In an unchanging environment, for example, an established firm that had succeeded in creating optimum administrative procedures and framing an optimum set of policies could operate successfully without any overt acts of ' central management ' at all; even new appointments could conceivably be made according to established regulations. Managerial and supervisory functions could be carried on by appropriate officials on different levels in the firm within the framework provided by the administrative organization and existing policy ' directives '.[1] In such circumstances, the administrative problem is ' solved ' once an appropriate administrative structure has been established.

Adaptation to change poses somewhat different problems. One type of problem is the adjustment to ' short-run ' conditions—the day-to-day, month-to-month decisions required in operations—and another is the adjustment to ' long-run ' changes and the making of ' long-range ' policies. While undoubtedly no clear dividing line can be drawn between the two types of problem, the former certainly requires many decisions that cannot be individually ' cleared ' with central management in the large firm; in consequence, organizational structures and procedures have been evolved which not only permit the making of such decisions on almost all administrative ' levels ' in the firm but also ensure at the same time a high degree of consistency among decisions. Similarly, techniques and procedures

Gordon. Cf. H. A. Simon, *Administrative Behavior* (New York: Macmillan, 1945), Chester Barnard, *The Functions of the Executive* (Cambridge: Harvard Univ. Press, 1938), Andreas G. Papandreou, ' Some Basic Problems in the Theory of the Firm ', op. cit., and R. A. Gordon, *Business Leadership in the Large Corporation* (Washington, D. C.: Brookings Institution, 1945).

[1] Compare the views, for example, of analysts as different as Nicholas Kaldor and Chester Barnard. Although Kaldor's frame of reference is that of the ' theory of the firm ' and thus fundamentally different from ours, nevertheless his conclusion, that ' the technically optimum size of the individual firm becomes infinite or indeterminate ' in equilibrium, rests on essentially the same conception of the administrative task as that set forth here. Op. cit., p. 71. Barnard on the other hand, points out that ' Systems of cooperation are never stable, *because of changes in the environment and the evolution of new purposes . . . adjustment of cooperative systems to changing conditions or new purposes* implies special management processes and, in complex cooperation, special organs known as executives or executive organizations '. Chester Barnard, op. cit., p. 37 (Italics added).

have been created to enable central management to deal with the longer-run problems without excessive congestion at the top.

Size and Administrative Co-ordination

The question has often been raised and is still debated, whether a firm can get 'too big' to enable both kinds of problem to be efficiently handled. At one time it was almost universally agreed that such a point would be reached as a firm grew in size, that management or 'co-ordination' was a 'fixed factor' which would necessarily give rise to diminishing returns and increasing costs of operation at some point. Behind this notion lay the common-sense deduction that consistency of behaviour requires 'single-minded' direction which is clearly limited in its possible scope simply because the capacity of any human being is finite. The conclusion that the limited capacity of the individual will limit the size of firms has not, however, been supported by events—at least not in any clearly discernible way. Now it seems likely that this 'single-mindedness' can be achieved through an appropriate form of organization inherited from the past and operated by people, also inherited from the past, who share a common tradition, who are accustomed to the organization and to each other, and who thus form an entity which works with sufficient consistency and efficiency in broad areas to make unnecessary any one individual having to comprehend and direct its detailed working. It is this capacity of the firm to alter its administrative structure in such a way that non-routine managerial decisions requiring real judgment can be made by large numbers of different people within the firm without destroying the firm's essential unity, that makes it so difficult to say with confidence that there is a point where a firm is too big or too complex to be efficiently managed.

At the present time at least it cannot be said that the large firms in the economy are unable effectively to compete with smaller firms nor that they tend to break up because of bureaucratic inefficiency and sheer inability of management to handle unwieldy size. On the contrary, the big firms appear extremely successful and there is no evidence at all that they are managed inefficiently when enough time has been given them to make the adjustments and adaptations of their administrative framework appropriate to increasing size. The techniques for decentralizing administrative organization have been developed to a fine point, and the task of central management is apparently not one of attempting to comprehend and run the entire organization, but rather to intervene in a few crucial areas and to set the 'tone' of the organization. Operating control is effected largely through accounting devices which, to be sure, are highly centralized, but which place the task of 'coordination' in an entirely different framework, and incidentally permit the use of extensively mechanized techniques in carrying it out.

Apparently what has happened as firms have grown larger is not that they have become inefficient, but that with increasing size both the managerial function and the basic administrative structure have undergone fundamental changes which profoundly affect the nature of the 'organism' itself. The differences in the administrative structure of the very small and the very large firms are so great that in many ways it is hard to see that the two species are of the same genus. We say they are because they both fulfil the same function, yet they certainly fulfil it differently, and it may be that in time the differences will become so great that we should consider in what sense they can both be called industrial 'firms'. In other words, I think the question whether firms can get 'too big' for efficiency is the wrong question, for there is no reason to assume that as the large firms grow larger and larger they will become inefficient; it is much more likely that their organization will become so different that we must look on them differently; we cannot define a caterpillar and then use the same definition for a butterfly.

Industrial Firms and Investment Trusts

To be more specific, consider the difference commonly held to exist between an industrial operating firm and a financial investment trust. The one organizes production, the other holds financial instruments. But as an industrial firm becomes larger and larger, and its operations become progressively more decentralized with the lines of authority becoming more tenuous, permitting greater autonomy in the constituent parts, is it not possible that the firm will increasingly acquire the characteristics of a financial holding company, lose those of an industrial firm, and finally become virtually indistinguishable from an investment trust? And if this does happen, can we safely assume that the principles that govern the growth of an industrial firm are equally applicable when the organization is metamorphosed into an essentially financial firm?

I do not think we can assume this; on the contrary, the techniques suitable for analyzing the growth of firms engaged in the actual organization of production and distribution are probably very different from those required for the analysis of the growth of a purely financial organization. It follows, therefore, that if we *define* the industrial firm with reference to its administrative framework within which industrial activities are co-ordinated, we can be concerned with its growth only as such an organization. It is the ' area of co-ordination '— the area of ' authoritative communication '[1]—which must define the boundaries of the firm for our purposes, and, consequently, it is a firm's ability to maintain sufficient administrative co-ordination to satisfy the definition of an industrial firm which sets the limit to its size as an industrial firm. Nevertheless, it cannot be presumed that if this limit is exceeded the organization has become ' inefficient '; it may merely have become a different type of organization to which a different type of analysis must apply.

'Authoritative communication' can consist on the one extreme of the actual transmission of detailed instructions through a hierarchy of officials and, on the other, of the mere existence among a group of people of observed and accepted policies, goals, and administrative procedures established at some time in the past. Difficulties arise when we consider whether various kinds of ' cross currents ' of ' authoritative communication ', particularly those arising from outside the firm, weaken the applicability of this criterion of the limits of the firm.[2] This is basically the problem of how the ' area of administrative co-ordination ' can be discovered in practice, in other words, how we shall determine the size of any given firm at any given time.

In earlier times, perhaps, before the predominance of the corporate form of enterprise, a firm was reasonably identifiable. The extensive and elusive lines of control in the modern business world, however, make it more difficult to decide what should be included within a given firm. The unincorporated individual proprietorship, the partnership, and the small corporation without subsidiaries create in general no trouble, but the large corporation with many subsidiaries over which it exercises some degree of control does. The concept of the firm developed above does not depend on

[1] The term is that of Chester Barnard, and is peculiarly appropriate because it leaves room for informal as well as formal ' communications ' which are accepted as ' authoritative '.

[2] See, for example, Papandreou's discussion, op. cit., pp. 194-5.

the ramifications of stock ownership or the mere existence of the power to control, although extensive stock ownership may, and probably should, be one important consideration in any attempt to apply it. On the other hand, long-term contracts, leases, and patent license agreements may give an equally effective control, and yet cannot easily be treated in the same way. If a corporation is controlled by, or because of stock ownership is classed as a subsidiary of, a larger corporation, it is part of the larger firm only if there is evidence of an administrative co-ordination of the activities of the two corporations—for example, if its production programme or its expansion plans are co-ordinated with those of the larger firm or if its financial decisions are made by or jointly with those of the larger firm. It should not be classed as part of the larger firm if it appears to operate independently of the *managerial* plans and *administrative* arrangements of the larger firm, for in this case any influence the larger firm exerts should be viewed as an extension of economic power and not as an extension of the co-ordinated planning of productive activity. Thus, although many industrial firms are more or less loosely bound together by a common source of finance or a strong element of common ownership, the mere existence of such connections is not of itself sufficient evidence that administrative co-ordination is effective and adequate enough to justify calling such a grouping a firm.[1]

Suppose, for example, one giant firm buys a strong minority interest in another giant sufficient to give it partial financial control, but makes no attempt to co-ordinate the productive activity of the other firm with its own. It may interfere at strategic points, but its power to do so may be no greater than that attaching to other relationships, for example, to the position of a powerful customer. Is the former firm bigger than it was before? The purchase may have been, from the point of view of the buyer, primarily a transformation of assets, say from cash to securities, and it is not even clear that the

[1] The National Resources Committee distinguished eight more or less clearly defined interest groups on the basis of interrelations between the corporations included in the group through interlocking directorates, minority stockholding, financial connections, etc. The largest, for example, it called the ' Morgan-First National group ', ' not because the separate companies are controlled by either J. P. Morgan and Co., or by the First National Bank of New York or by these two institutions in combination but rather because much of the interrelation between the separate corporations allocated to this group is brought about through these two institutions '. The eight interest groups included 106 of the 250 largest corporations and nearly two-thirds of their combined assets. See National Resources Committee, *The Structure of the American Economy*, Part I (Washington, D.C., 1939), pp. 160 ff.

buyer has extended its area of control, for financial ' size ' in terms of financial power over productive resources is not necessarily affected by such a transformation of assets.

It is essential to distinguish between the extent of economic power and the size of the industrial firm proper. For an analysis of economic power there is no doubt that the industrial firm is *not* the most relevant unit; indeed, individual men as well as corporations may extend their economic power by extending their ownership interests, and an attempt to define the firm according to power groupings would produce too amorphous a concept to handle; the analysis of ' growth ', of expansion and size would be of a very different kind. It is not clear in what economic sense a ' financial group ' can be called a ' firm ', or what reinvestment in such a ' firm ' would mean. The extension of power of this sort is largely a matter of legal opportunities, legal institutions and legal limitations; yet in some sense a firm, in extending its financial power, is continuing to ' grow ', but in another sense than ours; its growth still has economic significance, not so much for the organization of production as for the concentration of financial control and for the possibilities of using such control to manipulate the use of resources in the interest of the financial power of the controlling group. Public policy, or the hazards of financial speculation, and not conditions relating to the organization and administration of production, set the limits to this kind of growth.

Continuity in the ' History ' of a Firm.

Not only is it sometimes difficult to determine the boundaries of a particular firm at any given time; it is also sometimes difficult, in tracing the growth of a firm, to determine when a succession of legally different firms should be treated as events in the history of a single firm.

In practice the name of a firm may change, its managing personnel and its owners may change, the products it produces may change, its geographical location may change, its legal form may change, and still in the ordinary course of events we would consider it to be the same firm and could write the story of its ' life '. Whether the continuity was maintained by bankers in times of crisis or by the ingenuity of a clever promoter is irrelevent, provided that the firm neither suffered such complete disruption that it lost the ' hard core ' of its operating personnel, nor lost its identity in that of another firm. There may have been reorganizations, but a reorganization in itself generally requires a continuing group of at least the subordinate administrators to effect it. Just as in political life the state ' survives ' many changes of government and many reorganizations of its administrative organs, but not partition nor complete annexation by other states, so the identity of the firm can be maintained through many kinds of changes, but it cannot survive the dispersal of its assets and personnel nor complete absorption in an entirely different administrative framework.

A firm may fail to survive in any identifiable form without failing in a financial sense at all. A very successful firm may find it more profitable to merge with another firm, and thus lose its identity, than to continue independently. This may be classed as an expansion of the acquiring firm if the latter merely absorbs the former in its own administrative framework and maintains its own identity. Or the merger may be classed as a new firm if the change in the administrative structure of both firms is so extensive that it seems more appropriate to do so. In both cases firms have disappeared without failing. In one case a new firm is created, in the other not.

Survival in this sense is sometimes as much determined by the legal framework within which a firm operates as by the economic ' viability ' of the firm. The laws regulating bankruptcy and corporate reorganization as well as the attitude of the courts may be decisive in many cases. If the firm is a large one with extensive financial connections, the courts are prone to do everything possible to avert its failure as a going concern, and it may operate for years in an insolvent (' failed ') condition. Since any particular firm is a legal as well as an economic institution, these considerations should not be ignored; they are of great practical importance for the growth and size of many firms in the economy, but at the same time they make it extremely difficult to use survival as a test of ' comparative private costs ' or of adaptability to the environment, as some economists have attempted to do.[1]

Clearly all of these problems must be taken into consideration in any empirical study of the growth of firms. For our present purposes it is not necessary to be more precise; it is enough merely to indicate the nature of the unit with which we are concerned and

[1] See, for example, George Stigler, ' The comparative private costs of firms of various sizes can be measured in only one way: by ascertaining whether firms of the various sizes are able to survive in the industry.' George J. Stigler, ' Monopoly and Oligopoly by Merger ', *American Economic Review*, Vol. XL, No. 2 (May 1950), p. 26.

some of the criteria which should in practice be applied to define its boundaries. I doubt whether any ' rules ' could be laid down for the application of the criteria which would obviate the necessity of judgment in individual cases, with the consequent differences of opinion. In any event, in most empirical economic investigations the ability of the analyst to adopt a satisfactory definition is severely restricted by the form in which the data appear, and he usually has to make do with a rough approximation of the thing he really wants to measure. Consequently further abstract definition of the firm as an administrative unit would serve no useful purpose here.

THE FIRM AS A COLLECTION OF PRODUCTIVE RESOURCES

The cohesive character that an administrative organization imparts to the activities of the people operating within it provides the justification for separating for analytical purposes such a group from all other groups. The activities of the group which we call an industrial firm are further distinguished by their relation to the use of productive resources for the purpose of producing and selling goods and services. Thus, a firm is more than an administrative unit; it is also a collection of productive resources the disposal of which between different uses and over time is determined by administrative decision. When we regard the function of the private business firm from this point of view, the size of the firm is best gauged by some measure of the productive resources it employs.

The physical resources of a firm consist of tangible things—plant, equipment, land and natural resources, raw materials, semi-finished goods, waste products and by-products, and even unsold stocks of finished goods. Some of these are quickly and completely used up in the process of production, some are durable in use and continue to yield substantially the same services for a considerable period of time, some are transformed in production into one or more intermediate products which themselves can. be considered as resources of the firm once they are produced, some are acquired directly in the market, and some that are produced within the firm can neither be purchased nor sold outside the firm. All of them are things that the firm buys, leases, or produces, part and parcel of a firm's operations and with the uses and properties of which the firm is more or less familiar.

There are also human resources available in a firm—unskilled and skilled labour, clerical, administrative, financial, legal, technical, and managerial staff. Some employees are hired on long-term contracts and may represent a substantial investment on the part of the firm. For some purposes these can be treated as more or less fixed or durable resources, like plant or equipment; even though they are not ' owned ' by the firm, the firm suffers a loss akin to a capital loss when such employees leave the firm at the height of their abilities. Such human resources may well be on the payroll for considerable periods of time even though their services cannot be adequately used at the time. This may sometimes be true also of daily or weekly workers. They, too, may often be considered as a permanent ' part ' of the firm, as resources the loss of whose services would involve a cost—or lost opportunity—to the firm.

Strictly speaking, it is never *resources* themselves that are the ' inputs ' in the production process, but only the *services* that the resources can render.[1] The services yielded by resources are a function of the way in which they are used—exactly the same resource when used for different purposes or in different ways and in combination with different types or amounts of other resources provides a different service or set of services. The important distinction between resources and services is not their relative durability; rather it lies in the fact that resources consist of a bundle of potential services and can, for the most part, be defined independently of their use, while services cannot be so defined, the very word ' service ' implying a function, an activity. As we shall see, it is largely in this distinction that we find the source of the uniqueness of each individual firm.

Ideally, the size of a firm for our purposes should be measured with respect to the present value of the total of its resources (including its personnel) used for its own productive purposes. This is almost impossible to discover in practice, and in the absence of any really satisfactory measure of size we have a wide choice depending on our purpose. For the most part, though not always, the analysis of the growth of firms that is developed in the following chapters is most directly applicable to their growth measured in terms of fixed assets. This measure has its own disadvantages and there is no overwhelming reason for choosing it rather than another; adaptations of the analysis can be made to meet the requirements of nearly

---

[1] I am avoiding the use of the term ' factor of production ' precisely because it makes no distinction between resources and services, sometimes meaning the one and sometimes the other in economic literature.

any measure, and at appropriate points in the following pages various problems of measurement will be discussed. As I have indicated, however, the use of total assets may distort the size of the firm as a productive unit because it includes the ' placements '[1] of a firm which may be large simply because the firm is unable to expand its productive operations fast enough to make full use of its cash resources. This point will become clearer as we analyze the process of growth.

THE MOTIVATION OF THE FIRM

We cannot leave this discussion of the functions and nature of the firm without making a few remarks about the ' motivation ' of the firm—why it acts as it does. It is reasonable to assume that the people making decisions on behalf of a firm are acting in the light of some purpose, yet it is notoriously difficult to discover the true purposes of anyone. On the other hand, purposive behaviour cannot be understood if one does not know what the purpose is. Therefore if the economist is to understand the behaviour of firms he must make some assumption about why they do what they do. The more he believes that his assumption corresponds to the true motives, the greater will be his confidence in a theory designed to explain the behaviour of firms. It is possible that his theory may be very useful for analysis and for prediction, even if he is not very happy about the ' realism ' of his assumption, but the theory will not satisfy his desire to ' understand ', and his confidence in it will be correspondingly reduced.

Accordingly, a theory purporting to explain the process of growth of firms can be useful on two levels. It can be useful even if it only presents a logical model yielding conclusions which seem to correspond to actual events that can be ' observed ' in the growth of actual firms. But it will be even better if it helps us to understand the actions behind these events. For this, if we assume that firms act for a purpose, we must find an acceptable assumption as to *why* they act. In either case, the usefulness of the theory can only be tested against facts relating to particular firms.[2]

[1] This ingenious term was proposed by Joan Robinson to denote ' the purchase of titles to debts or shares ', and is used here to mean investments outside the firm which, though perhaps conferring some power to influence the behaviour of other firms, do not bring the other firms into the administrative orbit of the investing firm. See Joan Robinson, *The Accumulation of Capital* (London: Macmillan, 1956), p. 8.

[2] In this it differs fundamentally from the ' theory of the firm ', the primary usefulness of which lies in the extent to which it explains the response in the economy as a

The Profit Motive

The assumption on which this study is based is simply that the growth of firms can best be explained if we can assume that investment decisions are guided by opportunities to make money; in other words that firms are in search of profits. But then the further question arises, why should a *firm*, or more accurately the managers of a firm, always want to make more profits? The ' profit motive ' when applied to individuals is usually based on the psychological assumption that increases in income and wealth have personal advantages for the individual which will spur him to obtain what he reasonably can.[1] The profits of a firm do not confer such advantages on individuals unless they are paid out as income to individuals. From this it is often concluded that a firm is interested in making profits in order to pay out dividends to owners. To be sure, some dividends must be paid to maintain the reputation of the firm and, in particular, its attractiveness to investors as the source of future funds, but why should a firm ever want to pay out more than this if owners are not in a position to force it to do so?[2]

Almost every large firm to-day is appropriately classed as ' management controlled ', that is to say, most firms that have grown large (according to any of the commonly accepted criteria of what is large) have reached a size where either the ownership equity is widely shared, or the owners' control of operations is in practice effectively limited by the managerial bureaucracy.[3] Salaried managers

whole to those types of change which the theory leads us to believe will affect the price and output decisions of firms. The usefulness of this type of theory is not dependent upon whether or not it helps to explain the behaviour of any particular firm (although it may do so); consequently the appropriate test of its usefulness does not lie in its applicability to particular firms.

[1] For this reason, it has sometimes been held that the ' profit motive ' is weaker in the large corporations than in the small firm because the various managers of the former have less personal ' stake ' in the firm's profits. There may be some truth in this, but the extensive use of impersonal accounting records with which to judge the performance of the individual business executives in charge of the various operations of the large firms may have exactly the opposite effect; the ' profit motive ' may be sharpened simply because the personal preferences of the businessmen are more rigidly controlled in the interests of the firm.

[2] ' . . . the distribution of dividends . . . is a problem in the theory of the firm analogous to the problem of the distribution of a consumer's income between consumption and saving, and it presents similar analytical difficulties. From the point of view of the balance sheet a cash dividend represents a simple destruction of liquid assets. It is not an exchange, for no asset is created to correspond to the assets destroyed; it is, from the firm's point of view, an act of more or less voluntary consumption. It may be asked, therefore, why should the firm ever perform such an act?' Kenneth E. Boulding, *A Reconstruction of Economics* (New York: Wiley, 1950), p. 113.

[3] This is not only true in a country like the United States where firms have reached a very large absolute size, but also in some smaller countries as well. In the sample of

have little or nothing to gain by paying out more than is necessary to keep existing shareholders from complaining in force, to attract any additional capital that may be needed, and in general to build up or to maintain the reputation of the firm as a good investment. On the contrary, the managers of a firm have much more to gain if funds can be retained and reinvested in the firm.[1] Individuals thereby gain prestige, personal satisfaction in the successful growth of the firm with which they are connected, more responsible and better paid positions, and wider scope for their ambitions and abilities. On this view, dividends would be looked on as a cost to be kept to a level no higher than necessary to keep investors happy; providers of capital, like providers of labour services, must be remunerated, sometimes handsomely, but a desire to remunerate them as handsomely as possible is not a plausible explanation of the behaviour of modern corporations.[2] Even owner-managers often seem to be more interested in the growth of their firm than they do in the income they withdraw from it. Small businessmen frequently tend to identify themselves with their firm and to view it as their life's

large industrial firms that I studied in Australia, for example, not one was effectively owner-controlled in spite of the fact that no firm in Australia would be considered large in comparison with United States firms. The only exceptions were some of the wholly-owned subsidiaries of foreign corporations, and even here the influence of management was often very strong in all policy decisions.

[1] This does not mean that executives will keep their own salaries small in order to leave more for profits. On the contrary, the salaries of top executives will tend to get as high as the community will condone or as the conscience of the executives themselves will permit (and sometimes higher if the size of the remuneration can be concealed or ' justified ' by devices such as stock purchase options or other bonuses). The total remuneration of ' top ' executives in a large corporation will be such a small proportion of total profits that its effect on net profits has little practical significance, and the executives know this.

[2] It has been argued, for example, that an enterprise attempts to maximize net income to its owners, but that this is equivalent to maximizing the present worth of its assets, ' for the significance of the assets to the firm is their ability to contribute to the realization of the desired stream of dividends ', that is, ' the stream of cash payments (dividends) to owners (shareholders) having the greatest present worth '. N. S. Buchanan, *The Economics of Corporate Enterprise*. (New York: Holt, 1940), p. 209.

I am saying, on the other hand, that the enterprise must be considered separately from its owners from this point of view. In the calculation of the present value to owners of a dividend stream, dividend payments in the near future should be given more weight than dividend payments in the distant future. For the firm, however, dividend payments in the present may reduce funds available for investment and therefore reduce net earnings in the future, and there is no evidence at all that firms consider that the greater value of present cash payments to owners offsets in any degree the value to be attached to the prospect of higher earnings for the enterprise in the future. Furthermore, the ' significance of assets to the firm ' may just as well be considered to lie in their ' ability to contribute ' to meeting a ' desired ' payroll, a ' desired ' managerial bonus payment, or any other ' desired ' cost. Only if higher dividends in the present are expected to maintain or increase the availability of capital funds in the future will the firm have an incentive to make them.

work, as a constructive creation to which they can point with pride and which they can pass on in full strength to their children. To this end they often prefer to reinvest their profits in the firm rather than outside and to draw only moderately on profits for their personal consumption.

It seems reasonable, therefore, to assume that in general the financial and investment decisions of firms are controlled by a desire to increase total long-run profits.[1] Total profits will increase with every increment of investment that yields a positive return, regardless of what happens to the marginal *rate* of return on investment, and firms will want to expand as fast as they can take advantage of opportunities for expansion that they consider profitable.[2] On this assumption, we would expect a marked tendency for firms indefinitely to retain as much profit as possible for reinvestment in the firm; we would also expect that funds that could not be profitably used would be invested instead of being used substantially to raise dividends, unless higher dividends were required to attract further equity capital. In other words, profits would be desired for the sake of the firm itself and in order to make more profit through expansion. The proposition, thus baldly stated, may to some seem to imply extreme and almost irrational behaviour. Yet it is, to my mind, the most plausible of the various possible assumptions.[3]

Long-Run Profits and Growth

The assumption that the managers of firms wish to maximize long-run profits derived from investment in the enterprise itself

[1] Of course, no assumption about motivation will fit all firms. Indeed, there are many examples of firms that have been ' milked ' by those in a position to do so, and the firm destroyed because individuals in control were more interested in protecting their own interests than those of the firm or even of its owners. See, for example, the story of the destruction of the Amoskeag Manufacturing Company by a group of somewhat unscrupulous trustees. Alan Sweezy, ' The Amoskeag Manufacturing Company ', *Quarterly Journal of Economics*, Vol. LII (May 1938), pp. 473–512.

[2] It should be noted that this in no way gets around the ambiguities inherent in the notion of a ' most profitable ' course of action in an uncertain world where businessmen possess different degrees of optimism and different attitudes toward risk and uncertainty. These questions are discussed in the next chapter.

[3] Compare, for example, the views of one of the more ' popular ' writers on business matters. Speaking of large corporations Herrymon Maurer remarks, ' Such an enterprise is too big for any one owner or group of owners to control. It is run, therefore, not primarily for the stockholders, who have generally become used to a socially approved return on their investment, but for the enterprise itself. The aim of the enterprise is not immediate or even future maximum profits, once thought to be the goal of all enterprise, but healthy future existence, to which the size of profits is an important but secondary consideration '. Herrymon Maurer, *Great Enterprise: Growth and Behavior of the Big Corporation* (New York: Macmillan, 1955), p. 186.

has an interesting implication for the relation between the desire to grow and the desire to make profits. If profits are a condition of successful growth, but profits are sought primarily for the sake of the firm, that is, to reinvest in the firm rather than to reimburse owners for the use of their capital or their ' risk bearing ',[1] then, from the point of view of investment policy, *growth and profits become equivalent as the criteria for the selection of investment programmes*. Firms will never invest in expansion for the sake of growth if the return on the investment is negative, for that would be self-defeating. Firms will never invest outside the firm except eventually to increase the funds available for investment in the firm. To increase total long-run profits of the enterprise in the sense discussed here is therefore equivalent to increasing the long-run rate of growth. Hence, it does not matter whether we speak of ' growth ' or ' profits ' as the goal of a firm's investment activities.

There is no need to deny that other ' objectives ' are often important—power, prestige, public approval, or the mere love of the game—it need only be recognized that the attainment of these ends more often than not is associated directly with the ability to make profits. There surely can be little doubt that the rate and direction of the growth of a firm depend on the extent to which it is alert to act upon opportunities for profitable investment. It follows that lack of enterprise in a firm will preclude or substantially retard its growth, although ' enterprise ' is by no means a homogeneous quality, a problem to which we return in the next chapter.

[1] ' Payout, under an ideal dividend policy in a growth situation, should not exceed the minimum amount necessary to maintain the market position and integrity of existing debt and equity issues and of issues contemplated in the near future '. Harold Quinton, ' Financing Growth Industries in an Inflated Economy: Standards, Theory and Practice ', in *Long-Range Planning in an Expanding Economy* (American Management Association, General Management Series, No. 179), p. 29.

CHAPTER III

THE PRODUCTIVE OPPORTUNITY OF THE FIRM AND THE 'ENTREPRENEUR'

Growth limited by a firm's 'productive opportunity'. The role of enterprise and the competence of management. *Difference between entrepreneurial and managerial competence.* The quality of entrepreneurial services. *Entrepreneurial versatility. Fund-raising ingenuity. Entrepreneurial ambition. Entrepreneurial judgement.* The role of expectations in the productive opportunity of the firm.

The business firm, as we have defined it, is both an administrative organization and a collection of productive resources; its general purpose is to organize the use of its 'own' resources together with other resources acquired from outside the firm for the production and sale of goods and services at a profit; its physical resources yield services essential for the execution of the plans of its personnel, whose activities are bound together by the administrative framework within which they are carried on. The administrative structure of the firm is the creation of the men who run it; the structure may have developed rather haphazardly in response to immediate needs as they arose in the past, or it may have been shaped largely by conscious attempts to achieve a 'rational' organization; it may consist of no more than one or two men who divide the task of management; or it may be so elaborate that its complete ramifications cannot even be depicted in the most extensive chart. In any event, there need be nothing 'fixed' about it; it can, in principle, always be adapted to the requirements of the firm—expanded, modified, and elaborated as the firm grows and changes.

The productive activities of such a firm are governed by what we shall call its 'productive opportunity', which comprises all of the productive possibilities that its 'entrepreneurs' see and can take advantage of.[1] A theory of the growth of firms is essentially an

[1] The term 'entrepreneur' throughout this study is used in a functional sense to refer to individuals or groups within the firm providing entrepreneurial services, whatever their position or occupational classification may be. Entrepreneurial services are those contributions to the operations of a firm which relate to the introduction and acceptance on behalf of the firm of new ideas, particularly with respect to products, location, and significant changes in technology, to the acquisition of new managerial personnel, to fundamental changes in the administrative organization of the firm, to the raising of capital, and to the making of plans for expansion, including the choice of method of expansion. Entrepreneurial services are contrasted with managerial serviecs,

examination of the changing productive opportunity of firms; in order to find a limit to growth, or a restriction on the rate of growth, the productive opportunity of a firm must be shown to be limited in any period.

It is clear that this opportunity will be restricted to the extent to which a firm does not see opportunities for expansion, is unwilling to act upon them, or is unable to respond to them. We shall examine later the considerations determining the kind of opportunity a given firm will perceive, and determining its ability to take advantage of what it does see; but at the very least we have to assume that the firm is eager and willing to find opportunities and is not hindered in acting on them by 'abnormally' incompetent management. In other words the firms with which we shall be concerned are enterprising and possess competent management; our analysis of the processes, possibilities, and direction of growth proceeds on the assumption that these qualities are present in the firm.

It may be that most firms do not grow, that failure is more common than success, that over the long, long period, firms, like Schumpeter's lemmings, follow each other in succeeding waves into the sea and drown, or even that ' death and decay ' are ' inherent in the structure of organization '.[1] These things we do not know. We have neither the facts to disprove them nor convincing theoretical presumptions to support them.

We do know, however, that large numbers of firms *have* survived for long periods, and that there is at present no conclusive evidence that they have reached or are even near the end of the road—that they will not continue growing indefinitely. We know that other firms have been successfully established since the late 19th century,

---

which relate to the execution of entrepreneurial ideas and proposals and to the supervision of existing operations. The same individuals may, and more often than not probably do, provide both types of service to the firm. The ' management ' of a firm includes individuals supplying entrepreneurial services as well as those supplying managerial services, but the ' competence of management ' refers to the way in which the managerial function is carried out while the ' enterprise of management ' refers to the entrepreneurial function. The nature of the organization of a firm and the relationships between the individuals within it have often as important an influence on the competence and enterprise of management and on the kinds of decisions taken as do the inherent characteristics of the individuals themselves. The influence of ' organizational structure ' has been particularly stressed by the ' organization theorists '. See, for example R. M. Cyert and J. G. March, ' Organization Structure and Pricing Behavior in an Oligopolistic Market ', *American Economic Review*, Vol. XLV, No. 1 (Mar. 1955), pp. 129–139.

[1] As Kenneth Boulding has suggested in ' Implications for General Economics of More Realistic Theories of the Firm ', *American Economic Review* (Papers and Proceedings), Vol. XLII, No. 2 (May 1952), p. 40.

which, for our purposes, can be considered the beginning of the 'corporate age' marking the end of a necessarily close connection between the fortunes of firms and the fortunes of families. Many of the relatively young firms show the same characteristics which mark the successful older firms. These are the types of firms we are concerned with; and the fact that we deal only with enterprising firms possessing or able to attract competent management does not prejudge any part of our argument. It merely provides us with a class of firms which are capable of growing. In the absence of such firms there would be no need for a theory of growth.

Enterprise, or 'entrepreneurship' as it is sometimes called, is a slippery concept, not easy to work into formal economic analysis, because it is so closely associated with the temperament or personal qualities of individuals. This extremely personal aspect of the growth of individual firms has undoubtedly been one of the obstacles in the way of the development of a general theory of the growth of firms. It is important, therefore, to examine briefly the nature of 'enterprise' and to indicate its significance and the role it will play in our analysis.

THE ROLE OF ENTERPRISE AND THE COMPETENCE OF MANAGEMENT

There are probably many ways of defining enterprise, but for our purposes it can usefully be treated as a psychological predisposition on the part of individuals to take a chance in the hope of gain, and, in particular, to commit effort and resources to speculative activity. The decision on the part of a firm to investigate the prospective profitability of expansion is an enterprising decision, in the sense that whenever expansion is neither pressing nor particularly obvious, a firm has the choice of continuing in its existing course or of expending effort and committing resources to the investigation of whether there are further opportunities of which it is not yet aware. This is a decision which depends on the 'enterprise' of the firm and not on sober calculations as to whether the investigation is likely to turn up enticing opportunities, for it is, in effect, the decision to make some calculations. This is truly the 'first' decision, and it is here that the 'spirit of enterprise', or a general entrepreneurial bias in favour of 'growth' has perhaps its greatest significance.

The assumption that firms are 'in search' of profits already implies some degree of enterprise, for it is only in the special case where the profitability of expansion in a given direction is obvious and the decision to expand almost automatic that no particular quality of enterprise is required. One sometimes does hear businessmen insist that their firms ' just grew ', that there was no alternative —orders were coming in, demand was high and, pressed by circumstances, the firm simply ' had to expand '. Such conditions do not last indefinitely and the unenterprising firm ceases to expand as this type of opportunity declines. The enterprising firm, if it is a large one, will permanently commit part of its resources to the task of investigating the possible avenues for profitable expansion, acting on the general presumption, supported perhaps by past experience, that there are always likely to be opportunities for profitable growth, or that expansion is necessary in a competitive world. Smaller firms may only periodically be able to consider in what directions expansion might be profitable. In any case, the decision to search for opportunities is an enterprising decision requiring entrepreneurial intuition and imagination and must precede the ' economic ' decision to go ahead with the examination of opportunities for expansion.

Entrepreneurial versus Managerial Competence

' Enterprise ' is obviously closely related to ' ambition ', but even if a firm is not very ambitious it may nevertheless be competently managed. This is particularly true of those smaller firms where there is a close relation between the ' goals ' of owners and the ' goals ' of firms. There are many businessmen, and very efficient ones too, who are not trying always to make more profits if to do so would involve them in increased effort, risk, or investment. In many industries and areas there are a considerable number of firms which have been operating successfully for several decades under competent and even imaginative management, but have refrained from taking full advantage of opportunities for expansion. Many of these are ' family firms ' whose owners have been content with a comfortable profit and have been unwilling to exert themselves to make more money or to raise capital through procedures that would have reduced their control over their firms.

It is not reasonable to expect all businessmen to devote their last ounce of energy to making money. In wage theory, it is well recognized that after a point higher wages may reduce, or at least fail to increase, the supply of labour. There is no reason to assume that businessmen and workers are fundamentally different in this respect. Hence we should not assume that the prospect of higher profits will always call forth the necessary effort from *all* firms in a position to earn them. Very good businessmen may well possess a personal scale of values in which an income greater than that necessary to provide a comfortable position in the community has a relatively low claim on time and effort.

Such men may have a high degree of managerial skill and imagination; they may be hard and efficient workers, but the ambition that would drive other men in the same circumstances to expand their operations in an unending search for more profit, and perhaps greater prestige, may be lacking. There is no inconsistency here: a good businessman need not be a particularly ambitious one, and so long as a firm is dominated by men who are not ambitious always to make profits it is unlikely that the firm will grow very large. Entrepreneurial preferences of this sort provide exactly the same kind of restriction on a firm's growth as does entrepreneurial inability to perceive or to act upon opportunities for profitable growth, for the most effective restriction on the quality of entrepreneurial services is that which stems from a lack of interest in experimenting with new and alien lines of activity, or in moving into new geographic areas. I say that this is the most effective restriction because mere specialization of managerial knowledge and ability is not of itself a serious bar to a firm's branching out into new lines of activity if existing executives are sufficiently interested and imaginative to bring into the firm people possessing the relevant knowledge and ability. Thus, the managerial competence of a firm is to a large extent a function of the quality of the entrepreneurial services available to it.

THE QUALITY OF ENTREPRENEURIAL SERVICES

'Enterprise' is by no means a homogeneous characteristic, and the 'quality' of enterprise, that is to say, the particular types of entrepreneurial service available to a firm, is of strategic importance in determining its growth. Many of the most important services that a firm's entrepreneurs can produce are not the result of 'tempermental' characteristics of the individual men but are shaped and conditioned by the firm itself; this point will be taken up in the following chapters, for the 'production' within the firm of an important class of entrepreneurial services is a significant aspect of its changing productive opportunity. Here I want merely to discuss some of the 'temperamental' aspects of the quality of entrepreneurial services which are not amenable to economic analysis, but which nevertheless cannot be ignored; all we can do is to note them here and at appropriate points consider their effect; we cannot explain them in economic terms.

Entrepreneurial Versatility

Entrepreneurial versatility is a somewhat different quality from managerial or technical versatility. The latter two qualities are primarily questions of administrative and technical competence; the former quality is a question of imagination and vision, which may or may not be 'practical'. To the extent that entrepreneurial ideas are inherently impractical, they are of little use to a firm; but if they are commonplace and short-sighted they are equally useless, and firms whose entrepreneurs are 'dull' are by this fact alone restricted in their growth.[1] It often happens that the horizon of a firm, particularly of a smaller firm, is extremely limited. Content with doing a good job in his own field, the less enterprising entrepreneur may never even consider the wider possibilities that would lie within his reach if only he raised his head to see them. If occasionally he gets a glimpse of them, he may lack the daring or the ambition to reach for them, although he may be an ambitious, efficient, and successful producer in his chosen field or chosen geographical location. 'Specificity' of entrepreneurial resources means that some of the productive services most essential for expansion will not be available to the firm even though all managerial services which are required for efficient operation in a particular field are fully available.

There are many examples of firms with vigorous and creative management which have substantially altered their range of products, sometimes completely abandoning their original products and expanding their total output in spite of unfavourable demand conditions for the old products. But there are also many examples of other firms which have not been able to make the required adjust-

---

[1] Entrepreneurial services are probably required in some degree in most firms, for only if all the activities of a firm are carried out in a well-defined traditional way can one say strictly that no entrepreneurial function is being performed. It is, I think, important to recognize that there are varying degrees and qualities of 'enterprise'. The Schumpeterian 'entrepreneur', though more colourful and identifiable, is too dramatic a person for our purposes. Schumpeter was interested in economic development and his entrepreneur was an innovator from the point of view of the economy as a whole; we are interested in the growth of firms, and here the entrepreneur is an innovator from the point of view of the firm, not necessarily from the point of view of the economy as a whole.

ments. In such cases, failure to grow is often incorrectly attributed to demand conditions rather than to the limited nature of entrepreneurial resources.

The relation between 'demand' and the growth of firms is discussed later (Chapter V). Plainly, however, to the extent that a firm is capable of producing only a given range of products, any limitations on the market for those products will restrict the firm's opportunities for expansion. A versatile type of executive service is needed if expansion requires major efforts on the part of the firm to develop new markets or entails branching out into new lines of production. Here the imaginative effort, the sense of timing, the instinctive recognition of what will catch on or how to make it catch on become of overwhelming importance. These services are not likely to be equally available to all firms.[1] For those that have them, however, a wider range of investment opportunities lies open than to firms with a less versatile type of enterprise, although the mere existence of 'enterprise' is not sufficient, as we shall see, to enable a firm to move indiscriminately into any kind of activity.

It is not helpful to dismiss this lack of vision or of experimenting ambition as an example of a failure to attempt to 'maximize profits', for it is intimately connected with the nature of entrepreneurial ability itself and must be reckoned as a limitation on the supply of specific types of productive services.

Fund-Raising Ingenuity

Difficulties in obtaining capital are often given pride of place among the factors preventing the expansion of small firms, but this is legitimate in only a very limited sense. New, small, and unknown firms do not have the same facilities for raising capital as do established, large, and known firms. Of this there is little question. On the other hand, many small firms without adequate initial financial resources do succeed, do raise capital, do grow into large firms. And they do this, for the most part, by virtue of a special entrepreneurial ability. There are many examples testifying to the ingenuity of the superior businessman in obtaining the funds he needs, and

[1] The history of the Farr Alpaca Company provides an instructive example not only of the effect of enterprising leadership on a small firm's ability to raise capital, create markets, alter its product lines as conditions change, and grow large and powerful, but also of the effect on a successfully established firm of the advent of unenterprising and short-sighted leadership when its original 'productive opportunity' declines. Frances G. Hutner, *The Farr Alpaca Company: A Case Study in Business History* (Northampton, Mass.: Dept. of History, Smith College, 1951).

only if the requisite entrepreneurial ability is lacking can one safely say that a firm cannot attract the required capital.[1]

To be sure, the type of entrepreneurial service needed to raise capital may not be closely related to the type of services needed to run a firm efficiently, for successful raising of capital depends on an entrepreneur's ability to create confidence. Thus small firms have often relied on a division of labour between an inventor or a skilled production manager, and a ' businessman ' able to raise capital and buy on credit. The statement that ' shortage of capital ' is the cause of failure of small firms often means merely that a very particular and possibly very rare sort of entrepreneurial ability is required to launch successfully a new firm on a shoestring or to keep up the rate of net new investment required to enable it to reach a size and position where its general credit standing is well established. On the other hand, even firms with substantial financial resources but indifferent managerial resources can escape trouble only if their entrepreneurs are sufficiently flexible and imaginative to know the kind of management needed by the firm and to attract it. Capital is a problem for the small and new firm in much the same sense that ' demand ' is a problem—the same kind and quality of ' enterprise ' that might be successful in a known and established firm, may not be successful in ' selling ' a firm or its product to cautious and sceptical investors or consumers.[2]

It is, of course, true that ' capital-raising ingenuity ' is most

---

[1] Such, for example, was the ability of W. R. Morris (later Lord Nuffield), the well-known British automobile industrialist, to inspire confidence, that once when he asked for credit from a bank and was turned down, one of the directors of the bank threatened to sell his shares in the bank and finance Morris personally. Morris got the money, for, as Andrews reports, ' . . . in the last resort, what really interests a bank is just this sort of judgment of personalities [and] it was prepared to give way . . . '. P. W. S. Andrews and Elizabeth Brunner, *The Life of Lord Nuffield* (Oxford: Basil Blackwell, 1955), pp. 105–6.

[2] A prominent management consulting firm has stressed the same point: 'Among the resources which are scarce in the economic sense are certain psychological aptitudes including the spirit of enterprise and the ability to organize and run a new firm. There is reason to believe that only a small fraction of the working population possess these talents to an extent which is adequate for success. . . . The allocation of entrepreneurial skills is a controlling factor in the allocation of other scarce resources. A primary function of the entrepreneur is to persuade investors to put up their money. . . . If he does not possess adequate personal funds to launch the business he must then convince others that a differential advantage exists and can be exploited effectively at the proposed level of capitalization. *Thus the size of the capital requirement is not in itself a barrier if a genuine opportunity exists.* The larger the amount required, however, the smaller may be the number of prospective entrants who will be able to gain the confidence of investors either because of their persuasive powers or because of a personal record of success.' Alderson and Sessions, *Cost and Profit Outlook*, Vol. VII, No. 11 (Nov. 1954), p. 2. (Italics added).

easily recognized by its results, for it is difficult to say whether a given entrepreneur possesses the ability to raise capital if he has not yet demonstrated it by raising capital. Therefore it would not be very helpful, even if true, to say that small firms fail to raise capital because they do not have the ability to do so, and I do not mean to argue in this way. There is little doubt that the most ingenious and persuasive of entrepreneurs are at times unable to raise critically needed finance.[1] I want merely to draw attention to the fact that there is a relation between entrepreneurial ability and the finance a firm can attract, and that difficulties attributed to lack of capital may often be just as well attributed to a lack of appropriate entre-preneurial services, in the sense that a different entrepreneur in the same circumstances might well achieve different results.

Entrepreneurial Ambition

The fact that businessmen, though interested in profits, have a variety of other ambitions as well, some of which seem to influence (or distort) their judgment about the ' best ' way of making money, has often been discussed, particularly in connection with the controversial subject of ' profit maximization '. From our point of view it will be useful to distinguish two broad types of entrepre-neurial ambition, which are difficult to define with any precision, but which will be easily recognizable from a brief description of some of their characteristics.

There are some entrepreneurs who seem to be primarily inter-ested in the profitability and growth of their firm as an organization for the production and distribution of goods and services. These we might call ' product-minded ' or ' workmanship-minded ' entrepreneurs or ' good-will builders '. Their interests are directed towards the improvement of the quality or their products, the reduc-tion of costs, the development of better technology, the extension of markets through better service to consumers, and the introduction of new products in which they believe their firms have a productive or distributive advantage. They take pride in their organization, and from their point of view the ' best ' way to make profits is through the improvement and extension of the activities of this organization.

Another type of entrepreneur, whom we might call the 'empire-builder ' is of a different order. He is pushed by visions of creating

[1] For a discussion of the special problems of small firms see Chapter X below.

a powerful industrial 'empire' extending over a wide area. Though he may be concerned with product-improvement and development as a means of maintaining the competitive position of his firm, these activities are delegated to others in the firm, for he is much more interested in the extension of the scope of his enterprise through acquisition or the elimination of competitors by means other than competition in the market. He may hold fairly closely to a particular industrial field with the notion of obtaining a dominant position in that field, or he may range widely in his ventures, taking up anything that appears profitable. The successful empire-building entrepreneur must have initiative and be aggressive and clever in the strategy required to bargain with and successfully outmanoeuvre other businessmen; he requires a keen instinct for purely financial manipulations and a shrewd judgment in assessing not only the value of other firms but also the minimum costs at which they can be acquired, for often whole firms may be bought and sold merely for the ' quick profits ' to be obtained from them.[1] Above all, the empire builder, as the name implies, is a business politician and strategist—upon ability of this type his success depends.

The empire-builder will be of concern in this study only to the extent that he contributes to the process of growth of an industrial firm. Many empire-builders are, as individuals, nothing more than financial speculators, and the collection of firms they acquire never take on the characteristics of a single industrial firm as we have described it. We shall have occasion to examine the effects of ' empire-building ' on the process of growth of a firm, but for the most part the entrepreneurial services that will be of interest to us are of the ' product-' or ' workmanship-minded ' variety.

Entrepreneurial Judgment

Unlike ' versatility ', ' ingenuity ', and ' ambition ', the quality of entrepreneurial judgment is only partly a question of the personal characteristics or temperament of the individual. So far as it does turn on the personal ability of the entrepreneur, we can only treat it as we have treated other types of individual ability, and content ourselves with the observation that firms whose entre-

---

[1] From one point of view, perhaps, these two types of entrepreneur are analogous to the ' Stickers ' and ' Snatchers ' that Hicks has described with respect to pricing policy. The former are concerned with building up a steady business, the latter with quick profits. See J. R. Hicks, ' The Process of Imperfect Competition ', *Oxford Economic Papers*, New Series, Vol. VI, No. 1, (Feb. 1954), pp. 41–54.

preneurs are not capable of reasonably 'sound' judgments do not come within the class of firms with which we are concerned. That there are firms who consistently make mistakes, over-estimate what they can do, guess wrongly the future course of events, no one can doubt, but they do not interest us here; no theory of growth will explain their actions—only a theory designed to explain 'mistakes' or failure.

To a large extent, however, the problem of entrepreneurial judgment involves more than a combination of imagination, 'good sense', self-confidence, and other personal qualities. It is closely related to the organization of information-gathering and consulting facilities within a firm, and it leads into the whole question of the effects of risk and uncertainty on, and of the role of expectations in, the growth of firms. These aspects of the matter can be made an integral part of the analysis of the growth process, because the 'expectations' of a firm—the way in which it interprets its 'environment'—are as much a function of the internal resources and operations of a firm as of the personal qualities of the entrepreneur. This relationship we take up in the following chapters, but first a word about the significance of expectations.

THE ROLE OF EXPECTATIONS IN THE PRODUCTIVE OPPORTUNITY OF THE FIRM

Although the 'objective' productive opportunity of a firm is limited by what the firm is able to accomplish, the 'subjective' productive opportunity is a question of what it thinks it can accomplish. 'Expectations' and not 'objective facts' are the immediate determinants of a firm's behaviour, although there may be a relationship between expectations and 'facts'—indeed there must be if action is to be successful, for the success of a firm's plans depends only partly on the execution of them and partly on whether they are based on sound judgment about the possibilities for successful action. In the last analysis the 'environment' rejects or confirms the soundness of the judgments about it, but the relevant environment is not an objective fact discoverable before the event; economists cannot predict it unless they can predict the ways in which a firm's actions will themselves 'change' the relevant environment in the future. In any event, what the economist sees may be very different from what an individual firm sees, and it is the latter, not the former, that is pertinent to an explanation of a firm's behaviour.

Firms not only alter the environmental conditions necessary for the success of their actions, but, even more important, they know that they can alter them and that the environment is not independent of their own activities.[1] Therefore, except within very broad limits, one cannot adequately explain the behaviour of firms or predict the likelihood of success merely by examining the nature of environmental conditions.

Within the unknowable limits placed by the environment on successful action there is a wide scope for judgment. We shall be interested in the environment as an ' image ' in the entrepreneur's mind, for we want, among other things, to discover what economic considerations, as contrasted with ' temperamental ' considerations, determine entrepreneurial judgments about the environment. The factors affecting the relation between the ' image ' and ' reality ' are not being ignored, but for an analysis of the growth of firms it is appropriate to start from an analysis of the firm rather than of the environment and then proceed to a discussion of the effect of certain types of environmental conditions. If we can discover what determines entrepreneurial ideas about what the firm can and cannot do, that is, what determines the nature and extent of the ' subjective ' productive opportunity of the firm, we can at least know where to look if we want to explain or to predict the actions of particular firms. If we can further establish that there are significant factors expanding the productive opportunity of a firm and causing it to change in a systematic way over time with the operation of the firm, we are on the trail of a theory of the growth of firms.

[1] See my article ' Biological Analogies in the Theory of the Firm ', *American Economic Review*, Vol. XLII, No. 5 (Dec. 1952), pp. 814-15, and the subsequent *Rejoinder* to the *Reply* of A. A. Alchian, ibid. (Vol. XLII, No. 4 (Sept. 1953), pp. 600-609.

CHAPTER IV

EXPANSION WITHOUT MERGER: THE RECEDING MANAGERIAL LIMIT

Two basic assumptions: Some elasticity in supply of management, capital, and labour to the firm; some opportunities for profitable investment in the economy. The nature of the managerial limit on expansion. *The management 'team'. Release of managerial services. Growth of managerial services. The receding limit and the 'static' approach.* The effect of uncertainty. *Uncertainty and information. Risk and unavoidable uncertainty.*

Of the three classes of explanation why there may be a limit to the growth of firms—managerial ability, product or factor markets, and uncertainty and risk—the first refers to conditions within the firm, the second to conditions outside the firm, and the third is a combination of internal attitudes and external conditions. In this chapter we shall be concerned with the analysis of the fundamental and inescapable limits to the amount of expansion a firm can undertake at a given time when there is no rigid external barrier to its expansion, but we shall temporarily ignore expansion through acquisition and merger, reserving that for separate discussion.[1]

External barriers to expansion can be ruled out if we make two basic assumptions: First, that the supply to the firm of capital, labour, or management is not absolutely fixed—that there is not an effective limit to the amount of any kind of productive resource that the firm can obtain at a price; second, that there are opportunities for profitable investment open somewhere in the economy at existing prices and interest rates. These assumptions are, in general, fairly reasonable for many firms. In essence all they do is to ensure that the individual firm is not subject to the same restraints in the same degree as is the economy as a whole. It is reasonable enough to suppose that at any given time in any given economy the amounts of

---

[1] In spite of the fact that acquisition is one of the most significant and powerful methods by which firms do in fact grow, it is useful for analytical purposes to discuss growth by merger separately. In the first place, the factors limiting expansion by merger are much the same as those limiting 'internal' growth but they operate somewhat differently. Secondly, the process of expansion by merger raises difficult problems regarding the nature and function of the firm, and this in turn requires that the consequences of growth by merger be appraised somewhat differently from the consequences of growth by internal expansion.

labour, managerial services, and capital, and the opportunities for profitable investment are more or less fixed and not readily expansible, although they may increase over time. But one of the reasons for treating the individual firm differently from the economy as a whole is precisely that it is not constrained by the same supply or demand functions as is the economy. Different firms will be faced with different supply and demand conditions, and the profitability of investment in different directions will be affected accordingly.

A firm's managers may believe that they can acquire all the resources they want and can sell all the product they can produce at existing prices; alternatively they may recognize that some resources will be available in larger amounts only at higher prices and that some products can be sold in larger amounts only at lower prices or with higher selling costs. Increasing costs of some resources or declining average revenue for some products may make further expansion unprofitable in particular locations and in particular products. But a firm is not confined to particular products or locations by the supply of resources or the demand for products in the market, and provided that there are profitable opportunities open for the use of further or different resources obtainable in the market, the fundamental limit to the productive opportunity of the firm cannot be found in external supply and demand conditions; we must look within the firm itself.

We have to separate three problems: (1) the nature of the factors restricting expansion under the assumed conditions; (2) the influence of these restricting factors on the actual amount of expansion planned under different or changing conditions; and (3) the closely related problem of the composition of the expansion programme of a firm. Only the first of these will be dealt with in this chapter; consequently, while we shall deal with the factors limiting the rate of growth of a firm, we do not yet deal with *changes* in the rate of growth as the firm grows larger or as conditions change.

The Nature of the Managerial Limit

Expansion does not take place automatically; on the contrary, the composition and extent of an expansion programme, as well as its execution, must be planned. Planning implies on the one hand a purpose, and on the other, the organization of resources to accomplish this purpose in some desired manner. Specifically, the creation of an ' optimum ' plan for expansion requires that the resources available to a firm, whether already acquired by the firm or obtainable in the market, be used to ' best ' advantage.[1] It is obvious that if all necessary productive services, including managerial and entre-preneurial services, were available in unlimited amounts at constant prices, and if demand for products were infinitely elastic, no ' best ' plan could be constructed: a larger plan would always be better than a smaller one. It follows that there must be some limiting consideration to which the plan is anchored.

The assumption that a firm can obtain in the market any type of resource or quality of management implies that the specialized resources or managerial abilities it may need to take advantage of market opportunities are available to it. We assume that there are numerous opportunities for profitable production open to the individual firm. Nevertheless, the firm cannot, and in general will not attempt to, extend its expansion plans, and with them its ' management team ', in an effort to take advantage of *all* such oppor-tunities. It *cannot* do so because the very nature of a firm as an administrative and planning organization requires that the *existing* responsible officials of the firm at least know and approve, even if they do not in detail control all aspects of, the plans and operations of the firm; it *will not* even try to do so if the officials of the firm are themselves concerned to maintain its character as an organized unit.

The Management ' Team '

Since there is plainly a *physical* maximum to the number of things any individual or group of individuals can do, there is clearly some sort of limit to the rate at which even the financial transactions of individuals or groups can be expanded. In the present discussion, however, we are dealing with the rate of expansion of the firm as an administrative and planning organization. It follows that the existing officials of such an organization must have something to do with any operations that are to be treated as an expansion of that organization's operations; for to call a group of activities which are unconnected with a given organization an expansion of that organization is a contradiction in terms. This being so, the capacities of the *existing* managerial personnel of the firm necessarily set a limit to the

---

[1] The judgment regarding which of several alternative possibilities is ' best ' will, of course, for any given firm be influenced by the attitude of the firm's entrepreneurs towards risk and by their ideas about the kind of action appropriate to their firm. We need not inquire into these things for the present but merely assume that they remain unchanged from one planning period to the next.

expansion of that firm in any given period of time, for it is self-evident that such management cannot be hired in the market-place.

Businessmen commonly refer to the managerial group as a ' team ', and the use of this word implies that management in some sense works as a unit. An administrative group is something more than a collection of individuals; it is a collection of individuals who have had experience in working together, for only in this way can ' teamwork ' be developed. Existing managerial personnel provide services that cannot be provided by personnel newly hired from outside the firm, not only because they make up the administrative organization which cannot be expanded except by their own actions, but also because the experience they gain from working within the firm and with each other enables them to provide services that are uniquely valuable for the operations of the particular group with which they are associated.

These are services which make possible a working relationship between particular individuals making decisions and taking action in a particular environment, and they determine the efficiency and confidence with which action can be taken by the group as a whole. Unless such services are provided by its members, the group cannot function as a unit. It is for this reason that it is impossible for a firm to expand efficiently beyond a certain point merely by drawing up a management ' blueprint ' for an extensive organization and then proceeding to hire people to fill the various positions and carry out the functions laid down in detailed ' job descriptions '.[1]

If a group is to gain experience in working together, it must have work to do. The total amount of work to be done at any time in a

---

[1] The emphasis I am placing on managerial experience within a firm does not imply that ' outside ' experience is not also very valuable, especially for the ' chief executive ' of a large corporation. It should be remembered that the ' management group ' that we are discussing includes the entire managerial organization, subordinates as well as ' chiefs '. Herrymon Maurer, in his breezy and journalistic, but frequently shrewd discussion of the ' big corporation ', points out that decisions in the modern corporation are ' group ' decisions in which the president, or chief executive, of the corporation may take little direct part; his role being that of providing relatively unobtrusive guidance, lubrication, and conciliation. It is incidentally for this reason that, while the management group as a whole must be experienced in working together, a new ' leader ' from outside with the required personal qualifications and general experience, may very effectively preside over and ' lead ' the ' team '. See Herrymon Maurer, *Great Enterprise: Growth and Behavior of the Big Corporation*. (New York: Macmillan, 1955). Mabel Newcomer also stresses the contribution of outside experience to the successful functioning of the chief executives of large corporations. Her study dealt only with Presidents and Board Chairmen, but from the point of view of the problems of expanding an administrative organization these officials may be of less importance than their subordinates. See Mabel Newcomer, *The Big Business Executive* (New York: Columbia Univ. Press, 1955).

firm depends on the size of the firm's operations, which is in turn limited by the plans and actions of the past and thus by the managerial resources existing at the time the plans were made. Hence not only does existing management limit the amount of new management that can be hired (after all the services of existing management are required even to greet, let alone to install and instruct, the new personnel) but the plans put into effect by past management limit the rate at which newly hired personnel can gain the requisite experience.[1] Extensive planning requires the co-operation of many individuals who have confidence in each other, and this, in general, requires knowledge of each other. Individuals with experience within a given group cannot be hired from outside the group, and it takes time for them to achieve the requisite experience.[2] It follows, therefore, that if a firm deliberately or inadvertently expands its organization more rapidly than the individuals in the expanding organization can obtain the experience with each other and with the firm that is necessary for the effective operation of the group, the efficiency of the firm will suffer, even if optimum adjustments are made in the administrative structure; in extreme cases this may lead to such disorganization that the firm will be unable to compete efficiently in the market with other firms, and a period of ' stagnation ' may follow.[3]

[1] For example, in a report of the National Science Foundation it was noted that one chemical company in their survey ' has developed an optimum rate-of-growth factor expressed in terms of an annual percentage increase in personnel. The percentage is based upon the number of new employees the company believes can be successfully assimilated each year. This percentage is applied to the company's research staff, as well as to the other parts of the firm, but with modifications depending on the amount and kind of research considered necessary to assure overall company growth at the established rate.' National Science Foundation, *Science and Engineering in American Industry*: *Final Report on a* 1953–1954 *Survey* (Wash. D.C.: U.S. Government Printing Office, 1956), p. 48.

[2] The former director of the Tennessee Valley Authority, in discussing the problem of developing atomic energy quickly during the war and of putting production on an industrial basis, mentioned the various types of skills that were needed, and added ' most important of all, these three capabilities of research, industrial techniques and operation had to be *combined* in the same team, with experience in working together as a unit. To go out and create such an organization was out of the question. There was not time.' This was why it was necessary, he says, to turn to already established organizations, such as the Bell telephone system. David Lilienthal, *Big Business*: *A New Era* (New York: Harper, 1953), p. 102.

[3] One student of industrial organization has noted that ' . . . business enterprise today (as we must not cease to observe) is a corporate manifestation and its capacity to cope with larger outputs is not fixed but expands with its structure—and depends on the relation . . . between the governing members of the corporation. . . . Some firms will fail with size because of management, if the immediate jump in size which they attempt is too great; or if the management is incapable of adapting its structure . . .'. P. Sargant Florence, *The Logic of British and American Industry*. (London: Routledge and Kegan Paul, 1953), p. 64.

There is nothing novel about the suggestion that there are difficulties attendant upon the rapid expansion of the activities of a group of individuals bound together by intricate and delicate relationships. In a general way the notion has frequently been put forward in the literature.[1] I am giving so much attention to it in order to emphasize the significance of the experience gained by the personnel of a firm operating in a particular environment. In one form or another the experience of a firm's managerial group plays a crucial role in the whole process of expansion, for the process by which experience is gained is properly treated as a process creating new productive services available to the firm.

In Chapter II a distinction was made between resources and productive services. Managerial services of the type described here are as much productive services in a firm as are the services of engineers in the physical production process; and they are a necessary part of the ' inputs ' of which the productive activities of a firm are composed. Of all the various kinds of productive services, managerial services are the only type which every firm, because of its very nature as an administrative organization, must make use of. Since the services from ' inherited ' managerial resources control the amount of new managerial resources that can be absorbed, they create a fundamental and inescapable limit to the amount of expansion a firm can undertake at any time.[2] It is this as much as anything else that forces new firms to start on a small organizational scale unless they are built on existing firms or unless market conditions are such that they can afford to operate relatively inefficiently for some time.[3]

---

[1] The problem is more often mentioned in the literature of industrial organization than in ' theoretical ' economics, but even the latter has not ignored it. R. F. Harrod, for example, found the ' preponderating answer to the question why an entrepreneur does not move forward along his increasing returns curve ' to be in the fact that his ' enterprise is a delicate organism with complicated labour relations and managerial relations. There is an optimum rate at which labour can be diluted and management formalised in the way required for larger scale; to accelerate beyond this rate would not yield increasing returns '. R. F. Harrod, *Economic Essays* (London: Macmillan, 1952), pp. 184–185.

[2] It should be noted that this analysis applies only to the scale of organization of the firm, not necessarily to the scale of its production measured in terms of capital investment. As we shall see, in Chapter IX, for a given capital expenditure, the organizational problem may be reduced by the use of large-scale equipment and technical processes.

[3] See for example, C. Roland Christensen, *Management Succession in Small and Growing Enterprises* (Harvard: Harvard Univ. Press, 1953) for a good discussion of the managerial limits on the expansion of small firms. He stresses the time it takes to develop a good manager, the lack of experienced personnel in the small firm, and the relation between existing managerial abilities and the development of new men to take on managerial functions.

There are thus two aspects of the nature of the managerial limit on the rate of expansion of a firm: First, the services available from the existing managerial group limit the amount of expansion that can be planned at any time because all plans for expansion absorb some of the services available from this group, and the larger and more complex the plans the more services will be required to digest and approve them on behalf of the firm. Regardless of the extent to which a firm may use managerial and industrial engineering consultants and similar advisory services to improve its organization, to test markets, and to suggest possible avenues of expansion, all advice and proposed plans have to be considered and approved somewhere within the firm's own managerial hierarchy before action is taken. Secondly, the amount of activity that can be planned at a given time limits the amount of new personnel that can profitably be absorbed in the ' next period '.[1]

Release of Managerial Services

If the argument is accepted that a firm will expand only in accordance with plans for expansion and that the extent of these plans will be limited by the size of the experienced managerial group, then it is evident that as plans are completed and put into operation, managerial services absorbed in the planning processes will be gradually released and become available for further planning.

In practice, the planning of expansion, and expansion itself, takes place in a variety of different ways. In small firms where managerial services are supplied by from one to a half-dozen men who are fully occupied in running the firm, expansion sometimes depends on ' overtime ' spurts of activity which can only occur periodically. It may be necessary that each expansion programme be fully completed, the operating problems solved and the expanded firm as a

---

[1] Even when it has been recognized that the existing staff of a firm limits the amount of expansion it can undertake, the relation between the existing staff and the firm's past activities has not always been perceived. Robert Dorfman recognized, for example that ' Within a short time-period [the permanent and integrated staff of the establishment] limit absolutely the opportunities available to the firm, and in a dynamic context they limit the firm's rate of growth '; yet four pages later he commented, ' Dynamic models are particularly adapted to the study of self-contained organizations whose current activities are to a significant extent dependent on their own recent past. They do not appear to be readily applicable to the study of individual firms or industries which can procure necessary equipment from outside and can finance such procurement by recourse to external sources of credit.' Robert Dorfman, *Application of Linear Programming to the Theory of the Firm* (Berkeley: Univ. of California Press, 1951), pp. 86 and 90.

whole running smoothly before managerial services again become available for further planning, even on an ' overtime ' basis.

In the larger firm, on the other hand, the planning and execution of expansion is not a discrete ' step-by-step ' process, but a continuous one not always clearly separable from current operating activities. Plans are made and then revised as events command, and revision also absorbs managerial services. Small projects are constantly being created and executed, some of which are never considered in the higher reaches of management. Large programmes may be worked over by numerous committees for long periods of time and then put into effect gradually and revised in the process. The services of individual men, or all of the services of entire groups of men, are often used entirely in planning for expansion. Whole departments may be devoted exclusively to research into new products, new methods, new uses for old products, and new markets, envisaging the possibility that the firm might expand in new directions. On the other hand, a rapid obsolescence of methods, products, and materials, often forces firms not only to try to keep abreast of all new research, but if possible to lead in the introduction of new things, and the line between planning for expansion and planning ' defensive ' adjustments becomes difficult to draw. Since either type of planning requires that some productive services be free from current productive operations, a kind of ' vertical ' specialization is often effected, in the sense that planning and expansion at all levels are in the hands of personnel largely free of operating duties and more or less continuously occupied with planning.[1]

In any case, it is clear that the creation and execution of plans for expansion absorb managerial services, and that as these services are released they become available for still further planning of expansion if they are not needed to operate the expanded concern. If the amount of managerial services remains constant over time (or decreases) it might be possible for a firm so to organize their

[1] At this point I should like to thank W. W. Cooper for the suggestions and comments in his ' Discussion ' on the paper I presented at the December 1954 meeting of the American Economic Association. (*American Economic Review, Papers and Proceedings,* Vol. XLV, No. 2, May, 1955, pp. 559–565). His remarks were primarily directed to the organizational significance of my analysis but his criticism of my use of the ' traditional definitions and categories of cost ' and his approval of my introducing what he called ' hierarchical arrays of planning agents ' (which, I suppose, is one way of describing the type of organization mentioned above), made me re-think and revise some of my former propositions. On the other hand, I must reject, for reasons which will become clear presently, his criticism of my treatment of ' unused ' productive services.

use that some 'equilibrium' point could be reached in which all managerial services were used in the operation of the firm and none was available for expansion. A very slow rate of expansion with an increasing proportion of existing services devoted to operations and less to planning could conceivably reach this result.[1] Increments of expansion would deliberately have to be reduced as planning services could be absorbed into operating functions. It is not clear why any firm should adopt such a policy, especially if its actions are influenced by the considerations set forth in Chapter II. On the other hand, in small firms whose owner-managers want to substitute leisure for work, excess managerial services can easily be withdrawn from the firm if there is no desire to use them.

The Growth of Managerial Services

In most circumstances one would expect new managerial services to be created in the process of expansion and to remain available to the firm. Any substantial expansion normally involves both acquisition of new personnel and promotion and redistribution of the old. Not infrequently a new subdivision of managerial organization is effected and a further decentralization of managerial functions takes place.

As growth proceeds, the administrative structure of a firm changes—more and more authority becomes delegated 'down the line' and an increasing number of responsible officials with authority to act in defined areas is created. Delegation of *authority* may be virtually 'final' in the sense that the decisions of subordinates in their defined fields are rarely overruled, the officials being transferred if their decisions are not acceptable while the authority attaching to their old positions remains unchanged. But 'final' delegation of *responsibility* is impossible. Responsibility is cumulative in a firm —the very notion of a hierarchy of officials implies this—and must always accumulate in full measure at the 'top', even if in fact responsibility becomes divorced from effective 'authority' in the process.[2] This progressive decentralization of authority and of

---

[1] This possibility was suggested to me by Ralph Turvey. It has significance primarily for the argument to be presented later that unused managerial and other productive services provide an incentive for the expansion of the firm.

[2] Essentially the same point is made in the following statement: '. . . while authority may be divided many ways, responsibility can be only partially delegated. An executive can delegate the responsibility for doing a job, but he still retains the responsibility for seeing that the job is done. It is this complication, more than any other, that makes delegation so difficult. For it means that the top executive is fully responsible for

subordinate responsibility which leaves untouched the cumulation of ultimate responsibility is a necessary condition for continued growth beyond a relatively small size of firm. Its success depends upon a gradual building up of a group of officials experienced in working together. Although administrative ' organization charts ' and other formal statements of the ' lines ' of authority are doubtless an important adjunct to the process, they are, as we have seen, by no means sufficient to create a working team that can proceed efficiently and with confidence.

It is in this necessarily gradual process that new men brought in and the existing personnel of the firm all gain further experience. Not only is there likely to be a generalized improvement in skill and efficiency, but also the development of new specialized services. As was noted above, when men have become used to working in a particular firm or with a particular group of other men, they become individually and as a group more valuable to the firm in that the services they can render are enhanced by their knowledge of their fellow-workers, of the methods of the firm, and of the best way of doing things in the particular set of circumstances in which they are working.[1] Individuals taking over executive functions new to them will find that many things are problems merely because of their relative unfamiliarity. As executives become more familiar with their work and succeed in integrating themselves into the organization under their control, the effort required of them will be reduced and their capacity will therefore become less completely used, while at the same time that capacity will itself have increased through experience and general growth in knowledge.

The experience gained is not only of the kind just discussed which enables a collection of individuals to become a working unit, but also of a kind which develops an increasing knowledge of the possibilities for action and the ways in which action can be taken by the group itself, that is, by the firm. This increase in knowledge not

checking up on everybody below him, and on everything that might affect the company's success.' Perrin Stryker ' The Subtleties of Delegation ', *Fortune* Vol. LI, No. 3 (March 1955), p. 97. See also P. W. S. Andrews, *Manufacturing Business* (London: Macmillan, 1949), pp. 128 ff.

[1] Francis J. Curtis, vice president of Monsanto Chemical Company, is reported to have used the concept of ' value added by manufacture ' in discussing the increasing value of an executive as he gained experience in a firm and rose through the ranks: he is quoted as saying ' that a man 47 years old who had started his business career at 22 at a salary of $3,600 and had advanced to the second echelon from the top management post and a salary of $40,000 was worth to the company, at the very least, $425,000 '. Quoted in *New York Times*, March 29th, 1954.

only causes the productive opportunity of a firm to change in ways unrelated to changes in the environment, but also contributes to the ' uniqueness ' of the opportunity of each individual firm.

Knowledge comes to people in two different ways. One kind can be formally taught, can be learned from other people or from the written word, and can, if necessary, be formally expressed and transmitted to others. The other kind is also the result of learning, but learning in the form of personal experience. There is no easy way of sharply distinguishing these forms of knowledge in the abstract nor is there a satisfactory way of labelling them. The first form is what might be called ' objective ' knowledge. It is knowledge about things which is, conceptually at least, independent of any particular individual or group of individuals. It is, if you like, the ' state of the arts ' as well as the state of knowledge about markets, prices, tastes, etc. If the processes for the transmission of knowledge are not perfect, different groups of individuals may possess this knowledge in different degrees, but if so, it is due to the imperfection in what sociologists would call the ' communication system ' and is not inherent in the nature of the knowledge itself which, by its very essence, is transmissible to all on equal terms. In this it differs from the second form in which knowledge appears—the form I have called experience. Here emphasis is placed on the change in the services human resources can supply which arises from their own activity. Experience produces increased knowledge about things and contributes to ' objective' knowledge in so far as its results can be transmitted to others. But experience itself can never be transmitted; it produces a change—frequently a subtle change—in individuals and cannot be separated from them.

Increasing experience shows itself in two ways—changes in knowledge acquired and changes in the ability to use knowledge. There is no sharp distinction between these two forms because to a considerable extent the ability to use old knowledge is dependent on the acquisition of new knowledge. But it is not exclusively so dependent; with experience a man may gain in wisdom, in sureness of movement, in confidence—all of these become part of his very nature, and they are all qualities that are relevant to the kind and amount of services he can give his firm. Much of the experience of businessmen is frequently so closely associated with a particular set of external circumstances that a large part of a man's most valuable services may be available only under these circumstances.

A man whose past productive activity has been spent within a particular firm, for example, can, because of his intimate knowledge of the resources, structure, history, operations, and personnel of the firm render services to that firm which he could give to no other firm without acquiring additional experience. Let us imagine by way of illustration, that a man's productive services are A, B, C, D, E, F, and G. F and G may be useful only in a particular firm; C, D, and E only to a particular group of firms, B only in manufacturing industry, while A may be of such a general character that it would be useful in any type of productive activity.

Many of the productive services created through an increase in knowledge that occurs as a result of experience gained in the operation of the firm as time passes will remain unused if the firm fails to expand. Thus they provide an internal inducement to expansion as well as new possibilities for it. The unused services created in old as well as in newly acquired personnel through increases in both 'objective' knowledge and experience do not often exist in the open form of idle man-hours but rather in the concealed form of unused abilities. If there is not scope for the full use of the capacity of individuals in the firm to perform administrative services, to plan and execute production programs, to sell the firm's products, to test new ideas, a pressure to expand will be exerted on the firm.[1] A more complete use of the services of individuals is supposed to be made possible by promotion in rank, but this will eventually require enlargement of the firm's activities. While machinery after a point becomes less valuable and is 'downgraded', managerial resources may become more valuable and be 'promoted'. That promotion does not fully take care of the increase in services thus created is the common experience of many firms in periods when growth is slow. Pressure from younger executives for advancement sometimes even creates for the firm a problem of maintaining the morale of personnel and cannot be entirely explained by the hypothesis that individuals tend to over-estimate their own ability.

[1] P. W. S. Andrews has emphasized the same point: ' It has also to be recognized that a progressive business of any size will have another driving force making for this sort of expansion in the young up-and-coming men, pressing for promotion and looking for ways in which to achieve it. If they see a job which would be likely to be profitable and which they could add to their department, they will press for the consequent extension. This will make management more complex. . . .' P.W. S. Andrews, op. cit., p. 282.

The Receding Limit and the ' Static ' Approach

We have shown that there is a limit to the amount of expansion possible in any given period and that in this sense the productive opportunity of a firm can be considered ' fixed '. Thus a ' static ' analysis can be an appropriate method of exploring the conditions of ' equilibrium '. The productive opportunity of the firm *will* be fixed if we assume that no change takes place in external conditions, nor any change in knowledge and, as a consequence, no change in the internal supply of productive services.

These are the traditional static assumptions and by themselves they guarantee that increasing costs of production for all products produced by the firm must at some point set in. So-called managerial diseconomies *must* eventually come into play if it is assumed that there is no change in knowledge and hence no change in the quality and type of managerial service; for it is widely agreed that the only reason managerial diseconomies do not arise is because it is possible for firms to effect a progressive subdivision of function and decentralization of operation. Such a subdivision and decentralization is equivalent to a change in the input of managerial services, and some of these services become available only *after* experience has been gained of a given organization. The assumption that there is no change in knowledge or the state of the arts rules out any change in the quality of managerial services through experience as effectively as it rules out changes in ' objective ' knowledge, for both changes have the same type of significance for the productive services effectively available to the firm. Hence among the unchanged conditions postulated by the static assumptions is the given level of experience of businessmen. The supply of managerial services is thus fixed. The new and unique types of service that come only with experience in a given environment cannot arise. In a static analysis they must be dealt with, in effect, as changes in the parameters of the system.

The assumption of ' complete rationality ' or ' perfect knowledge ' does not change the matter. This assumption has never been held to mean that all men have experienced everything, or that all is known that ever will be known, but only that men ' are supposed to know absolutely the consequences of their acts when they are performed, and to perform them in the light of the consequences.'[1]

[1] Frank H. Knight, *Risk, Uncertainty and Profit* (Boston and New York: Houghton Mifflin, 1921), p. 77.

In addition, perfect knowledge implies that what we have called 'objective' knowledge is uniformly accessible to all. This is all, and under such conditions managerial services unaltered by experience become a fixed factor and diminishing returns must eventually set in.

Once it is recognized that the very processes of operation and of expansion are intimately associated with a process by which knowledge is increased, then it becomes immediately clear that the productive opportunity of a firm will change even in the absence of any change in external circumstances or in fundamental technological knowledge.[1] New opportunities will open up which did not exist at the time expansion plans were made. The factors determining the nature of these opportunities and therefore the direction of expansion will be examined in the next chapter. But first we must analyze the relation between the managerial limit on expansion and the existence of uncertainty and risk, for these are among the most widely accepted explanations of the limits to the expansion plans of firms.

THE EFFECT OF UNCERTAINTY AND RISK

The fact that the future can never be known with accuracy means that the planning of business firms is based on expectations about the future which are held with varying degrees of confidence; furthermore, the expectations are themselves essentially estimates of various possible outcomes in the future of a given action or series of actions. 'Uncertainty' refers to the entrepreneur's confidence in his estimates or expectations; 'risk', on the other hand, refers to the possible outcomes of action, specifically to the loss that might be incurred if a given action is taken.

The question therefore arises what is the effect of uncertainty and risk on the expansion plans of a firm. The most common simple approach to this question assumes that entrepreneurs merely make allowances in their cost and revenue calculations by deliberately and somewhat arbitrarily using lower estimates of demand or higher estimates of costs than those they consider most likely to prevail. Such allowances can deal with both risk and uncertainty,

---

[1] This fact, of course, in no way interferes with the usefulness for price and output analysis of the 'static' assumptions. As we have seen in Chapter II, the 'size' of the firm—that is, the output of a given commodity—in the so-called 'theory of the firm' need not be materially affected by the process described here.

for the estimates on which action is finally taken may take into consideration not only the chance of failure as the entrepreneur sees it, but also the effect of the uncertainty with which he views his estimate of the chance of failure. The result is a reduction of expected profit at every level of output, and in consequence a reduction of planned expansion.[1] If the allowances for either risk or uncertainty increase as the size of expansion plans increases—as they may do if more predictions about the future or longer-range predictions are implicit in the plans—then any tendency for expected revenues to increase or cost to fall as output is expanded is at least partly offset by the effects of risk and uncertainty.

' Risk ' includes both the chance of loss and the significance of whatever it is that might be lost. Thus the ' risk ' to me of gambling $1 is less than that of gambling $100 even though the chance of losing my gamble is the same in both cases, not simply because $100 is more than $1, but because the loss of $100 endangers something other than money that is not endangered by the loss of $1. If I were a millionaire, for example, I might feel as indifferent to losing $100 as to losing $1, and the ' subjective risk ' of the gamble would be the same in both cases—merely my estimate of the probability of loss. But since I am not a millionaire the loss of $100 would endanger my ability to pay my debts, my ability to borrow more funds, or the feeling of security a bank account gives me. I ' can't afford ' to lose $100 for it would endanger my financial position as a whole, whereas if I lose $1 I am not going to care much one way or the other. In the one case the ' risk ' to me is higher than in the other even though the chance of loss is the same.

This is essentially the ' principle of increasing risk ' which has been put forward in different forms in the literature.[2] As a firm expands its investment, the risk to it of a given chance of loss becomes more serious with each increment of investment—its ' wealth ' position becomes endangered if it operates on borrowed money; its liquidity, or ability to meet unexpected demands for cash, becomes precarious as it depletes its own reserves and if its ability to raise money is affected by its heavy illiquid investment. Hence it

[1] In this discussion we shall not be concerned with how the ' optimum ' output, or the ' maximum-profit ' output, should be calculated by the rational entrepreneur under conditions of uncertainty. This is the usual issue under discussion in the economic literature on risk and uncertainty, but is designed to explore problems rather different from the ones raised here, as will become clear presently.

[2] See especially M. Kalecki, ' The Principle of Increasing Risk,' *Economica*, New Series, Vol. IV (Nov. 1937), pp. 440–447.

is concluded that a firm's expansion plans are restricted by ' increasing risk '.

Thus, unless a firm is willing to bear an indefinite amount of risk and cares nothing about uncertainty, risk and uncertainty will, according to accepted theory, necessarily restrict the expansion plans of the firm. In this approach the entrepreneur is treated as a passive ' risk bearer ', for it is implicitly assumed that there is nothing he can do to reduce the uncertainty or risk attached to any course of action; he is faced with it and must bear it or shrink from it depending on his temperament. Uncertainty and risk become a limit to expansion which is ' given ', as it were, and to which the entrepreneur must adjust but which he cannot affect; they therefore become the same type of explanation of the limits to expansion as those which stress the state of demand or the availability of capital.

But is this passive acceptance of risk and uncertainty the only possible entrepreneurial response? Are there not ways open to the entrepreneur of reducing uncertainty and avoiding risk which will enable him to use fully all of the managerial resources at his disposal? If there are such ways, uncertainty and risk, though affecting the amount of expansion that a firm will plan, will affect it only to the extent that managerial resources are unavailable to deal with it. If we admit that uncertainty and risk can limit the amount of expansion and if we agree that managerial resources can also limit the amount of expansion, which one of these provides the effective limit will depend on which comes into operation first. To postulate risk and uncertainty as the fundamental limit on expansion, we should have to show that these alone could be expected to force firms to use their managerial resources at less than full capacity. We shall look first at uncertainty.

Uncertainty and Information

If one is concerned with the effect of uncertainty on the behaviour of a firm, one is concerned with ' subjective ' uncertainty—with the state of mind of the entrepreneur—and with subjective estimates of the risk of disappointment. Subjective uncertainty about the future and, in particular, about the weight to be given to various possible outcomes, can be traced to two sources: ' temperament ' (for example, self-confidence), and an awareness on the part of the entrepreneur that he possesses insufficient information about the factors which might be expected to determine the future course of events. Uncertainty resulting from the feeling that one has too little information leads to a lack of confidence in the soundness of the judgments that lie behind any given plan of action. Hence one of the most important ways of reducing subjective uncertainty about the future course of events is surely to obtain more information about the factors that might be expected to affect it; and it is reasonable to suppose that one of the most important tasks of a firm in an uncertain world will be that of obtaining as much information as is practicable about the possible course of future events.

To obtain information requires an input of resources, and to evaluate the information requires the services of existing management. Therefore one of the important effects of subjective uncertainty is to induce a firm to devote resources to what might be termed ' managerial research '.

Clearly the amount and kind of information required to instil sufficient confidence will vary between firms according to the temperament and even competence of their management (whether entrepreneurs are optimistic or pessimistic by nature, hesitant or self-confident, careless or calculating), but will not necessarily reflect their ' aversion to risk '. A firm requiring a great deal of information may still be willing to accept considerable risk once it believes it has evaluated a situation reasonably accurately. But only the incompetent and thoughtless will act before making an attempt to acquire information on which to base judgments. Similarly there will be differences in the extent to which managerial groups will be willing to act on the advice of ' outsiders ' without examining it. Both general reasoning and discussions with businessmen lead to the conclusion that, unless his own judgment has been involved, a businessman does not like to take responsibility for action in areas he considers within his competence; on other matters he may accept the judgment of people he knows and trusts and who can explain the basis of their judgment, especially if these people also share a general responsibility for the outcome. This is one of the functions of management as a ' team '. The smaller the team and the smaller their combined area of competence, the smaller will be the total of the activities they will be willing to undertake; conversely, the larger the group and the more they are willing to accept each other's judgment and to subdivide areas of competence, the greater can be the absolute amount of activity planned.

As the managerial group becomes larger with the growth of a

firm, the influence of the 'temperament' and personal attitudes of individual men tends to decline as the role of 'group action' rises in importance. The amount and type of information required often becomes relatively standardized and planning becomes subject to defined procedures. The requisite level of confidence in the information and judgments embodied in plans for action become a question of how adequately they meet fairly well-defined standards of planning techniques known and accepted by all members of the managerial group. The improvement of methods of collecting and analyzing information and the emergence of consultant organizations specializing in this type of work and in giving advice to the management of industrial firms not only reduces the managerial effort required of an expanding firm but also goes far to reduce subjective uncertainty.[1]

In principle, therefore, uncertainty which a firm's entrepreneurs refuse to tolerate because it arises from a lack of confidence in the completeness of planning, and which they believe could be eliminated by further information and more detailed planning, will limit expansion only to the extent that managerial resources are limited. When more resources become available, more information can be obtained, more uncertainty eliminated, and more expansion planned. Yet no amount of obtainable information can completely eliminate uncertainty for any expansion plan; and information has no effect on risk. Hence, we have to examine risk and unavoidable uncertainty.

Risk and Unavoidable Uncertainty

As planning proceeds, the point will be reached where a firm believes it is either impossible or too expensive to attempt to obtain further information.[2] At this point the firm must decide

[1] Jacob Schmookler has suggested to me that the progressive development of highly systematic and precise planning techniques may have led to a substantial improvement in firms' notions of what is likely to happen in the future, and thus to a reduction in the incidence of mistakes, especially on the part of the large modern corporations.

[2] The fact that managerial research undertaken to reduce uncertainty involves expenditures to improve the prospects of successful growth, is of some relevance for the economic effects of a profits tax. This has nothing to do with the present discussion, but it has frequently been argued that the imposition of a progressive profits tax will tend to reduce the willingness of a firm to undertake the more risky investments. If, in this context, 'risk' includes both risk and uncertainty, as is reasonable, then the effect of such a tax may be substantially to increase expenditures designed to reduce uncertainty, both because the marginal profit may become of less interest to the firm than before the imposition of the tax, and because expenditures reduce taxable profits. If one of the purposes of a firm in attempting to increase its profits is to provide funds for reinvestment in the firm, as we have argued in Chapter II, there is clearly an increased incentive to disguise such reinvestment as expenditure, if by doing so tax payments can be reduced.

how far, if at all, it should commit resources to the activity in question in the face of the irreducible uncertainty and of its estimates of risk. There is little question that for any given direction of expansion there will be some reasonably definite limit beyond which the firm will not feel that the chance of gain really justifies the risk.

But the expansion plans of a firm are not necessarily limited to any particular type of product or market. Having decided how much it wants to expand in one direction, there is nothing that necessarily prevents it from turning attention to other types of activity, and then to still others. Each new activity requires an increased input of managerial services, not only to obtain sufficient information and develop sufficiently well-worked-out plans to reduce uncertainty to the required level, but also to organize and execute the expansion.[1] As the new activities become less familiar, more effort is required of management, and there is no reason at all to presume that the enterprising firm will reach the point where it refuses to take further action because of the risk of expansion before it has exhausted the capacity of management to deal with new things.

There remains, however, the problem of the increasing risk to the financial position of the firm as expansion proceeds. For the analysis of this problem it is important to distinguish two broad types of response to risk and unavoidable uncertainty. One type leads a firm to adopt conservative financial policies and to restrict its expansion programmes to the extent permitted by funds obtainable from specified sources; the other leads a firm to arrange its expansion plans to minimize the risk. ' Risk-avoidance ' is the goal of the entrepreneur in both cases, but the effect on the expansion programme of the firm is very different.

---

[1] In discussing the problems of expansion with the responsible executives of business firms I made a special point of trying to discover what they felt was the ultimate limit on the expansion they would undertake. In a fair number of cases, the firms voluntarily limited their access to capital, either refusing to borrow at all or borrowing only for limited purposes. In almost all other cases, businessmen agreed that managerial capacities set the limit to expansion. If I was told that expansion was not warranted in existing lines for a variety of reasons and I asked why they did not go into new fields, I was almost invariably told, in effect, ' We are—slowly. We don't know enough to go outside our field too fast. We can hire experts, but we have to know a bit about these things ourselves.' As we shall see later (Chapter VIII), even expansion through acquisition is generally related in some way to the existing activities of the firm, although one advantage of acquisition as a method for expanding into new fields is that a firm can acquire not only assets but an experienced managerial group as well. Furthermore, mergers are often preceded by considerable managerial planning of the selection of companies to be acquired and in the execution of the merger.

The methods of handling risk and unavoidable uncertainty often become more or less part of the tradition of a firm, changed only rarely under the impact of special circumstances. Some firms are known for their preference for large liquid reserves, others for their refusal to borrow outside funds, but still others for the boldness of their financial and expansion policies. Characteristic ways of handling risk often tend to persist in the same firm through generations of managers, although occasionally ' new blood ' may be brought in when a firm lets its tradition stultify its enterprise to such a degree that its standing in the business world deteriorates.

If a firm accumulates and retains liquid reserves to enable it to bear the financial strain should events turn out unfavourably, or if it voluntarily limits its access to capital by refusing to borrow above certain amounts, the amount of capital funds is restricted, sometimes even to those generated within the business itself. But in such cases there is no more reason to attribute the firm's financial conservatism to risk than to the quality of enterprise, provided that there are alternative methods of dealing with risk. It makes little difference, for example, whether a firm refuses to borrow because it is conservative and dislikes risk or because it believes the running up of debts is immoral. The effect on expansion is the same in both cases. We have already seen that for many reasons the quality of enterprise will have a significant effeçt on the expansion plans of firms. Enterprise and attitude towards risk are, in this context, opposite sides of the same coin, for enterprise includes the willingness to take risks. But enterprise includes much more than this; it also includes the willingness to search for ways of avoiding risk and still expand.

Any individual firm may insist on financial policies which will restrict its expansion plans, even refusing to take on the most promising ventures if borrowed money is required, but this is essentially lack of enterprise. On the other hand, even the most enterprising entrepreneur (if he is reasonable) will at some point baulk at accepting further risk, but he will proceed to search for ways of expanding without increasing risk. There are a variety of ways in which firms can arrange the composition of their expansion plans such that the chance of loss is less for a larger programme as a whole than for any part of it. They can, for example, diversify their activities to spread risk, or protect themselves by backward or forward integration; or they can adopt short-run flexible programmes easily changed when conditions change;[1] or they may, as a means of limiting their own liability, set up subsidiaries able to borrow money on their own account to take on some of the more speculative activities.

Practically all of the various ways of reducing risk have the same effect on the demand for managerial services as do the ways of reducing uncertainty. The greater is risk or uncertainty, the more difficult will be the managerial task. Hence the expansion plans of a firm are necessarily restricted by the capacity of management to deal with the increased problems with which they are confronted. But as the management group increases in size, more can be undertaken. Thus it is not easy to untangle the effect of risk and uncertainty on the amount of expansion from the effect of the limited availability of managerial services. A distinction is possible only when it can be shown that managerial services are inefficiently used because expansion is held up not only by attitudes towards risk which are themselves responsible for extremely conservative financial policies, but also by an absence of enterprising attempts to reduce the risk of further expansion. The same ' unwillingness to bear risk ' has a different effect on expansion depending on the other qualities of enterprise with which it is associated.

A firm has a given amount of experienced managerial services available at any one time. Part of these are needed for ordinary

---

[1] Short-run ' flexible ' planning is apparently one of the more common ways in which firms deal with the problems of change. A. G. Hart has a good theoretical discussion of this type of action in Chapter IV of his *Anticipations, Uncertainty, and Dynamic Planning* (New York: Kelley, 1951). And one empirical investigation of the investment plans of a sample of firms in a large industrial area found that: ' Firm capital investment plans are typically limited to a few months. Quick and unpredicted changes in such plans are the order of the day '. Walter W. Heller, ' The Anatomy of Investment Decisions ', *Harvard Business Review*, Vol. 29, No. 2 (March 1951), p. 99.

Incidentally, the importance of management as a brake on expansion was clearly brought out in the same study by Heller. In addition to the curbs on capital investment created by the ' fetish of prosperous companies for internal financing and the inability of limping companies to get outside financing ', he found that ' One of the unforseen —and most interesting—investment barriers encountered was the bottleneck in top engineering and management talent. In more than half of the companies studied, it was flatly stated that either (1) the postwar pace of capital expansion had been too fast for top management and engineering staffs to handle efficiently and digest thoroughly, and a pause for digestion was now in order, or (2) the rate of capital expenditure had been, and still was being, held down to what the very scarce factor of ' brains '— engineering and managerial—could handle. One executive put this point particularly effectively:

' Perfecting a layout involves a minimum amount of managerial and technical work that you can't escape. You have to handle expansion projects in a series, because you simply don't have the necessary number of men of the required caliber around to keep up a doubled-up pace,' Ibid., p. 102.

operations; the rest are available for planning and executing expansion programmes. The effect of uncertainty is to require that some of these available services be used to gather information, digest it, and reach conclusions about the possibilities of action in which the firm has confidence. These conclusions will include estimates of the risk and unavoidable uncertainty attached to the various courses of action. If this is so high that the firm refuses to act, or acts only in a very limited way, then the managerial services which would otherwise have been used in perfecting and executing expansion plans either remain unused or are devoted to alternative plans, including plans for programmes which reduce total risk. If managerial services are fully used, clearly their limited supply is just as much a limit on expansion as is risk and uncertainty. If they are not fully used (and there are no other ' bottlenecks '), then, but only then, can risk and uncertainty alone be identified as the final limiting factor.

Risk and uncertainty clearly do affect the amount and variety of managerial services *required* for expansion, both because they force firms to obtain certain types of information before acting and because they affect the composition of its expansion plans—the variety of products, the time ' structure ', even the type of process used. Thus, for any given amount of experienced managerial services, risk and uncertainty will effectively limit expansion. On the other hand, for any degree of uncertainty, the supply of managerial services will determine the amount of expansion undertaken by the enterprising firm. The overcoming of uncertainty has its cost, which could conceivably be expressed in terms of the managerial services required for the task. But its restraining effect on expansion depends on the resources available to meet it.

CHAPTER V

'Inherited' Resources and the Direction of Expansion

Types of inducement to expand. The continuing availability of unused productive services. *Indivisibility and the 'balance of processes'.* The specialized use of resources. *The heterogeneity of resources. Interaction between material and human resources. The creation of new productive services.* ' Demand ' and the productive resources of the firm. *What is the relevant demand?* The direction of expansion.

The emphasis of our analysis now shifts from the limits on expansion to the direction of expansion. At any time a firm will have a variety of inducements to expand in one or more specific directions; but at the same time there will be a variety of difficulties to be overcome in planning and executing an expansion programme in any given direction. The inducements as well as the difficulties may be outside the firm, in the external world, or within the firm—in the ' internal world ' so to speak. They create conditions enhancing or restricting the profitability or practicability of expansion in particular directions.

The external inducements to expansion are well known and require little discussion. They include growing demand for particular products, changes in technology which call for production on a larger scale than before, discoveries and inventions the exploitation of which seems particularly promising or which open up promising fields in supplementary directions, special opportunities to obtain a better market position or achieve some monopolistic advantage, and similar conditions and opportunities. They also include changes which might adversely affect a firm's existing operations and against which it could protect itself through expansion in particular directions, for example through backward integration to control sources of supply, diversification of final products to spread risk, or expansion of existing or allied products to preclude the entry of new competitors.

External obstacles to expansion are equally well known. They include keen competition in markets for particular products which makes profitable entry or expansion in those markets difficult or necessitates expensive selling efforts and the acceptance of lower profit margins; the existence of patent rights and other restrictions on the use of knowledge and technology; high costs of entry into new areas; or difficulties of obtaining raw materials, labour, or specialized technical or managerial personnel.

While external inducements and difficulties have been widely discussed, little attention has been paid, in a systematic way at least, to the equally important internal influences on the direction of expansion. Internal obstacles arise when some of the important types of specialized service required for expansion in particular directions are not available in sufficient amounts within the firm—in particular when not enough of the managerial capacity and the technical skills required for the planning, execution, and efficient operation of a new programme can be had from among existing experienced personnel. Internal inducements to expansion arise largely from the existence of a pool of unused productive services, resources, and special knowledge, all of which will always be found within any firm. Most of this chapter will be devoted to the explanation of why there will always be unused productive services within a firm, and to a discussion of the significance of the existence of such services for the ' external ' opportunities for expansion as perceived by the firm.

We should note in passing that it is important to discuss separately the nature of the inducements and obstacles to expansion instead of simply ' net inducements to expand ', because different kinds of inducements and difficulties influence differently both the direction and the method of expansion chosen. If, for example, the external inducement to expand is the profitability of a new and growing market, but there is an external obstacle to entry in the form of, say, patent rights, the external inducements and obstacles may both be high and the only feasible method of expansion may be acquisition of another firm. Or, if the incentive to expand is the fear of adverse changes in the external world the effects of which might be offset by diversification, the problem will be one of finding suitable fields in which neither the external nor the internal obstacles to expansion are great. On the other hand, a firm may have a strong internal inducement to expand provided by the presence of an energetic and ambitious entrepreneur with many ideas, but if at the same time the firm lacks the managerial abilities or technical skills to carry his ideas into action, a significant internal obstacle to expansion exists which again will influence the direction, and in particular, the method of expansion chosen. This type of problem will be taken up in the chapters on diversification, merger, and the factors affecting the rate of growth of firms.

THE CONTINUING AVAILABILITY OF UNUSED PRODUCTIVE SERVICES

Resources were defined in Chapter II to include the physical things a firm buys, leases, or produces for its own use, and the people hired on terms that make them effectively part of the firm. Services, on the other hand, are the contributions these resources can make to the productive operations of the firm. A resource, then, can be viewed as a bundle of possible services.

For any given scale of operations a firm must possess resources from which it can obtain the productive services appropriate to the amounts and types of product it intends to produce. Some of the services will be obtained from resources already under the control of the firm in the form of fixed plant and equipment, more or less permanent personnel, and inventories of materials and goods in process; others will be obtained from resources the firm acquires in the market as occasion demands. Although the ' inputs ' in which the firm is interested are productive services, it is *resources* that, with few exceptions, must be acquired in order to obtain services. For the most part, resources are only obtainable in discrete amounts, that is to say, a ' bundle ' of services must be acquired even if only a ' single ' service should be wanted.[1] The amount and kind of productive services obtainable from each *class* of resource are different, and sometimes, particularly with respect to personnel, the amount and kind of service obtainable from each *unit* within a resource-class are different. Having acquired resources for actual and contemplated operations, a firm has an incentive to use as profitably as possible the services obtainable from each unit of each type of resource acquired.

It follows, therefore, that as long as expansion can provide a way of using the services of its resources more profitably than they are being used, a firm has an incentive to expand; or alternatively, so long as any resources are not used fully in current operations, there is an incentive for a firm to find a way of using them more fully. Unused productive services available from existing resources

[1] Even those raw materials which are in principle finely divisible must usually be acquired in minimum-sized bundles because to acquire less than the ' standard unit ' is usually disproportionately expensive. However, this type of indivisibility is probably not of much practical importance.

are a 'waste', sometimes an unavoidable waste (that is to say, it may not pay to try to use them) but they are 'free' services which, if they can be used profitably, may provide a competitive advantage for the firm possessing them.

The next question to explore is whether or not it is likely that a firm will ever reach a position in which it will have no incentive to expand in order to use the productive services available from its existing collection of resources more profitably than they are being used. In the language of traditional theory, can we say that a firm will ever reach an 'equilibrium position' in which there is no further internal incentive to expand?

The attainment of such a 'state of rest' is precluded by three significant obstacles: those arising from the familiar difficulties posed by the indivisibility of resources; those arising from the fact that the same resources can be used differently under different circumstances, and in particular, in a 'specialized' manner; and those arising because in the ordinary processes of operation and expansion new productive services are continually being created.

Indivisibility and the 'Balance of Processes'

The 'balance of processes' or the 'principle of multiples' has been explicitly discussed by economists for over 100 years with respect to the optimum size of plant.[1] It is an application of the principle of the 'least common multiple'. If a collection of indivisible productive resources is to be fully used, the minimum level of output at which the firm must produce must correspond to the least common multiple of the various maximum outputs obtainable from the smallest unit in which each type of resource can be acquired. The principle has usually been applied to machines, and even in this case it has been pointed out that it may be necessary to plan production on a very large scale in order to use all machines at their most efficient level of operation.[2]

---

[1] In 1832 Charles Babbage pointed out: 'the extent of a factory . . . ought to consist of such a number of machines as shall occupy the whole time of one workman in keeping them in order, and in making any casual repairs; if it is extended beyond this, the same principle of economy would point out the necessity of doubling or tripling the number of machines, in order to employ the whole time of two or three skilful workmen'. Charles Babbage, *On the Economy of Machinery and Manufactures* (London: Charles Knight, 1832), p. 175. So far as I know, E. A. G. Robinson was the first to use the term 'balance of processes'. *The Structure of Competitive Industry* (New York: Harcourt Brace, 1932), pp. 31–35. P. Sargant Florence uses the term 'principle of multiples', *The Logic of British and American Industry* (London: Routledge and Kegan Paul), p. 51.

[2] See, for example, E. A. G. Robinson, op. cit., p. 33.

If we consider the *full* range of resources used in any firm of even moderate size, including its various grades of management personnel, its engineers and other technical specialists, the minimum sales force needed to reach its market and sell its products, its financial specialists, and even its research personnel, it is clear that this ' least common multiple ' may call for an enormously large and varied output. This is, of course, the result of the indivisibility of the units in which resources can be acquired; even though a firm may not need a full-time salesman, engineer, or ' trouble shooter ', it is often impossible, or at best difficult and disproportionately expensive, to acquire a part-time one, and for a given scale of operations it may be preferable to acquire a resource and use it only partly than to do without it.

From our point of view, the significance of indivisibility does not lie so much in the fact that large units of equipment or large-scale processes may be most efficient in certain types of production —the traditional examples being railways, public utilities, mass production industries, etc. It lies rather in the fact that a large number and variety of indivisible resources are used. None of these need be very large, but if each is capable of rendering not only different amounts, but also different *kinds* of services, a combination that achieves the full utilization of all of them may perforce call for an output much larger and more *varied* than can be organized by a firm in any given period of time.

We have seen that there is a limit on the amount of expansion a firm can undertake at a given time. Obviously the output that will fully use the productive services available from every one of the firm's resources can be reached only if there is no limit short of this output on the availability of any of the productive services required to produce that output. If we take into account all of the resources used by a firm, the limit on the amount of expansion it can plan may well force it to forgo the use of many of the services available to it. In other words, in putting together the jig-saw puzzle of resources required in an expansion programme, the firm may find that a number of awkward corners persist in sticking out.[1]

[1] For example, an industrial engineer in charge of product development in a firm is quoted as having stated: ' Every time we make something, we have something left over, and have to find something to do with that. And when we find something to do with it we usually find that leaves us with something else. It is an endless process.' A. D. H. Kaplan, *Big Enterprise in a Competitive System* (Washington D.C.: Brookings Institution, 1954), footnote, p. 191.

On the other hand, we have also seen that the limit on expansion is a receding one; in the next period the firm can undertake still more. But in the process of expansion the firm will acquire still further resources, and the individual units of many of these will vary in the amount and type of service they can provide. Thus the 'multiple' will again be changed, and further expansion may be called for; the firm may be aware that this will be the case even before it undertakes the expansion, but be unable to do anything about it; the firm needs the resources it acquires, but at the same time it cannot plan a programme large enough to use all of them fully.

The jig-saw puzzle becomes more complicated when we consider imperfections of the market, whether they arise from transport costs, monopoly positions, competitive differentiation of products, or the necessity of incurring selling costs. The full use of important resources in the process of production may, under such conditions, require some diversification of output because further expansion of some existing product lines may not be warranted by market conditions at the time, even though further growth in demand for these products may be expected in time.

When, however, a firm embarks on a programme of diversification, new types of resources rendering services quite different from those required to produce its older products will be added to the firm's collection of resources, and the problem of 'balancing processes' may carry the firm off in entirely new directions.[1] Examples of this process will be given in Chapter VII, which deals with the economics of diversification.

Since attempts to achieve a 'balance' in the utilization of resources can never reach the continually receding goal, some resources will always be only partly used and some will be used less efficiently than they would have been in the absence of the restriction on the firm's expansion. 'Idle' services range from those available from resources which could be by-products but which are in fact treated as waste-products and thrown away or dumped (because the

---

[1] For a good discussion see P. Sargant Florence, op. cit., pp. 74 ff. He summarizes his argument as follows: 'The economy of integration due to common costs boils down to this, that if a manufacturer has a certain unused capacity in equipment or in research or in finance (or brains of himself and staff), it may pay to "balance up" by taking on as a side line new processes or products using that idle capacity. As a summary to the American survey puts it under the heading of utilization of resources, "diversification may result from an attempt to make full use of managerial or manufacturing capacity"'. op. cit., p. 76. The 'American survey' referred to is that of the Temporary National Economic Committee, *The Structure of Industry*, Monograph 27 (Wash., D.C., 1941).

firm cannot organize the profitable exploitation of them and is unable to sell them) to idle man- or machine-hours at various points in the production process and in the managerial staff.[1] By-products and certain other types of potential joint-products have in fact provided an important basis for expansion for some firms, once the energies of management could be released from the task of expanding the firm's primary lines.

The Specialized Use of Resources

The avoidance of ' idleness ' in resources is only one aspect of the problem posed by the indivisibility of resources and by the logical implications of the ' principle of multiples ' for the planning of the most efficient scale of a firm's operations. A firm has an incentive not only to engage in operations large enough to eliminate pools of idle services, but also to use the most valuable specialized services of its resources as fully as possible. A small firm may employ a chemist to test products in the process of production even though his services as a chemist are required only a few hours a day. The rest of his time may be used in checking inventories or in sending out accounts; he is not ' idle ', but neither are his most valuable services fully used because the firm's output is too small to permit their use. In general, the extent to which a firm can employ the most advantageous division of labour depends on the scale of its operations; the smaller its output the less can resources be used in a specialized manner.

That increasing division of labour is promoted by large markets, and that division of labour makes possible a more efficient use of resources, are among the most firmly accepted of the principles of economics. An increase of efficiency in the use of resources through the specialization of firms on narrowly defined products or processes was early seen to be a characteristic of the ' industrial revolution '.[2] But just as the division of labour in the economy as a

[1] Not all ' idle ' or ' free ' services, however, provide genuinely profitable opportunities. The problems of expanding on such a basis—sometimes called ' burden absorption ' or ' creep ' are discussed in Chapter VII.

[2] See, for example, Allyn Young, ' Increasing Returns and Economic Progress ', *Economic Journal*, Vol. XXXVIII, No. 152 (Dec., 1928), pp. 527–542. The increasing scope for the division of labour led to a disintegration of industry in the sense that different processes became concentrated in separate specialized firms. There is no technological or organizational necessity for division of labour to take this form; it could just as well have taken the form of a division of function between different establishments of the same firm or different parts of the same establishment, and if there were no restrictions on the rate of growth of firms I should expect this to have occurred. One reason for the limit to the rate of expansion of firms was the difficulty of obtaining

whole is limited by the demand for goods and services, so within a firm the division of labour, or the specialization of resources, is limited by the total output of the firm, for the firm's output controls its ' demand ' for productive services. If the chemist in our example were used only as a chemist, then other workers would have to be employed to check inventories and to send out accounts, but the employment of these new personnel becomes profitable only if the scale of operations is enlarged.[1]

Thus specialization can take place within a firm only to the extent that the output of the firm is large enough to justify it. In other words, increasing advantages from further division of labour within a firm are available to the firm only if it can grow. By the same token, to expand efficiently, a firm must effect a division of labour appropriate to the size of the expansion it wants to undertake.

An extreme illustration of this was given earlier in another connection where it was pointed out that if the manager of a small firm is unwilling to relinquish any of his functions to others he creates a bottleneck which will effectively restrict further growth. In general, it can be said that when the demand for specialized services is sufficient to justify the specialization of resources, a failure on the part of a firm to effect at least a minimum degree of specialization will lead to such inefficiency that even firms in highly protected positions will run into serious administrative or technical trouble with a consequent severe increase in costs. A firm with only half a dozen administrative personnel would hardly consider a type of organization where there was no division of labour at all between the administrators, each doing a bit of everything in turn.

As a firm grows in size, therefore, it will reorganize its resources to take advantage of the more obvious opportunities for specialization. As a result, a higher level of output will be required if full use is to be made of resources. In consequence, the process of growth which itself necessitates, at least up to a point, increasing specializa-

capital for expansion by the individual firm, particularly in the days before the corporation or joint-stock company was the normal form of industrial enterprise and equity markets little developed. But in addition the fact that the rate of internal expansion of firms is limited under any circumstances encourages specialization of firms in periods of rapidly growing demand. This limit on expansion was even more restrictive in the 19th century than it is to-day, for acquisition and merger were not common means of expansion before the ' corporate age '.

[1] There are many discussions of the relation between specialization and the scale of operations of firms and there is no need to give an extensive review of the subject here. Among the more comprehensive discussions is that of P. Sargant Florence in the works already cited.

tion, gives rise at the same time to higher and higher 'lowest common multiples' with respect to the output which will fully use the specialized services of the resources acquired. This has been called the 'virtuous circle' in which 'specialization leads to higher common multiplies, higher common multiples to greater specialization'.[1]

The mere fact, however, that a higher level of output is called for does not mean that a firm can plan the amount of expansion necessary to produce it. To the extent that the problem is primarily one of attaining the lowest-cost scale of production for a given product, it seems probable that a point will be reached where no further gains are to be obtained from specialization. But the process is a good deal more than this, for the advantages of using the specialized services of resources may themselves lead a firm to diversify its final output. It often happens, for example, that there are 'stages' in the processes of production in which significant economies can be obtained if sufficient use can be made of specialized resources. This may promote diversification of final output by encouraging a firm to produce a group of products which require the same productive services at some stage, for example, products that use raw materials processed in common, or products that are sold through the same channels of distribution. In other words, if a group of products have costs in common, specialization at the point of common cost may reduce the cost of production of any one of them. And once new products are added, new types of specialized resources may be required at other stages of production or distribution, and a new series of advantages from further specialization in still different directions may become obtainable.

The new resources required are, of course, not only managerial, but include other types of personnel, such as engineers and salesmen, as well as physical resources, such as plant and equipment. Moreover, with larger outputs it becomes profitable to use different kinds of resources and processes. In particular, it becomes profitable to employ expensive capital equipment instead of, or in addition to, specialized labour resources, and to undertake activities unprofitable at smaller scales of operation, such as extensive advertising, market analysis or other research. The total of the productive services available to the firm is again enlarged, and the 'jig-saw' puzzle changes in size. But there is every reason to assume that the problem

[1] P. Sargant Florence, op. cit., p. 52.

of fully using all resources will never be solved, partly for the reasons discussed above, but partly also because *new* services will become available from existing resources—services which were not anticipated when the expansion was originally planned. Why new services from managerial resources will be created has already been demonstrated; but the change in the services of managerial resources also changes the nature of the productive services available from other resources, as well as the significance to the firm's management of existing services. Let us see how.

The Heterogeneity of Resources

Productive services are not ' man-hours ', or ' machine-hours ' or ' bales of cotton ', or ' tons of coal ', but the actual services rendered by the men, machines, cotton, or coal in the productive process. Although it is manifestly services in this sense that are the actual (physical) ' inputs ' in production, a less specific or more indirect definition is usually required when services must be expressed as measurable homogeneous *quantities*, for example, if it is desired to measure the *cost* of certain productive services or to construct technological production functions for certain outputs. In the theory of production, therefore, man-hours, machine-hours, acre-years, or the units in which a resource is acquired, are themselves often treated as the productive services of the resource.[1] Such generalized definitions of services are sufficient where it is the *homogeneity* of the services per unit of any given resource that is relevant for the analysis; they are not useful where the *heterogeneity* of the services contained in resources makes a fundamental difference.

For many purposes it is possible to deal with rather broad categories of resources, overlooking the lack of homogeneity in the members of the category. Economists usually recognize this, stating that for convenience alone resources are grouped under a few heads—for example, land, labour and capital—but pointing out that the sub-division of resources may proceed as far as is useful, and according to whatever principles are most applicable for the

[1]As a matter of fact, no consistent principle other than practical convenience has been adopted. In some circumstances the service itself can be expressed in homogeneous units (BTU's for coal, haulage-miles for trucks) and these units may be used; in others a unit of the resource itself has to be used (bales of cotton, pounds of sulphuric acid). The chief problem is to obtain a classification related to the nature of the resource within which the required degree of homogeneity exists. When a choice of units is feasible, measures that reflect most directly the actual services rendered tend to be preferred.

problem in hand.[1] There are many resources of which each unit is so much like every other unit that a homogeneous category can be established which includes a large number of units. This is true of many materials. With respect to other resources, however, each unit may be so unique that any classification, except one that makes each unit a separate resource, must disregard some heterogeneity; this is the case for human beings, land, and certain other types of resources.

The lack of homogeneity within any classification of resources does not much matter if we are concerned only with the analysis of the supply of particular services (as is true for the most part in the theory of production) and if there is a reasonable relation between the amount of service supplied and the measure of the service in terms of the resource. For some productive services even this is lacking: entrepreneurial services are the classic example and many economists have refused to include entrepreneurs among the ' factors of production ' since the heterogeneous nature of entre-preneurial services is such that no ' unit ' of input can be devised. The number of entrepreneurial man-hours has surely very little relation to the ' amount ' of service rendered. This is equally true of research personnel, of the higher grades of managerial personnel, and similar types of human services. In all these cases, not only is each resource unique, but many of its services are unique in the sense that the same service is not repeatable. An idea produced, a decision made, an important employee grievance settled, are each a unique operation of value in the organization of production— services performed which cannot be repeated. There is no supply curve or production function into which such services can be fitted, but they are nevertheless inputs in production.

The fact that most resources can provide a variety of different services is of great importance for the productive opportunity of a firm. It is the heterogeneity, and not the homogeneity, of the productive services available or potentially available from its resources that gives each firm its unique character. Not only can the personnel of a firm render a heterogeneous variety of unique services, but also the material resources of the firm can be used in different ways, which means that they can provide different kinds of services.

[1] The subdivision cannot go so far that each input is defined as a separate resource, however. The only purpose of devising a ' unit ' of resources or services is to enable us to measure the number of units within a given category. If this number is always one, no purpose is served by the classification.

This kind of heterogeneity in the services available from the material resources with which a firm works permits the same resources to be used in different ways and for different purposes if the people who work with them get different ideas about how they can be used. In other words there is an interaction between the two kinds of resources of a firm—its personnel and material resources—which affects the productive services available from each.

Interaction between Material and Human Resources

For physical resources the range of services *inherent* in any given resource depends on the physical characteristics of the resource, and it is probably safe to assume that at any given time the known productive services inherent in a resource do not exhaust the full potential of the resource. In other words, it is likely that increases in knowledge can always increase the range or amount of services available from any resource. Of the services available, only a few can be profitably used by a given firm at a given time. Some of the services may be alternative uses of the resource—if used for one purpose the resource cannot be used for another; some of them may be suitable only for products which the firm, because of cost and demand conditions, cannot profitably produce under the circumstances; some of them may be useful only in combination with other types of services which the firm cannot obtain at the time.

The possibilities of using services change with changes in knowledge. More services become available, previously unused services become employed and employed services become unused as knowledge increases about the physical characteristics of resources, about ways of using them, or about products it would be profitable to use them for. Consequently, there is a close connection between the type of knowledge possessed by the personnel of the firm and the services obtainable from its material resources.

That the knowledge possessed by a firm's personnel tends to increase automatically with experience means, therefore, that the available productive services from a firm's resources will also tend to change. In addition, there is likely to be an increase in what, for want of a better term, I have in Chapter IV called ' objective ' (or transmissible) knowledge. ' Objective ' knowledge does not automatically increase in the same sense that the experience of a firm's personnel will automatically accumulate as the firm operates. The search for ' objective ' knowledge is, in a way, deliberate and voluntary, but at the same time it is so much a part of the normal operations and thinking of businessmen that it cannot safely be left outside our system of explanation. Economists have, of course, always recognized the dominant role that increasing knowledge plays in economic processes but have, for the most part, found the whole subject of knowledge too slippery to handle with even a moderate degree of precision, and have made little attempt to analyze the effect of changes in the traditional economic variables upon changes in knowledge.[1] We cannot afford to avoid such an analysis here because not only are the significance of resources to a firm and the productive services they can yield functions of knowledge, but—and this is the crucial fact—*entrepreneurs are fully aware of this*. Surely extensive questionnaires are not required to convince us that able businessmen are well aware that the more they can learn about the resources with which they are working and about their business the greater will be their prospects of successful action.

A firm is basically a collection of resources. Consequently, if we can assume that businessmen believe there is more to know about the resources they are working with than they do know at any given time, and that more knowledge would be likely to improve the efficiency and profitability of their firm, then unknown and unused productive services immediately become of considerable importance, not only because the belief that they exist acts as an incentive to acquire new knowledge, but also because they shape the scope and direction of the search for knowledge. If there are circumstances in which a businessman acquainted with the properties of the resources at his disposal (including his own abilities) says to himself regarding a particular resource, ' there ought to be some way in which I can use that ', and subsequently proceeds to explore the possibilities of using it, then we can fairly conclude that he believes there are productive services inherent in that resource about which as yet he knows little or nothing. The effort to discover more about the productive services of a resource may take the form of research into its characteristics or of research into ways of combining its known characteristics with those of other resources.

---

[1] The argument that the patent system stimulates invention implies that increased knowledge is a function of prospective profits. The economics of the argument have never been developed with any rigour but it remains one of the few economic ' models ' in which knowledge becomes a function of an economic variable. See E. T. Penrose, *Economics of the International Patent System* (Baltimore: Johns Hopkins Press, 1951), pp. 34 ff.

If ways of using resources which are not profitable at a given time may nevertheless influence the behaviour of firms, we are justified in adopting a concept of ' economic resources ' that is wider than the concept traditionally used in economic analysis. Resources or services without value are ' free ' goods and are universally excluded from any ' productive ' classification because they have no ' causal relation to conduct '.[1] It is the traditional view that ' superabundant elements in production ' should be taken ' absolutely for granted ' and ignored. ' Only the "possibility" of a situation arising in which a thing would not be superabundant can give it significance or lead to its being consciously considered in any way '.[2] Under the assumptions of the familiar equilibrium analysis, and for the purposes for which it is used, this procedure is undoubtedly correct. From the point of view of the present analysis the fact that here are ways of using free goods in production—air is the classic example—has considerable significance for the conduct of the firm. Some materials required in some types of production are in fact obtained from the air. If we assume that the state of the arts is not fixed and, in particular, that knowledge acquired by one firm is not immediately available to all firms, then the fact that a 'good' is freely available may encourage innovations which use its services in production. The free resource may never become a valuable good in the economic sense, but it may still powerfully influence economic conduct, partly because the services it can render are not free in the same sense that the resource is free.

The Creation of New Productive Services

The import of the above argument is, essentially, that both an automatic increase in knowledge and an incentive to search for new knowledge are, as it were, ' built into ' the very nature of firms possessing entrepreneurial resources of even average initiative. Physically describable resources are purchased in the market for their known services; but as soon as they become part of a firm the range of services they are capable of yielding starts to change. The services that resources will yield depend on the capacities of the men using them, but the development of the capacities of men is partly shaped by the resources men deal with. The two together

[1] Frank H. Knight, *Risk, Uncertainty, and Profit* (Boston: Houghton Mifflin, 1921), p. 61.
[2] Ibid., p. 97.

create the special productive opportunity of a particular firm. The full potentialities for growth provided by this reciprocal change will not necessarily be realized by any given firm, but in so far as they are realized, growth will take place which cannot be satisfactorily explained with reference only to changes in the *environment* of the firm.

The process is one by which new productive services are continually becoming available to a firm, and the new services are not just those of its managerial and other personnel, but also of the physical resources with which a firm works. If these services can profitably be used only in expansion, the firm will have an incentive to expand. Again, it is clear that a firm may be unable to take advantage of all the opportunities that are created by the new services available to it, since the amount of expansion it can plan is limited. But for the enterprising firm, even in the absence of changes in the external world, there is a continuous impelling pressure to expand, arising from the continuous opening up of new areas of profitable expansion.

To be sure, experience of the external world is part of the experience of a firm's personnel. We have concentrated on experience and increasing knowledge of the productive possibilities inherent in the resources of the firm; we should not ignore the effect of increased experience and knowledge of the external world and the effect of changes in the external world. Clearly external changes may also become part of a firm's ' stock of knowledge ' and consequently they may change the significance of resources to the firm. Knowledge of markets, of technology being developed by other firms, and of the tastes and attitudes of consumers, are of particular importance. Moreover, many developments in technological knowledge become available to firms not simply as new knowledge, but physically embodied in the form of the capital equipment they buy.[1]

Many changes in the external world are appropriately treated as environmental changes affecting the rate of growth of firms through their effect on entrepreneurial expectations about productive possibilities. I have placed the emphasis on the significance of the resources with which a firm works and on the development of the

[1] A study of the significance of the fact that new technology becomes embodied physically in capital equipment has been made by W. E. G. Salter in a monograph to be published by the Cambridge Institute of Applied Economics.

experience and knowledge of a firm's personnel because these are the factors that will to a large extent determine the response of the firm to changes in the external world and also determine what it 'sees' in the external world. This is particularly evident when we recognize that changes in the knowledge possessed by the managerial personnel of a firm will not only change the productive services of other resources, but will also change the 'demand conditions' as seen by the firm.

'Demand' and the Productive Resources of the Firm

Within rather wide limits it is reasonable to suppose that consumers' tastes are formed by the range of commodities which are available to them or, at least, about which they know. Business firms have believed this for a long time. The really enterprising entrepreneur has not often, so far as we can see, taken demand as 'given' but rather as something he ought to be able to do something about. Until the disturbing problems of advertising and sales efforts crept into the framework of formal economic analysis along with the theory of monopolistic competition, this fact was largely ignored. The analytical techniques provided by the later developments in theory enabled economists to deal more readily with the fact that very few industrial firms can be in a position closely approximating that of 'pure competition', and led to a clearer realization of the essentially subjective nature of demand from the point of view of the firm. Both when selling expenses are incurred and when possible retaliatory action of rivals is considered, a firm recognizes that the demand for its product can be affected by its own actions. Neither case is of a cumulative expansionary nature. In the former, the cost of selling increases as the firm attempts to reach more and more customers, until the additional revenue no longer justifies further expansion; in the latter, the problem is merely whether there exists a determinate equilibrium price and output or whether fluctuations will occur indefinitely as the firms jockey for position.

What is the Relevant Demand?

When we move from the problem of determining 'equilibrium' with respect to cost and revenue curves for given products (which represent the 'firm' in the 'theory of the firm') to the problem of the growth of firms treated as administrative organizations free to produce any products they choose, we must go further into the meaning of ' demand '. Once it is recognized that the ' demand ' with which an entrepreneur is concerned when he makes his production plans is nothing more nor less than his own ideas about what he can sell at various prices with varying degrees of selling effort, then we ought to consider what influences the development of those ideas. For if entrepreneurial notions about what consumers ought to like have some influence on what is offered to consumers and therefore on what they do in fact like, or learn to like, a mere inquiry into the ' state of demand ' will not enable us to understand the productive activity of entrepreneurs and, in particular, their innovating activity.[1] In a historical sense it is quite correct, though tautological, to say that consumers' demand has determined productive activity, since in the end it is consumers' acceptance of products that decides the matter. For an analysis of the process of change, however, it is necessary to enquire where entrepreneurs get their ideas about what they should produce.[2]

' Demand ' from the point of view of an individual firm relates not only to the amounts of its given products it could expect to sell at varying prices but also to the kinds of product it could expect to sell profitably.[3] The traditional assumption that the first aspect of demand—how much can be sold by the firm—is independent of costs of production for an individual firm has, of course, long been challenged in the theory of monopolistic competition. But even

[1] For example, Alderson and Sessions, marketing and management counsellors, have pointed out that ' . . . it is essential to distinguish between what the economist has called the elasticity of demand and the *more fundamental* factor of plasticity. The intended difference is suggested by the common meaning of the words. " Elastic " refers to something that can be stretched, and " plastic " to something that can be molded. Economics long ago pointed out that demand can be stretched to include more units of a product by the simple expedient of reducing the price. Much less attention has been devoted to the fact that demand can often be remolded into quite different forms. The investigation of plasticity of demand has generally been left to the market analyst rather than to the economist. The re-molding of demand to make a place for new products has proceeded to a spectacular extent in the United States. To make use of the innate plasticity of demand means to find ways of changing the habits and attitudes of consumers. Changing a buying habit means, among other things, making it as convenient as possible for consumers to buy the new product. Changing buying attitudes means *supplying consumers with reasons for preferring the new product* '. *Cost and Profit Outlook*, Vol. 5, No. 8 (Aug. 1952). Italics mine.

[2] In fact, when one considers the almost appalling efficiency with which market specialists, using psychological and sociological information and techniques developed in universities and elsewhere, are learning to manipulate consumers (in the guise, of course, of meeting their unexpressed needs and desires), one almost wonders if in time the whole of the economist's theory of the market will not have to be completely reversed and no place at all left for the notion of independently formed consumer demand. Here, eventually, may lie the real origin of the ' Brave New World ' to come.

[3] Cf. the comment of Alfred Sherrard in 'Advertising, Product Variation, and the Limits of Economics ', *Journal of Political Economy*, Vol. LIX, No. 2 (April 1951), p. 134.

more important for the growth of a firm is the dependence of the
second aspect of demand—what products to consider—on the
possibilities of supply, that is, on the resources and productive
services available to the firm. It has already been pointed out above
that if resources were completely non-specific, a firm could in
principle produce anything. In reality no firm does produce just
anything that happens to be in strong demand at any time in the
economy. It is obvious that the relevant demand for any particular
firm is not defined by the entire range of goods and services being
bought and sold in the economy, or even in the relevant geographical markets. Each firm is concerned only with a limited range of
products and focuses its attention on particular product-markets
selected from the total market. The selection of the relevant product-
markets is necessarily determined by the ' inherited ' resources of the
firm—the productive services it already has.[1] This is true even in
the extreme case of the prospective new firm with no resources at
all other than the entrepreneur himself and what capital he can
raise; the particular productive activities to be undertaken by such
a firm must be chosen from among the alternatives suitable to the
abilities, finance, and preferences of the entrepreneur.

There is no doubt that the growth of demand for a firm's
existing products, as expressed through price changes and other
sorts of market information, is a powerful influence on the direction
of productive activity and on the expansion of firms. The possibilities of expanding such demand by advertising and other sales efforts,
and the effect of such efforts on the productive opportunity of the
firm are not to be underestimated. Other things being equal, it is
usually cheaper and less risky to expand the production of existing
products than to enter new fields. When, therefore, the market
demand for existing products is growing and entrepreneurs expect
continued growth, ' demand ' will appear as the most important
influence on expansion, and current investment plans may be
closely tied to entrepreneurial estimates of the prospects for increasing sales in existing product-lines. If expectations are disappointed,
a sharp curtailment of investment plans may follow. In an expanding
economy, therefore, a large proportion of the growth of existing

---

[1] The point can of course, be expressed in terms of cost: those products for the
production of which a firm is thoroughly unsuited can only be produced at prohibitive
or ' infinite ' cost. This is not a convenient way of looking at the matter, however,
partly because businessmen don't think in these terms about products they don't think
about at all.

firms may be closely related to increased demand for their original types of product in much the same market area. Conversely, in periods of contraction, the decline in demand for existing products will show up in curtailed expansion plans: demand for a firm's existing products will, therefore, have an important influence on the rate of growth of firms,[1] and studies of the investment plans of particular firms at particular times would be expected to show that ' demand '—entrepreneurial expectations regarding the amounts of existing products they could reasonably hope to sell at varying prices—is the controlling influence on expansion.[2]

On the other hand, very few of the older and larger firms in the economy have continued to produce the same type of product throughout their lifetime, even when the demand for that product has risen substantially over the period. Conversely, where demand for the original products has fallen or disappeared, firms have still continued to expand. The growth of almost all large firms has been accompanied by far-reaching changes in the *composition* of the ' demand ' which the firm has considered relevant for its operations. Somehow or other, in spite of the apparently controlling influence on expansion of demand for existing products in the shorter run, the 'product-mix' of firms changes substantially over the longer period.

When firms get into the production of products about which consumers know nothing, and for which there is no market expression at all of consumers' ' wants ', overt demand is clearly irrelevant.[3]

---

[1] We return to this point in Chapter IX.

[2] There have been a number of such studies. See, for example, Robert Eisner, ' Determinants of Capital Expenditures: An Interview Study ', *Studies in Business Expectations and Planning*, No. 2 (Urbana: Univ. of Illinois, 1956). Unfortunately the more extensive study of influences on the investment decisions of firms by John R. Meyer and Edwin Kuh, *The Investment Decision: An Empirical Study* (Cambridge: Harvard Univ. Press, 1957) could not well take into account anticipated demand for a firm's products because of the fact that such anticipations could not easily be related statistically to any of the ' observed ' variables with which the study was concerned. It is, therefore, of no help to us here.

[3] Joseph Schumpeter has stated ' That new commodities or new qualities *or new quantities* of commodities are forced upon the public by the initiative of entrepreneurs . . . is a fact of common experience . . .'. ' The Instability of Capitalism ', *Economic Journal*, Vol. 38 (1928), p. 379. G. H. Evans, Jr., has taken exception to this view, arguing that ' . . . the entrepreneur has been essentially an economic opportunist. . . . This hypothesis is in sharp contrast to the assumption that change in consumers' taste is incident to, and brought about by producers' action.' 'A Theory of Entrepreneurship ', *Journal of Economic History*, Vol. II (1942), p. 142. One may, however, at the same time hold that the entrepreneur is an ' opportunist ' and that he moulds the tastes of consumers if the ' opportunities ' to which he responds arise, not from the market, but from some other source.

Ventures into new products or into the development of new uses for old products are originated by entrepreneurs who believe that they could produce products with the uses of which consumers are as yet unacquainted, but which consumers (whether households or other firms) would find useful and would be willing to buy at prices and in quantities that would be profitable to the producer. Steadfast in their conviction that their products are really useful to consumers, firms may even go into production in the face of active consumer resistance.[1] To be sure, the anticipation of consumer acceptance is a necessary condition of entrepreneurial interest in any product, but the original incentive to a great deal of innovation can be found in a firm's desire to use its existing resources more efficiently. The type of product in which the consumer might be interested is in effect very often suggested to the entrepreneur by the firm's resources, and the possibilities of successfully introducing it largely depend upon them. The general direction of innovation in the firm (including innovation in production) is not haphazard but is closely related to the nature of existing resources (including capital equipment) and to the type and range of productive services they can render. An explanation of the extent and nature of diversification becomes, therefore, an important part of the explanation of the growth of firms, and for this we shall find that ' demand ' is no more important, and is perhaps less important, than the existing resources of the firm.[2]

The significance of all this lies in the fact that ' demand ', in the sense of the *composition* of selling opportunities relevant to a firm's planning, will undergo important changes as the firm grows if growth itself alters the significance and character of the resources

[1] The early struggles of the aluminium industry provide one of the many examples of this. Great difficulties were experienced by the new firm in getting its product recognized and accepted. It was early brought up against ' . . . the greatest truth in all business: that no matter what you have to offer, it takes a vast amount of study and ingenuity to fit it into the world's needs and an unbelievable amount of persistent argument and shoe-leather to sell it '. An official of ALCOA quoted by Robert R. Updegraff in 'Aluminum Tells Its Story ', *The Magazine of Business*, Vol. I, 56. (Aug. 1929), pp. 123-125.

[2] Several writers concerned with the study of the business firm have, of course, made this same point. For example: ' The clue to successful formulation of objectives [for the firm] is to think in terms of what the company can *accomplish* through use of its resources rather than in terms of what products it may happen to find.' Thomas A. Staudt, ' Program for Product Diversification,' *Harvard Business Review*, Vol. 32, No. 6 (Nov.–Dec. 1954), p. 124. And A. D. H. Kaplan speaks of the firm as ' a pool of resources, the profitable use of which requires that products and processes be revised and machines be improved if they are to win and retain market acceptance.' Op. cit,, p. 157.

of the firm, that is, the productive services they can render. This is exactly what happens, as we saw in the previous section. For demand from the point of view of the firm is highly subjective— the opinion of the firm's entrepreneurs.[1]

THE DIRECTION OF EXPANSION

The emphasis of this chapter has been on the relation between the existing resources of a firm and the kind of expansion it undertakes. In planning expansion a firm considers two groups of resources—its own previously acquired or ' inherited ' resources, and those it must obtain from the market in order to carry out its production and expansion programmes. At the very least, some services of the firm's existing management are required, and usually the services of a large number of other ' owned ' and familiar resources as well. There is a close relation between the various kinds of resources with which a firm works and the development of the ideas, experience, and knowledge of its managers and entrepreneurs, and we have seen how changing experience and knowledge affect not only the productive services available from resources, but also ' demand ' as seen by the firm. Such changes, together with the various special advantages accruing to a firm because of the availability of unused productive services within it create the special productive opportunity of a given firm. Unused productive services are, for the enterprising firm, at the same time a challenge to innovate, an incentive to expand, and a source of competitive advantage. They facilitate the introduction of new combinations of resources —innovation—within the firm. The new combinations may be combinations of services for the production of new products, new

---

[1] One businessman has stated frankly that attempts ' to determine what is wanted by the consumer and developing value to meet this want . . . can be based only on opinion. Very often this opinion is that of a few individuals with strong, and perhaps strongly subjective, reactions and rarely is it based on factual data.' In fact he considered this approach ' uneconomical and wasteful of time and money ', preferring free to develop new products from research, and then to sell them to consumers by developing markets using ' adequate techniques '. Quoted in *Research Operations in Industry*. (David B. Hertz, editor). Papers delivered at the Third Annual Conference on Industrial Research. June, 1952. (New York: King's Crown Press, 1953), pp. 232-33.

Even the opposite approach, the ' evaluation of sales intelligence ', is often not really a question of discovering what consumers actually demand, but one of what they ought to demand. ' . . . sales intelligence is the nexus of communication between buyer and seller, guiding the seller toward those areas where ingenuity and sweat can most profitably be expended. . . . The buyer may not even realize that they are problems. But many an industry has been founded on a seller's alert perception of an unnoticed need—that is, his skill in gathering and evaluating his sales intelligence '. Editors of *Fortune, Why Do People Buy?* (New York: McGraw-Hill, 1953), p. 168.

processes for the production of old products, new organization of administrative functions. There is no warrant for assuming, even under unchanging external conditions, that combinations of services that will be effectively available to a firm to-morrow are available to it to-day. Firms, like individuals, occupy at any moment of time a given position with respect to the external world. This position is not only determined by time and space but also by the ' intellectual ' horizon, so to speak; it provides the frame of reference from which external phenomena are approached and the point of origin of all plans for action.

The point of origin for the plans of any firm is circumscribed by the firm's resources and by the services they can render. Although this follows from our definition—since we include ' entrepreneurs ' among the resources of the firm and the range of ideas of entrepreneurs among the services rendered—it gains substantive significance from the fact that no resources, not even entrepreneurial resources, are of much use by themselves; any effective use for them is always viewed in terms of possible combinations with other resources. Hence no firm ever perceives the complete range of services available from any resource, because the range of services recognized is for the most part confined by the management's existing ideas as to possible combinations.

We have said little about the external influences on a firm's choice of product although there can be no question that external influences may be the decisive factor in determining the particular direction of expansion of a given firm. We have ignored them in order to show in what sense they may be decisive. If there are profitable opportunities for increased production anywhere in the economy they will provide for some firm an external inducement to expand. But this alone tells us nothing about their significance for any given firm. New inventions, changes in consumers' tastes, growing demand for particular products are external inducements to expand only for what might be termed ' qualified ' firms—firms whose internal resources are of a kind either to give them a special advantage in the ' profitable ' areas or at least not to impose serious obstacles. On the other hand, there are industries into which entry is so easy that almost any firm can take up production; ' qualifications ' are minimal, the rate of entry very high—particularly of small firms—and mortality also high. In these cases we have to examine not only the characteristics of firms that enter such industries, but also the factors which determine whether they can remain and grow in the industry.[1]

Whether we want to answer the question what external opportunities for expansion are relevant for a given firm, or the question what firm will respond to a given external opportunity, we must examine the productive services available within firms. For in a very significant sense unused productive services are a selective force in determining the direction of expansion.

At all times the productive opportunity of a firm is being shaped by the circumstances mentioned at the beginning of this chapter— internal and external inducements, and internal and external obstacles. In a certain sense each one is decisive, but nothing can be determined by looking at one of them in isolation. The significance of existing resources may not be noticed by particular firms when their management is preoccupied with satisfying the demand for existing products, but it becomes very much in evidence when demand falls off or when entrepreneurs no longer want to put all of the resources available for expansion into existing product lines. But internal inducements to growth are not by themselves profitable opportunities for expansion, nor are external inducements by themselves, as we shall see when we analyze the economics of diversification and examine the interplay of internal and external inducements to expand as well as the effect of both internal and external obstacles. Before turning to this subject, however, we ought to make a slight detour to analyze somewhat more closely the relation between the ' internal economies of growth ' that are implied in this discussion and the economies of ' size '.

[1] An analysis of this question will be made in Chapter X.

CHAPTER VI

THE ECONOMIES OF SIZE AND THE ECONOMIES OF GROWTH

The economies of size. Technological economies. Managerial economies. Economies in operation and expansion. The economies of growth. Disappearing versus enduring economies.

The proposition that enterprising firms have a continuous incentive to expand and that there is no limit to their absolute size (other than that imposed by our conception of the nature of an industrial firm) stands in sharp contrast to the notion of an ' optimum ' size of firm. We have argued that the expansion of firms is largely based on opportunities to use their existing productive resources more efficiently than they are being used. In so far as a firm's opportunities are not based on the possession of gross monopoly power to exploit suppliers or consumers, expansion that uses resources more efficiently may be an efficient process from the point of view of society as a whole as well as from the point of view of the firm. As a result of the process, firms become larger and larger, and the question arises whether the large firms, because they are larger, are more efficient than smaller firms would be. The biggest firms in the economy to-day will continue to grow; does this justify the assumption that they will become more efficient as they grow, that each of their product-lines will tend to become cheaper, of better quality, or more adapted to the wants of consumers because they are produced within the administrative framework of a larger organization? Are there economies still to be obtained which relate directly to the increased size of the firms? Growth is a process; size is a state. Our task now is to examine whether there may be economies from the point of view of the efficient utilization of the resources of society which relate to the process but which do not pertain to the ' state ', to the size that is the by-product of the process.

I shall first describe very briefly the nature of the economies of size as they are usually presented. I shall not go into detail, or attempt to evaluate the relative significance of the different kinds of economies or the conditions under which they arise. The economies of size have been extensively and competently described by others, and my purpose in the following summary is merely to provide a background for some important distinctions and relationships between the economies of size and those of growth.[1]

THE ECONOMIES OF SIZE

Economies of size are present when a larger firm, because of its size alone, can not only produce and sell goods and services more efficiently than smaller firms but also can introduce larger quantities or new products more efficiently. In discussions of the economies of size, so-called 'technological economies', derived from producing large amounts of given products in large plants, are commonly distinguished from 'managerial' and 'financial' economies, derived from improved managerial division of labour and from reductions in unit costs made possible when purchases, sales, and financial transactions can be made on a large scale. Moreover, one can distinguish the economies of size applying to plants from those applying to firms, but the distinction between plant and firm is not coterminous with the distinction between technological and managerial economies.[2] The size of plant is not independent of managerial and financial economies; nor is the size of firm independent of technological economies, although technological economies relate most directly to the organization of plants.

Technological Economies

A plant, unlike a firm, is necessarily confined to a given geographical location. From the point of view of the present discussion

---

[1] Nearly every economist concerned with the operations of industry has at some point discussed this subject from Babbage in 1832, through Marshall, both in the *Principles* and in his *Industry and Trade*, up to the modern discussions of E. A. G. Robinson in *The Structure of Competitive Industry* (New York: Harcourt Brace, 1932), and P. Sargant Florence in *The Logic of Industrial Organization* (London: Kegan Paul, 1933) and *The Logic of British and American Industry* (London: Routledge and Kegan Paul, 1953). Abba Lerner in *Economics of Control* (New York: Macmillan, 1944) and Fritz Machlup in *Economics of Sellers' Competition* (Baltimore: Johns Hopkins Press, 1952) have useful theoretical discussions. A recent review of the empirical work on the subject as well as a penetrating analysis of the theoretical and conceptual problems can be found in Caleb Smith, 'Survey of the Empirical Evidence on Economies of Scale', in *Business Concentration and Price Policy* (New York: Princeton Univ. Press for the National Bureau of Economic Research, 1955), pp. 213 ff. Many competent industry studies, too numerous to list, are also available.

[2] P. Sargant Florence, for example, discusses the economies of large-scale operation in a very generalized form, recognizing that the same fundamental principles lie behind all kinds of economies regardless of which type of organization they apply to. He analyzes three basic principles: the 'principle of bulk transactions'; the 'principle of massed (or pooled) reserves'; and the 'principle of multiples'. *The Logic of British and American Industry*, op. cit., pp. 50–51.

a ' plant ' or ' factory ' is characterized chiefly by the fact that the activities contained within it and the products produced by it, are technically related to each other in the process of production.[1] Technological economies arise, when, under given conditions, for given products, changes in the amounts and kinds of resources used in production permit a larger output to be produced at lower average cost. Thus, technological economies arise when costs can be reduced through an increase in the specialization of labour; the introduction of automatic machinery, assembly-line techniques, or mechanized internal transport systems; the installation of large units of equipment capable of producing larger quantities at lower unit cost if used to capacity; and other similar technical alterations in the organization of production.

The effect of any of these technological changes on costs depends not only on the physical productivity of the combination of ' inputs ', but also on the prices of the factors of production required. Hence the ' technically optimum ' size of plant is as much a function of prices as of technology, and the concept of technological economies of scale can only mean that with given prices of productive resources a larger scale of output permits changes in the productive techniques or resources used which reduce the average cost of output.[2] If the change in the type of input required to produce a larger output of given product in a larger plant calls for an increased use of more expensive resources, costs may not fall as the scale of production is enlarged; while if the same resources were cheaper, the larger size of plant could produce at lower cost. Thus, where capital equipment, or the skilled labour necessary to operate it, is relatively expensive, the introduction of more capital-using mass-production techniques may not reduce costs, and the most efficient size of plant will be smaller than it would have been if capital had been cheap and skilled labour less scarce and expensive. Furthermore, if

[1] Where this is not true, the mere fact that a variety of productive activities are carried on in close geographical proximity does not provide an economic reason for calling the collection of activities a single plant.

[2] It should also be noted that changes in the price of the final product change the opportunity cost of resources used in its production and therefore their value to the firm. This has relevance not only for the optimum size of plant in an industry, but also for the scale on which each of the particular products of a multi-product firm will be produced. In addition, even if an important resource used is specific to a single product and has no opportunity cost to the firm, its value will change with the price of the product and rent should be imputed to the resource and added to the cost of production. This, too, will change the optimum size of plant. For a full discussion of this point see Fritz Machlup, op. cit., pp. 288-299.

transportation costs of either the raw materials or product are high, a given plant may be faced with increasing costs on this account as output expands, and the most profitable size will be appropriately limited.

Moreover, management varies in ability, and the size of plant that can be operated most efficiently by one type of management may not be an efficient size for another type. Small plants run by unspecialized and relatively untrained men may compete successfully with larger plants run by highly skilled, specialized, but more expensive managers, if the lower cost of management offsets the technical disadvantages of the smaller plants.[1]

Nevertheless, it often happens that when the scale of output is increased technological considerations are of such overwhelming importance that changes in managerial or transport costs may be of negligible significance. In this case we may neglect them, and plants taking advantage of technological economies will always be able to produce at lower costs than plants that do not, and will therefore tend to dominate the industry. It may be that this is a fairly common situation in some industries, particularly in the large-scale mass-production industries, such as automobile assembly, and in industries in which the most efficient units of productive machinery are very large. Thus, where technological economies of size are very great and can be achieved without the aid of exceptionally scarce managerial or other productive factors, and when they more than offset any increases in transport costs as output increases, the size of plant that can survive in an industry will have to be large enough to take advantage of the production methods which make possible the bulk of the economies. Technological economies will affect the minimum size of plant, and therefore of firm in such industries. Furthermore, where a large plant is necessary to achieve low-cost production, the minimum amount of expansion planned by firms will have to be fairly large.

The size of plant can be measured in different units, with different results. A measure of plant size in terms of employment will understate the effects of increasing mechanization, while a measure in terms of capital equipment will distort comparison of plant sizes between regions where the relative prices of labour and capital are

---

[1] This is not a fanciful illustration. Executives of a large firm will often tell you of smaller firms—sometimes very small firms—that can produce one of the large firm's products at the same, or lower cost merely because the small firm does not have the managerial overhead of the larger.

different, or between periods of time in which the 'utilization' of plant has changed.[1] Within the same industry, the volume of output is the simplest measure, but between industries 'outputs' are difficult to compare and some other measure must be adopted. In considering the effect of the size of plant on the size and growth of firms we must, of course, measure plant size in the same units as we do the size of firms and, as we shall see in Chapter IX, if we measure both by the capital equipment employed, there is reason to believe that the amount of expansion a given firm can plan is greater when the most profitable plant requires a large amount of capital.

Managerial Economies

Large firms are for the most part multi-plant firms, and economies of multi-plant operation must in general be sought in other sources than technology—in what are known as 'managerial economies' which, in the broadest sense, include marketing, financial, and research economies. Managerial economies are held to result when a larger firm can take advantage of an increased division of managerial labour and of the closely allied mechanization of certain administrative processes; make more intensive use of existing managerial resources by the 'spreading' of overheads; obtain economies from buying and selling on a larger scale; use reserves more economically; acquire capital on cheaper terms; and support large-scale research.[2]

When the scale of production is sufficient to justify a specialized production manager, a sales manager, a financial expert, or a specialist in raw-material buying, for example, each function is performed more efficiently than it would be if all of them were performed by one person. An excellent plant manager may make a poor financial

---

[1] W. Baldamus, in a very interesting article, has attempted to explain the trend in plant size in a variety of industries in Britain in terms of the relative influence of 'mechanization' and 'utilization'—the former being an increase in output by expansion of plant, the latter, by more intensive utilization of existing plant. He found that in the 'newer' industries, mechanization, i.e., 'technical progress', tended to be largely responsible for rapid increases in the size of plants. 'Then there comes a point when utilization takes over as the dominant principle controlling expansion, because it is no longer possible or profitable to carry through radical technological innovations.' W. Baldamus, 'Mechanization, Utilization and Size of Plant', *Economic Journal*, Vol. LXII (March 1953), p. 68.

[2] The reader will notice the similarity between the discussion of the economies of size and our earlier analysis of the significance of unused productive services. Since the two discussions are merely different ways of analyzing the same problem, some repetition is inevitable but will help to bring out the relation between the economies of size and those of growth.

manager indeed. For any given degree of specialization, further economies may often be obtained by the spreading of managerial overhead cost, thus reducing average cost as output increases. This may be possible because existing personnel have been used below capacity or because a given function or service required for one scale of operation need not be increased proportionately for larger outputs. For example, if a firm employs a specialized market-analyst, a research staff, specialized salesmen, etc., it may be able to plan an output appreciably larger than the minimum that would justify their original employment, thereby reducing their cost per unit of product. The same market forecast may be as applicable to an output of 500,000 units as for an output of 50,000 units.

When a larger output can be produced more cheaply than a smaller output without any change in the basic techniques of production, simply because at the larger scale of operations it is possible to employ specialized managerial talent and so to improve the efficiency of operations that savings are made in materials cost, labour cost, fuel or any other cost, these savings may properly be classed as a managerial economy.

If some of the reduced cost can be attributed to basic changes in production techniques (e.g., to increased mechanization), managerial economies may in some sense be part of the total economies of the changed scale of operation, but they could never be identified. This is, of course, the more usual case in reality. Managerial and technological reorganization proceed *pari passu* with increasing size of firm, and an increased division of managerial labour is often necessary to keep costs from rising at higher levels of output; it is an adaptive procedure undertaken to permit economies to be achieved elsewhere. Average cost of output may fall, but average managerial cost may remain constant or even rise as additional managerial personnel are acquired to fulfil more and more specialized functions. Even when it is possible to prevent the emergence of managerial diseconomies by appropriate distribution of the various managerial functions among a larger number of people, it does not necessarily follow that any part of the lower cost of the greater output can be traced to managerial economies.

Economies in selling come from the increased efficiency resulting when specialized sales personnel can be employed and from producing on a scale sufficiently extensive to use their full selling capacity. There may also be economies in large transactions and in handling bulk quantities; in maintaining an advertising programme sufficiently extensive to ensure not only that all potential consumers are aware of the kind and quality of product available, but also to persuade them that they need the particular brand of product produced; and in maintaining a sales organization that reaches well forward towards the final consumer.

A great deal of the superior selling strength of large firms as compared with small firms is undoubtedly of a ' monopolistic ' variety in the economist's sense. This is especially true of advertising and certain types of sales technique. Yet, given the natural imperfections of the market—the difficulties consumers have in knowing what is available at what prices and where, the physical arrangements necessary to bring seller and buyer together, the education and instruction of the consumer in the use and care of products, and similar problems—selling efforts on a sufficient scale to meet the real needs of consumers are surely an economy for the consumer as well as an economy of scale for the firm. There is little doubt that the smallest firms often cannot support sales organizations and programmes that can serve consumers as effectively in such matters as do those of larger firms.

A firm needs a variety of ' reserves ' for its operations, whether they be financial reserves, inventory reserves, or labour reserves. With large-scale operations, economies may be obtained in the use of reserves because the proportion of total reserves to total operations can be reduced. This is perhaps most clearly seen in the case of inventories. A small repair shop, for example, may have to carry reserves of parts of all kinds but cannot easily adjust the size of the stock of each part to requirements because the small scale of operations makes it difficult for the firm to predict with any accuracy the demand for any particular part. The larger shop, on the other hand, can, because of the ' law of large numbers ', predict demand for each kind of part more successfully and can more accurately trim its inventories accordingly.[1]

---

[1] This principle has been particularly stressed by P. Sargant Florence under the name of ' massed (or pooled) reserves '. He points out that it appears in ' . . . many apparently unrelated branches of economic life . . . in schemes for the decasualization of labour at the docks and underlies all forms of insurance and banking; the reserves that are economized may in fact be labour, liquid monetary resources, stocks of goods and materials or any other factors in production, when the demands upon these factors are somewhat uncertain in their incidence.' It illustrates ' the statistical theory of large numbers, based on probable error, that the greater the number of similar items involved the more likely are deviations to cancel out and to leave the actual results nearer to the

As to financial economies and the ability to support research, the advantages of the large firm are self-evident. The greater security offered to investors, the easier access to capital markets, the greater public knowledge of the firm's existence and operations, the fact that it is often cheaper within limits to borrow large than small amounts of funds, all combine and interact to place the larger firm in a better financial position than the smaller firm. When research personnel and laboratories are expensive, the large firm can support more of them than can the small firm; when research operations require a large organization, the larger firm can administer them with greater ease than can a smaller firm. We shall have more to say in the next section about the question of treating the ability to support research as an ' economy of size '.

Economies in Operations and Economies in Expansion

Clearly the several economies of size refer to different types of operation: some economies apply to the large-scale production of given products in large plants; some relate to the improved utilization of an administrative organization and have no relevance to any particular products; some are economies in expanding into new fields. But when we speak of ' economies ' that apply to different sets of existing products, or to new products yet to be created or produced, we have departed a considerable distance from the traditional economies of large-scale production, commonly called ' increasing returns '.

The theoretical analysis of the economies of large-scale production has been developed most rigorously within the context of the ' theory of the firm ' or ' theory of the industry ' and refers, not to the growth of an administrative organization producing many products, but rather to the production of a given product on an increasing scale. In this context, the costs of production as the ' firm ' grows in size, as well as the costs of production of different ' firms ' in the same ' industry ', are always comparable because ' firm ' and ' industry ' are defined as producers of a given product. Within a firm the existence of economies of scale can be shown by a ' reversible cost curve ' that declines as output increases in volume (i.e., the ' firm ' increases in size) and rises as one traces the curve backwards to smaller outputs.

expected results. The probable deviation in orders for similar items that a reserve guards against is thus proportionately less when orders are many, and the cost of reserves per unit of output falls correspondingly '. P. Sargant Florence, op. cit., pp. 50–51.

In the more descriptive analyses, on the other hand, many of the economies of size apply to firms defined differently and presumably influence the cost of any number of products; further, some of them, notably economies in the ability to support research and certain economies of selling, apply primarily to the development or introduction of new products. The word ' economies ' implies that in some sense output is ' cheaper ', and this in turn implies a comparison with some other output of the same or very similar products. Here we have two possibilities: first, the average cost of a larger output produced by a firm may be compared with the cost of a smaller output produced by the same firm. If the cost of the larger output is lower, economies of large-scale production are present and we can unequivocally say that the same firm is more efficient when it is larger than when it is smaller. Second, the average cost of additional output may be compared with the cost of the same output in some other firm. Here the ' additional output ' may consist of products very different from those the firm has been producing and the appropriate comparison is with the cost of producing the additional output in some other firm. If this cost is cheaper in a larger firm than in a smaller one, where size is the only variable, then economies of size are present, though not necessarily economies of large-scale production, for the lower cost of the additional output may be due only to the size of the firm that undertook it and not to the scale on which the new output itself is produced. In this case we can say that a large firm is more efficient than a smaller firm, but we cannot say that the same firm is more efficient when it is larger than it was when it was smaller.

Economies of operation refer to the average cost of production and distribution of additional output *after* an expansion has been completed. Here we can compare the average cost of the new output by one firm either with the cost of the same firm's previous output, or with the cost of similar products in another firm. Economies of expansion do not refer to the costs of production after production has been established, but only to the cost of effecting an expansion. This includes the cost of establishing additional production on a smoothly operating basis and of enlarging or creating the market for the additional output. Here the appropriate comparison is only with the cost that another firm would incur if it undertook to initiate the production and marketing of the same products, though not necessarily on the same scale. Needless to say, if the volume of output of two firms is different, cost per unit of output must be compared. If a large firm, because of its size alone, would be able to take up production at a lower average cost than that of any smaller firm, then economies of size are present; and this would be true even if after the new productive activities were well established by the larger firm they could be separated from it and carried on independently at no increase in cost.

In including among the economies of size such things as the ability to support research, the ability to capture the confidence of consumers through extensive advertising that is made possible only because the firm is large, or merely the financial security which is not easily acquired by smaller firms, I have not departed from the customary treatment.[1] Yet there is a fundamental difference between these and the economies of large-scale production and operation that depend essentially on the efficiency with which resources are used for the production and distribution of existing products.

To illustrate, suppose a firm, large enough to support an extensive research organization, perfects a new product and proceeds to introduce it. Assume that the product could not have been perfected or introduced by a smaller firm, but that it is produced by a separate division in separate plants of the large firm. Once the investment to manufacture and distribute the product is made and the product clearly established in the market, it may well be possible to separate the production of the new product from the firm, thus reducing the size of the firm, without causing any increase in the costs of production in any part of the firm. Or again, suppose expansion of the production of a given product has been made possible because of an advertising programme so extensive that only a large firm could have undertaken it. This is an economy to the firm (and perhaps also to consumers if the product could not have been made so widely known in the absence of the selling effort of the firm); but again, once the product is established, no increase in the cost of producing or distributing it need follow if production is transferred to a separate firm.

Thus, economies attributable to the size of firms may, up to a point, not only be responsible for lower costs in the production and distribution of the existing products of larger firms, but also for lower costs and competitive advantages enabling larger firms to

[1] See, for example, E. A. G. Robinson, op. cit., pp. 39–40; and P. Sargant Florence, op. cit., p. 52.

expand in certain directions. These latter are economies of size whenever their existence is directly correlated with the size of the firm enjoying them. They would not be available if firms were sufficiently reduced in size; but they are economies which are applicable only to the process of growth and, once taken advantage of, their fruits may remain in existence and be enjoyed by society even if separated from the tree that bore them—a subsequent reduction in the size of the firm need not lead to increased costs of production or distribution of any of its existing products.[1]

The distinction between economies in operations and economies in expansion throws light, I think, on some of the difficulties with the notion of an ' optimum ' size of firm. Economies of large-scale production or operation have traditionally been associated with the concept of an optimum firm—a firm large enough to take full advantage of all economies of size but not so large that it runs into net diseconomies. Diseconomies of size arise from excessively diminishing returns to scale, but diminishing returns depend upon the existence of a ' fixed factor ' in the operations of the firm. As we have earlier noted, management has often been treated as the ' fixed factor ' giving rise to increasing costs; while this may be legitimate for many particular firms, it is not appropriate for all firms. Under competition, and in the presence of economies of large-scale production and operation, there may be a *minimum* size of firm, but we have rejected the proposition that there is for every firm some *optimum* size beyond which it will run into diseconomies. Only for firms incapable of adapting their managerial structure to the requirements of larger operations can one postulate *an* optimum size.

For any given product there may be decreasing costs as the scale of production is increased, but after a point costs must increase when all costs, including the opportunity costs of resources, are taken into consideration.[2] In other words, there may be an ' optimum ' output for each of the firm's product-lines, but not an ' optimum '

---

[1] I am not suggesting that the persistent removal of the fruit would not reduce the future supply of fruit; I am only concerned to make clear the distinction between the two types of economies of size. Incidentally, that there may be economies in expansion without enduring economies of size often helps to explain the voluntary reduction in the size of a firm when it sells one of its ' businesses ' to another firm. See the discussion below in Chapter VIII of the ' Purchase and Sale of Businesses That are Not Firms '.

[2] The significance of this is discussed more fully in the next chapter, which deals with the economics of diversification.

output for the firm as a whole.[1] In general we have found nothing
to prevent the indefinite expansion of firms as time passes, and clearly
if some of the economies of size are economies of expansion, there
is no reason to assume that a firm would ever reach a size in which
it has taken full advantage of all these economies. But the notion
of ' decreasing costs ' is inapplicable to economies of expansion
unless, after an expansion has been completed, one can compare the
new output with the old and find it cheaper.

THE ECONOMIES OF GROWTH

Economies of growth are the internal economies available to
an individual firm which make expansion profitable in particular
directions. They are derived from the unique collection of productive services available to it, and create for that firm a differential advantage over other firms in putting on the market new
products or increased quantities of old products. At any time the
availability of such economies is the result of the process, discussed
in the previous chapter, by which unused productive services are
continually created within the firm. They may or may not be also
economies of size.

Economies of size do not provide economies of growth for
firms that are unable to expand sufficiently to obtain them. If there
are substantial economies in the large-scale production of particular
products, but if at the same time there are already in existence large
firms whose selling prices reflect the low costs of production obtainable only at large outputs, small firms may survive in the interstices
of the market, but their expansion in competition with the larger
firms may be precluded if the amount of expansion required to
obtain the lower costs of large-scale operation is beyond their
ability to plan or to execute.

Thus, it is not necessarily capital that prevents the expansion of
the small firms often found on the fringes of an industry; it may
just as well be that the organization and execution of an expansion
on the required scale is only possible for firms already large.[2] The

---

[1] It should be clear, once again, that in rejecting the notion of an optimum size of
firm in this context we are not quarrelling with the concept of the optimum size of
firm as it appears in the ' theory of the firm ', since the ' optimum firm ' in that context
is merely the optimum output of a given product. Furthermore, the above discussion
refers only to the firm, and not to the plant—there probably is in any particular economy
an optimum size of plant for many industries.

[2] Essentially the same point is made by E. A. G. Robinson with respect to the costs
of selling: ' The cost of selling is only in part, and in certain conditions, a cost of production. At other times and in other conditions, it is a cost not of producing but of

small firms may survive because of some small advantage in some special market, but they will not in such circumstances become large producers in the industry. New entrants to the industry, if any, will consist of large firms, usually from related industries, which are able to undertake the necessary expansion.

All of the economies of size that we have discussed—whether they be economies of larger-scale production or operation, or economies of expansion—also provide economies of growth for any firm that can take advantage of them. On the other hand, economies of growth may exist at all sizes, and some of them may have no relation either to the size of the firm before it undertakes an expansion based on them, or to any increase in efficiency due to a larger scale of production. Economies of size do not exist if smaller firms could produce or introduce the same products at no higher cost than larger firms when size is the only factor considered. Nevertheless, under given circumstances, a particular firm may be able to put additional output on the market at a lower average cost than any other firm, whether larger or smaller. In this case, economies of growth are present, but not economies of size. A firm may find it profitable to expand even though, after its expansion, it may have no advantages other than those that would have accrued to any other larger or smaller firm that had had equivalent productive services available at the time. For one of the significant characteristics of the economies of growth is that they depend on the particular collection of productive resources possessed by the particular firm, and the exploitation of the opportunities provided by these resources may be quite unrelated to the size of the firm.

Obviously expansion always implies an increased size of firm, but even the firm itself may see no particular advantage in being larger, and in fact may deplore the increase in size which necessarily follows the exploitation of a profitable opportunity, because size creates administrative problems the firm would have preferred to avoid.[1] One does often find that a firm expanded because it was

growing. For once the market has been won, it can be retained at a lower selling cost than is necessary to secure it initially. We have, then, two quite distinct questions to which we must give an answer. First, is a larger firm more efficient than a smaller firm? Second, will it pay to grow from being smaller to being larger? The high cost of selling may be, paradoxically, at the same time a source of economy, making the already large firm more efficient than the smaller firm, and a cost of growth which makes it unprofitable for the small firm to grow up to its most efficient size.' E. A. G. Robinson, op. cit., p. 67.

[1] For example, the executives of one prominent United States firm that I studied felt strongly that increased size brought nothing but administrative headaches; at the same time they knew they could not afford to pass up promising opportunities for expansion.

aware that a larger size of operation was necessary for the effective exploitation of its opportunities; but in firms already large, the economies perceived relate primarily to the particular opportunity being exploited and not to the increased size of the firm as a whole. It is only in relatively small firms that management itself seems to think that a greater size of the firm as a whole would lead to more efficient production.[1]

Disappearing versus Enduring Economies

Economies of growth that are not at the same time economies of large-scale production and operation are essentially transient economies. Almost by definition economies available only in expansion disappear when the expansion has been completed; they can only be obtained if the firm grows larger, but they disappear once the firm has become larger. This means not that the firm has no competitive advantages in its new operations, but that these advantages do not rest on the fact that the new activities are part of the activities of a large firm. Taking advantage of internal economies of growth, firms may go into new products, sometimes founding new industries, or they may build (or acquire) plants in new locations at home and in foreign countries. Often these operations are organized in new subsidiaries, new divisions, new branches, or some similar unit. Once established, they, too, proceed to grow in the same manner as the rest of the firm, in response to economies of the same sort, constrained by managerial limitations, unable to use all the services of the resources they acquire, creating new productive services, and expanding as their managerial constraints recede. The process we have described for the single firm applies, *mutatis mutandis*, to all parts of it.[2] Whenever these parts are reasonably self-contained, even though they use staff services, research help,

---

[1] On the other hand, many large firms insist on the social advantages of their large size, largely, I suspect, because they feel they must justify their existing state. Even if size is no advantage, no firm wants to be broken up by outside action.

[2] Sometimes the ' evolutionary process ' takes place in such a way that the new activities are no longer desired by the firm. For example, in 1920 General Motors Corporation organized a consolidation of several manufacturers of plate glass as part of the Fisher Body Corporation, a subsidiary of General Motors, because at that time Fisher Body was having trouble obtaining adequate supplies of plate glass. In 1931 General Motors reported: ' Through evolution the situation has changed and the point was reached at which it became essential for the Corporation to enter into the manufacture and general distribution of plate glass and allied products, or to retire from the field and turn its interest over to others. For that reason it was decided to sell the productive properties of the National Plate Glass Company to the Libby-Owens-Ford Glass Company.' 1931 *Annual Report*, p. 11.

and similar aids provided by the firm, and in turn pay a share of the overhead, there is the possibility that they could operate as efficiently independently of the firm as they do within it.

The explanation of this apparent contradiction lies in the process of growth itself. When an expansion is based on internal economies of growth which are related to unused knowledge and productive services already existing within a firm, the efficiency of the expansion may rest on advantages that will tend to disappear with the establishment and further growth of the new activities, especially if these activities involve the production of types of product new to the firm or the establishment of plants and subsidiaries in new geographical areas. The original economies may disappear if (a) the resources used in the new activities become specialized in their new use and are no longer significantly connected with any of the older activities of the firm; and (b) if the original advantage was primarily an ' entry advantage '. This is likely to happen when the primary internal inducement to expansion is knowledge, managerial ability, or the general reputation of the firm. In such cases it may well be that once solidly established, the new operations of the firm could be split off from the original firm without any loss of efficiency. Both the original firm and the ' splinter ' firm would still possess unused productive services and would develop new ones; they would both continue to grow, sometimes in much the same directions. There is no reason to assume that splitting the enlarged old firm would reduce or increase costs—the big firm or the two smaller firms may be equally efficient producers.

An imaginary example will illustrate the point. There are economies of scale in the manufacture of glass bottles. Assume a given firm builds a large plant in a particular location. Bottles are not cheap to transport, and the optimum size of plant is determined by the size of a regional market under such circumstances. The experience of the established firm together with its managerial capacity may make it easier and cheaper for this firm than for any other to set up another glass bottle plant in another location to serve another market. Even from the point of view of society this may be the most efficient way of establishing the new plant. But once both plants are set up and in operation, it does not follow that costs of production will necessarily be lower in either plant than they would be if the firm were split up and each plant operated by a separate firm.

On the other hand, economies of growth will remain as economies of size if a reorganization of the older activities of the firm is required to take advantage of them, or if they apply jointly to the old and new activities. Thus if the association between the old and new activities is such that they use the same resources at any stage of production (from purchasing raw materials to selling the finished product) and if at that stage a reduction in the scale of operations would increase costs, the economies of growth are also economies of size.

In practice, of course, it is difficult to compare costs of different firms; and even when one can put costs on a comparable basis it is difficult to attribute any differences found to any particular variable. Different firms of much the same size in the same ' industry ' produce different collections of products, use different collections of resources, are located in different places, and are organized differently. In a reasonably competitive economy, if the size of firm made a significant difference to efficiency, one could presume that firms of inefficient sizes would be rare; but if the size of the firm does not make much difference, at least above a moderate size, the mere fact that an economy is dominated by large firms, and that existing firms are efficient producers and seem to grow ever larger, is not sufficient evidence to allow us to infer that economies of large-scale production and organization are the primary forces at work.

We have, therefore, an interesting paradox: The growth of firms may be consistent with the most efficient use of society's resources; the result of a past growth—the size attained at any time—may have no corresponding advantages. Each successive step in its growth may be profitable to the firm and, if otherwise under-utilized resources are used, advantageous to society. But once any expansion is completed, the original justification for the expansion may fade into insignificance as new opportunities for growth develop and are acted upon. In this case, it would not follow that the large firm as a whole was any more efficient than its several parts would be if they were operating (and growing) quite independently.

CHAPTER VII

THE ECONOMICS OF DIVERSIFICATION

Meaning of diversification. Areas of specialization. Specific opportunities for diversification. Importance of industrial research. Significance of selling effort. Importance of a technological base. Some examples. The role of acquisition. The role of competition. The necessity of continued investment in existing fields. Full-line diversification. Competition and diversification into new areas. Diversification as a solution to specific problems. Temporary fluctuations in demand. Permanent adverse changes in demand. The direction of diversification. Diversification as a general policy for growth. Vertical integration. The firm as a pool of resources.

Of all of the outstanding characteristics of business firms perhaps the most inadequately treated in economic analysis is the diversification of their activities, sometimes called 'spreading of production' or 'integration', which seems to accompany their growth. It has often been pointed out that this process is likely to be 'inefficient' in the sense that productivity is likely to be smaller the greater the number of activities to which a given collection of resources is devoted.[1] 'Efficient' production of given products is the economist's criterion of satisfactory performance, and the primary justification for a large size of firm; yet the most successful and evidently highly efficient firms in the business world are heavily diversified, producing many products, extensively integrated, and apparently are always eager to take on more products. A variety of *ad hoc* explanations ranging from market imperfections and uncer-

[1] Nicholas Kaldor, for example, concludes that ' "spreading of production" is always attended with some cost; i.e. the physical productivity of a *given* quantity of resources calculated in terms of *any* of the products will always be less, the greater the number of separate commodities they are required simultaneously to produce.' He gives the following as 'evidence' for his proposition: 'That this is the case for a large proportion of jointly produced commodities is shown by the fact that the development of an "industry" is always attended by "specialization" or "disintegration", i.e. the reduction of the number of commodities produced by single firms.' Nicholas Kaldor, 'Market Imperfection and Excess Capacity', *Economica*, Vol. II (New Series), 1935, p. 48.
And P. Sargant Florence writes: 'Integration within a plant or a firm must be suspected therefore of small-scale inefficient production till it is proved innocent.' *The Logic of British and American Industry* (London: Routledge and Kegan Paul, 1953), p. 74.

tainty to the dead hand of the past have been presented, and are true enough so far as they go, but they do not go very far.

It may be true for many (if not most) lines of production that productivity and costs would *ceteris paribus* tend to be lower in the more specialized than in the more diversified firms, and that in favourable periods profits on investment would tend to be higher. The proposition cannot be adequately tested, for each individual firm has different productive services available to it, the products of each differ either technically or in the eyes of the consumer, accounting systems are not only different but whenever there are a variety of products produced there will be arbitrary elements in the calculations of costs, and so on. Even if the proposition were valid, however, it has but limited relevance for the determination of the most profitable use of its resources by an individual private-enterprise firm under conditions of change. This is only partly because a specialized firm is highly vulnerable in an environment of changing technology and tastes, and can often make more profitable use of its resources over a period of time by spreading production over a variety of products; it is largely because the changing nature of the productive opportunity of the firm continually presents new opportunities for new investment of which it is profitable for the firm to take advantage while at the same time maintaining, and even expanding, those lines of production to which it has already extensively committed its resources.

So-called 'market imperfections' as an explanation of diversification rest largely on the declining profitability of existing markets as output expands. This is, of course, one aspect of the matter, but there is no reason to assume that it is generally the most important. It is a special case of the changing opportunity cost to the firm of its own resources. It is not necessary that existing markets become less profitable in themselves, only that they become *relatively* less profitable for any new investment the firm wants to undertake. This can just as well occur because of the rise of new opportunities for investment as because of the decline of the old, or because markets for existing products do not grow fast enough to provide scope for the firm's internal capacity for growth. As we have seen, new opportunities are related not only to changes in prices, tastes, and other market conditions, but also to the special kinds of productive services and knowledge developed within a firm.

Although new opportunities for expansion may be related to

changes in external conditions or to changes within the firm itself, competition of a certain kind links these changes together. The expected actions of competitors are a part of the external environment of an individual firm, and the techniques adopted by the firm to maintain its position in the face of competition have themselves a significant influence on the kind of new productive services that are created within the firm. The relationship between competition and the internal supply of productive services is of particular significance wherever the individual firm must keep abreast of new technical developments to compete successfully, and where the continued profitability of the firm is likely to be associated with the possibilities of innovation. The result of such conditions of competition has been the almost universal adoption by larger firms of the industrial research laboratory, which immeasurably speeds up the creation of productive services and knowledge within the individual firm. The Schumpeterian process of ' creative destruction ' has not destroyed the large firm ; on the contrary, it has forced it to become more and more ' creative '.

In the United States, where the process seems to be most highly developed, a kind of ' competition in creativity ' has become a dominant motif in the pattern of competitive behaviour in many industries, where consumers and producers alike are caught up in an almost compulsive obsession for that which is ' new '. In the extreme case the individual firm is forced constantly to remould its products—to create the ' new ' and ' improved ' either in performance or design. To a large extent the new products are superior in performance; to a considerable extent they are merely new and different and can be sold only if the consumer can be convinced that the ' newest ' is the ' best '. Once this conviction takes hold, an almost senseless circular process can develop in which the consumer must have a new model every year and every producer must therefore produce one. But regardless of the ' sense ' or lack of it that one may find in such a process when carried to extremes,[1] it has considerable significance for the pattern of growth of firms. On the one hand it intensifies the vulnerability and restricts the prospects of growth for firms that confine themselves to a narrow range of products; on the other hand, it compels firms to specialize in a relatively narrow range of basic areas of production and restricts

---

[1] The process finds great favour in the eyes of those who see it as an important means of sustaining investment in a highly developed capitalist economy.

the rate at which they can diversify their fundamental activities. We shall pay considerable attention to the relation between diversification and competition, but before going further we must discuss the meaning of diversification and the kinds of opportunity that induce it.

MEANING OF DIVERSIFICATION

The ambiguity inherent in the concept of a ' product ' or an ' industry ' has often been commented on; the same difficulties necessarily beset the concept of ' diversification '. It is common for firms to be characterized as ' single-product ' firms or ' multi-product ' firms, as ' highly ' diversified or as ' undiversified ' firms, etc. Precisely what the terms mean will depend on the grouping of commodities defined as a single product that is significant for the analysis at hand. Thus for some purposes a firm producing only shoes may be considered ' undiversified ', while for other purposes, a firm that produces all sizes and varieties of shoes for all ages and sexes of people may be considered significantly diversified. It is not possible, nor indeed desirable, to try to establish any ' absolute ' meanings for such words. In consequence, not only is a comparison of the ' extent of diversification ' of different firms likely to be meaningless in itself, but statistical studies of the number of different ' products ' produced by firms are also of very limited usefulness, especially if one does not know the identity of the firms referred to.

The Temporary National Economic Committee, for example, produced an extensive study of the product structure of fifty large manufacturing companies in the United States, with elaborate tables giving a variety of different kinds of information about the number of products produced and the importance of each product to each company.[1] This study, though giving much useful information, is of no help in our analysis (nor could any such study be) because the ' number of products ' produced by a firm has no general significance in the absence of detailed information about that firm and its products. The definition of a product is at best arbitrary; to be useful for inter-firm comparisons the criteria for defining a product must have the same significance from one firm to another and must be related to the reasons for discussing the number of products in the first place. Census classifications of

[1] Temporary National Economic Committee, *The Structure of Industry*, Monograph No. 27 (Wash. D.C.: 1941) Part VI, ' The Product Structures of Large Corporations '.

'products' cannot possibly satisfy these conditions. In the modified census product classifications used by the T.N.E.C. study, for example, a product was sometimes defined with respect to the type of raw material used (all-wool blankets and 90 per cent wool blankets being different products); sometimes with respect to the type of user (girls' and children's shoes being separate products from youths' and boys' shoes); sometimes by the process ('stitch-down' and 'welted' shoes are different products); sometimes by the combinations in which goods are sold (a three-piece suit with extra trousers being a different product from a two-piece suit with extra trousers), and so on.

If we are told that Firm A produces 20 products and Firm B produces 4 products, can we sensibly conclude that Firm A is the more diversified? And would our judgment be changed if we knew that the 20 products of Firm A were 20 kinds of shoes while the four of Firm B were tractors, radios, airplane engines, and automobiles?

More recently the Federal Trade Commission has come out with a comprehensive report on product diversification in the 1000 largest manufacturing companies in the United States in 1950.[1] For these companies the report presents statistics on the diversity of their activities measured by the number of 'product-classes' produced. Some useful information about the differences between companies of different size is presented; but again, because of the ambiguity and non-comparability of product classes, one cannot appraise the significance of the comparative diversification of different companies.[2] Difficulties of this sort interfere with attempts to compare statistically the 'product-structure' of different firms, but they do not interfere with an analysis of the economics of diversification so far as it is concerned with the *process* taking place within firms, or even with the significance of diversification for an analysis of market and production relationships, provided we know the kind of firm we are dealing with.

For the purpose of analyzing the process of diversification we can say that a firm diversifies its productive activities whenever,

[1] *Report of the Federal Trade Commission on Industrial Concentration and Product Diversification in the 1,000 Largest Manufacturing Companies,* 1950 (Wash. D.C., 1957).

[2] The report gives a brief discussion of the limitations of product-class enumerations as a measure of the diversity of a company's manufacturing activities, pointing out the uneven refinement of the classifications, the conceptual difficulties in the meaning of 'diversity of activity', and the different significance of different products from the point of view of the manufacturing process. Ibid., pp. 25–26.

without entirely abandoning its old lines of product, it embarks upon the production of new products, including intermediate products, which are sufficiently different from the other products it produces to imply some significant difference in the firm's production or distribution programmes. Diversification thus includes increases in the variety of final products produced, increases in vertical integration, and increases in the number of ' basic areas ' of production in which a firm operates. This last type of diversification is of especial importance, and cannot be measured by the number of different kinds of final or intermediate products produced. If a firm previously producing air brakes of various kinds, for example, enters the production of electronic equipment, it is certainly diversifying its productive activities (provided it does not abandon its air brake production entirely), although at the same time it may reduce the varieties of air brakes produced and in consequence the absolute number of different kinds of products. This points out once again the futility of attempting to measure the ' extent ' of diversification as such, for there is no single all-purpose measure. Is the air brake-electronics firm less diversified because the total number of separate products is reduced? Clearly the *type* of diversification is different, and for a study of the growth of firms the type of diversification and the reasons for it are of more relevance than the ' amount ' of diversification, whatever that may mean.[1]

' Areas of Specialization '

Diversification may take place within a firm's existing areas of specialization or it may result in a firm going into new areas. At all times a firm has a foothold in certain types of production and in certain types of market, both of which are here called ' areas of specialization ' of the firm.

Each type of productive activity that uses machines, processes, skills, and raw materials that are all complementary and closely associated in the process of production we shall call a ' production base ' or ' technological base ' of the firm, regardless of the number or type of products produced. A firm may have several such bases,

---

[1] Nor can the difficulty be evaded by trying to distinguish diversification into different *products* (or product-classes) from diversification into different *industries*, because the same problems plague the attempt to define an industry. If, for example, the elasticity of substitution in consumption is the criterion for defining an industry, then women's and children's shoes belong to entirely different industries, for surely the elasticity of substitution is close to zero. If raw materials are the criterion, then canvas and leather shoes are different industries. Clearly we are no better off than we were before.

and even when they are related to each other by common elements or knowledge or technology, they will be treated as different bases if there are substantial differences in their technological characteristics. The particular group of activities to be treated as a single production base will vary for different firms. The significance of distinguishing such groupings lies in the fact that a movement into a new base requires a firm to achieve competence in some significantly different area of technology.

A firm may sell in a variety of different markets even though it has only one production base. Markets, from this point of view, are conveniently classified according to the kind of buyer they serve, since some of the most important opportunities for diversification arise as a result of the relation between a firm and its customers. Each group of customers which the firm hopes to influence by the same sales programme is called a ' market area ', regardless of the number of products sold to that group. Thus occupational groups (such as housewives, farmers, or industrial firms), distributive organizations (such as different types of retailers, or wholesale houses), geographical groups (for firms whose existing markets are geographically limited), different income and social groups, etc., may each be a different ' market area ' if different selling programmes are required to influence them. The appropriate criteria for the delimitation of market areas are different for different firms; the significance of the boundaries lies in the fact that a movement into a new market area requires the devotion of resources to the development of a new type of selling programme and a competence in meeting a different type of competitive pressure.

A wide variety of products may be produced for each market; and a wide variety of markets may be served from the same production base. Diversification within the same area of specialization refers to the production of more products based in the same technology *and* sold in the firm's existing markets. Diversification that involves a departure from the firm's existing areas may be one of three kinds: (1) the entry into new markets with new products using the same production base; (2) expansion in the same market with new products based in a different area of technology; and (3) entry into new markets with new products based in a different area of technology.[1] These categories do not, of course, include diversification

---

[1] The same physical product from a production point of view may be a different product from the selling point of view, and a firm, by entering new markets with old

by increasing the number of products produced for the firm's own use, a category that is best discussed separately.

Many firms have diversified in all of these ways both within and beyond their existing areas of specialization, others in only one or two ways. There are very few, if any, completely undiversified firms if ' product ', and especially ' intermediate product ', is defined narrowly. In any given circumstances, including the state of technology and the existing organization of competing firms, much diversification is almost a necessity, in the sense that no firm would expect to compete successfully if it did not produce at least a minimum product line or a minimum of its own intermediate requirements, the number of products involved depending on the circumstances.

There are a few studies in which the ' causes ' of diversification are listed; such lists provide convenient classificatory boxes into which any given collection of examples can be sorted, but they are of limited usefulness for an analysis of the relation between diversification and the process of growth. Here we shall link diversification with the changing internal and external circumstances which affect the productive opportunity of the firm, discussing not only the forces promoting diversification but also those limiting the firm's freedom of action in this respect.

THE SPECIFIC OPPORTUNITIES FOR DIVERSIFICATION

Opportunities to produce new products arise from changes in the productive services and knowledge available in the firm of the kind we have explored in earlier chapters, and from changes in external supply and market conditions as perceived by the firm. A single ' opportunity ' in the sense used here is merely one of the components of the whole productive opportunity of the firm as defined earlier. In other words, it is one of a number of possible uses of the resources of the firm, in each of which the firm believes it could make profit, ' profit ' being calculated without reference to the ' opportunity cost ' of its resources (that is to say, the firm calculates the possible profit for each opportunity without reference to whether it is more or less profitable than available alternatives).

products, may achieve results similar to those achieved by diversification. In order to avoid overloading the concept of diversification and thereby confusing the reader we have not included this kind of ' market diversification ' in our definition, but probably most of the considerations influencing diversification from the same production base are relevant to the entry of a firm into new markets with old products.

Thus, any specific opportunity to diversify is merely an opportunity, not yet the most profitable course of action—the firm may pass it over, believing other things would be more profitable or considering that the action required is not worth the risk or does not justify the amount of resources that would have to be committed.

There is no need here to repeat our earlier analysis of the pervasive existence of unused productive services within firms and of the process by which they are continually created by the normal operations of the firm. It is easy to understand, in the light of that process, how and why a firm may find it profitable to alter and add to the kind of products it produces. In the following discussion we shall explore the characteristics of some of the more important general sources of new opportunities for diversification.

The Importance of Industrial Research

Industrial research, the deliberate investigation of the as yet unknown properties of the materials and machines used in production (or as yet undeveloped ways of using them) for the express purpose of improving existing or creating new products and productive processes, has probably existed in some form wherever industry has existed. But the systematic and extensive development of the industrial research laboratory is of very recent origin, and only in this century has it reached such proportions that the normal activities of large firms cannot be discussed without reference to it.[1] Many entrepreneurs very early perceived the possibilities for improving the long-run profitability of their own firms through systematic research into the properties of the materials and equipment they dealt with, partly because they dreamed of new things, partly because they saw in such research a way of improving their existing products and widening their opportunities.

But quite apart from the dreams or motives of entrepreneurs or the actual historical processes which led to the development of the industrial research laboratory, it is the logical response of the individual firm to the challenge inherent in the Schumpeterian ' process of creative destruction '. After all, the specialized firm is vulnerable. Its profitability and very survival as a firm are imperilled by adverse changes in demand for the type of products it produces

---

[1] For a perceptive discussion of research and innovation as an ' ordinary ' business activity see Carolyn S. Solo, ' Innovation in the Capitalist Process ', *Quarterly Journal of Economics*, Vol. LXV, No. 3 (Aug. 1951), pp. 417–428.

and by increased competition from other producers. Its growth is limited by the growth of the market for its existing products or by the share of the existing market it can succeed in obtaining. On the other hand, as we have shown, its opportunities are largely determined by its existing resources. Its entrepreneurial and managerial personnel work within the framework provided by these resources and their interests and abilities are conditioned by them. Except in those instances where firms are dominated by entrepreneurs of the roving ' empire-building ' sort, there is a strong tendency for each firm, in the first instance at least, to concentrate on the profitable development of what it has.

A firm may attempt to entrench itself by destroying or preventing effective competition by means of predatory competitive practices or restrictive monopolistic devices that relieve it of the necessity of either meeting or anticipating serious competitive threats to its position. In such circumstances a firm may grow for a considerable period depending on the demand for its products, harassed neither by price competition nor by the fear that competitive developments will make its products or processes obsolete. Examples of growth over long periods which can be attributed *exclusively* to such protection are rare,[1] although elements of such protection are to be found in the position of nearly every large firm.

Even when a firm exploits to the fullest possible extent the opportunities for monopolistic gain available to it, the protection afforded, though often extensive, can neither be complete nor absolutely certain. For many, if not most firms, the more effective long-run protection both against direct competition as well as against the indirect competition of new products will lie in the firm's ability to anticipate, or at least to match, threatening innovations in processes, products, and marketing techniques. In a society characterized by a widespread ' spirit of enterprise ' and a highly developed technology, the threat of competition from new products, new techniques, new channels of distribution, new ways of influencing consumer demand, is in many ways a more important influence on the conduct of existing producers than any other kind of competition.[2] Its primary effect is to force a firm wanting to maintain itself

---

[1] I am not here concerned with the growth taking place during the *process* of acquiring such monopoly positions through extensive merger but with the growth that takes place *after* such a position has been obtained.

[2] This is, of course, precisely what Schumpeter maintained: ' But in capitalist reality as distinguished from its textbook picture, [the] . . . kind of competition which counts

in the market for any given product to learn all it can about the product, its market and, in particular, the relevant technology, and to endeavour to anticipate the innovations of other firms.[1]

Industrial innovations come, for the most part, from industrial firms, and those firms that introduce them first are likely to have a competitive advantage because they can obtain patent protection or otherwise prevent imitation, or merely because they are first. Of this, firms are very much aware, and if one wants to examine the influence of ' environmental ' factors on the growth of firms, here is one of the most important to note. We have already indicated that the environment exerts its influence primarily through its effects on entrepreneurial judgments; if a firm believes that the advantages which create its own ' business opportunity ' are likely to be temporary because new things will inevitably be introduced by other firms, it will respond by an active ' innovation policy ' of its own.[2] Even if the primary purpose is to develop ways of reducing the costs and improving the quality of existing products, the exploration and research involved will certainly speed up the production of new knowledge and the creation of new productive services within the firm.[3]

There is no reason to assume that the new knowledge and services

[is] the competition from the new commodity, the new technology, the new source of supply, the new type of organization . . . it is hardly necessary to point out that competition of the kind we now have in mind acts not only when in being but also when it is merely an ever-present threat. It disciplines before it attacks.' Joseph Schumpeter, *Capitalism, Socialism and Democracy* (New York: Harper, 2nd ed. 1947), pp. 84–85.

[1] In a recent survey of industrial research in the United States in which officials of firms were asked about the factors inducing their firms to undertake research, the role of competition was prominent: ' Research officials in virtually all industries cited competition as an important consideration—often an overriding one—in appraisals of company research needs.' A common refrain was ' we have to do some research to stay in business'; and the importance of research for ' growth ' and for ' diversification objectives ' was stressed. National Science Foundation, *Science and Engineering in American Industry: Final Report on a 1953–1954 Survey.* (Wash. D.C.: U.S. Government Printing Office, 1956), pp. 43–44.

[2] For example, in a recent survey of 110 companies rated as ' excellently managed ' by the American Institute of Management, almost nine-tenths of the respondents to a questionnaire expressed the opinion that ' staying abreast or out ahead in the innovative race is more important to their long-range business success than a " defensive " policy of basing prices closely on costs.' James S. Earley, ' Marginal Policies of " Excellently Managed " Companies ', *American Economic Review*, Vol. XLVI, No. 1 (March 1956), p. 59.

[3] The research laboratory is itself one of the most important sources of new ideas for further research. In one survey of 121 outstanding industrial research laboratories, questions were asked about the frequency with which research projects originate from various sources. It was found that 50 per cent came from existing research activities, including commercial research. David B. Hertz (ed.), *Research Operations in Industry* (New York: King's Crown Press, 1953), p. 122.

will be useful only in the production of a firm's existing products; on the contrary, they may well be useless for that purpose but still provide a foundation which will give the firm an advantage in some entirely new area. A firm's opportunities are necessarily widened when it develops a specialized knowledge of a technology which is not in itself very specific to any particular kind of product, for example, knowledge of different types of engineering or industrial chemistry.[1]

Thus whether research be originally undertaken merely because the firm is convinced that profitable new opportunities will come out of it, or because it is considered necessary for survival in a competitive world, it enables at least the large firms to turn aside the process of 'creative destruction' and to thrive on the novelty which might otherwise have destroyed them. The spectacular results of industrial research were bound, of course, to stimulate that imitative response which follows any important innovation, and firms of all descriptions have become convinced that a research laboratory is the panacea for their difficulties. The vision of unlimited opportunity thus invoked is a mere mirage for many.[2] New knowledge may be gained, but at great expense, and for the small firm the use of its resources for 'research' in general is as likely to be wasteful as it is to be profitable unless the firm has specific and reasonably original ideas upon which it is working. The appraisal of the results of research is extremely difficult and methods of appraisal are still in a primitive state.[3] The amount of funds to be devoted to research is often determined on some arbitrary basis (for example, some per cent of sales), for there is as yet no reasonably accurate way of determining in advance how much investment in any particular type of research will

[1] For example, the chief products of Schenley Distillers Corporation required a knowledge of grains, fermentation processes, and moulds. When antibiotics began to be developed, the firm found that its knowledge and research gave it a 'better understanding of the fundamental nature of the complex fermentation processes involved' and hence an important advantage in this new and rapidly growing industry. (*Annual Report*, 1948).

[2] For criticism of the notion that research is necessarily a great advantage, see J. Jewkes, 'Monopoly and Economic Progress', *Economica* Vol. XX (New Series), No. 79 (Aug. 1953), esp. p. 206.

[3] Only about one-fourth of the officials interviewed in the National Science Survey of some 200 United States corporations reported that 'their companies have a formal method of estimating the financial return on research expenditures. And a few said that their companies make no attempt to appraise the results of their research and development effort', op. cit., p. 49.

turn out to have been justified. Research is essentially speculative activity, frequently adopted under necessity or as a matter
of faith.[1]

The Significance of Selling Efforts

Opportunities for the production of new products arise not only
from the productive activities of a firm, including its technological
research, but also from its selling activities. This second source of
opportunity is important for all kinds of firms, but it is perhaps of
greatest importance for firms whose productive processes are either
highly specialized with respect to the kind of product for which
they are suitable, or are simple and easily imitated and of a kind
where research yields little that provides particular firms with any
competitive advantage—for example, some types of food processing
such as milk production or flour milling, tobacco processing, and
some types of textile production.

Whenever a firm adopts policies under which the sale of its
products is associated with the advertisement in one way or another
of the firm itself, the demand, not only for existing products, but
also for other products of the firm is likely to be affected; the productive opportunity of the firm is changed by the demand-creating
process itself. It makes a great difference for the prospects of
diversification whether competition in a given market forces the
cutting of prices (or absorption of transport costs) or requires the
exertion of selling efforts. The former is an impersonal market

[1] In England the Manchester Joint Research Council, in reporting the results of a
survey, stated: ' One of the questions a firm considering the formation of a research
department must ask itself is: ' What is it going to cost, and what will the firm derive
in material benefit ? '
   ' There have been many attempts to answer this question, both here and abroad,
but so far as is known none has proved wholly satisfactory. Although it is quite
possible to estimate the capital cost of establishing a modest research section and to
budget for its annual upkeep, it has generally been found impossible to produce a
profit and loss account to show to what extent a research department is paying its way.
So many of the advantages of such a department are so intangible that it is, perhaps, not
surprising that this survey has not brought to light any new ideas as to how such a
balance can be struck, nor how the value of such a department can be assessed. There
is nothing which can be pointed to as an infallible indication that a firm needs a research
department, or that it will be profitable to found one. Perhaps not unexpectedly,
wherever a research department was found to exist it was thought by the board and
management to be a most important aspect of the firm's activities, and the best means of
keeping abreast of progress. The decision to institute research can only be taken after
mature consideration, but even so, it will still be largely a matter of faith, and a belief
that the scientific method has advantages over those of trial and error.' Manchester
Joint Research Council, *Industry and Science* (Manchester: Manchester Univ. Press 1954)
pp. 48–49

response leaving the identity of the seller of no significance to the buyers. The latter will almost of necessity be connected not only with the product but also with the name or trademarks of the seller, and the identity of the firm emerges as a significant competitive factor. The firm having to create new markets for its products, for example, is virtually always in this position, for it is rarely possible to advertise or otherwise push sales of a product without at the same time advertising the source of supply, if not to the final consumer, certainly to the wholesaler or retailer.[1]

When a significant part of the market-creating process consists of the personal sales efforts of a firm's staff, several important changes take place. A relationship is established between the firm and its customers which, other things being equal, places the firm in a preferred position compared to complete newcomers. Frequently this relationship goes much further than a friendly and personal confidence of one man in another and extends to ' technical ' matters. For example, the selling firm makes special efforts to adjust the quality and characteristics of its products to the customers' requirements, and the buying firm makes special efforts to inform the seller of its peculiar requirements in order to get the seller's help in meeting them and in solving its own problems. This tends to give a firm that has succeeded in establishing such relationships an ' inside track ' with the buyer should it become interested in supplying other products quite different from those it is selling at the time. Consequently after a firm has established such relationships with customer firms it is faced with a different set of productive opportunities. These opportunities may continue to grow as the firm learns more, not only about its markets, but also about the technical potentialities of it own resources.

The other general method of establishing a market is through various forms of advertising in the several popular and technical media of public communication. Just what type of advertising is deemed most effective depends on the product, the type of competition, and the customs of the trade. But again it is often the firm itself that is advertised as well as, and sometimes more than, the product. For non-durable consumer goods where quality is either

---

[1] In many cases, the actual name of the seller may not be so important as the fact that the seller of one product is also the maker of some other well-known product. Advertisements often emphasize the fact that the product in question is produced by the makers of some other widely accepted product.

of little importance or is reasonably evident from untutored inspection, the reputation of the firm makes little real difference, although even here the customer can often be led to choose the products, otherwise equal, of the better-known firm or of the firm producing the better-known products. For goods whose quality is difficult to judge or where service, dependability, and continuity of supply are really part of the ' utility ' the customer purchases when he buys the product, the reputation of the firm is of great importance whether the customer is a manufacturer, a dealer, or simply the household consumer.

The Importance of a Technological Base

Although the possibilities of successful diversification based on strength in the market are often given pride of place, it is a mistake to stress them to the neglect of the concomitant development of the technological base of the firm. As will be shown in the section concerned with the significance of competition for diversification, a strong market position without technological competence is as precarious as is strong technological competence but weak selling ability. Furthermore, when a firm's strength is not closely related to its technological strength, but rests primarily on a dominant position in important markets, it is more difficult for the firm to move into entirely new basic areas of specialization. Not only is such a firm unlikely to develop abilities that would give it a substantial technological advantage in an entirely new field, but it is also handicapped in the acquisition of other firms in fields where technology is substantially different.

In the first place, in the absence of strong legal protection, the mere fact that a firm with no technical superiority can establish a dominant market position is *prima facie* evidence that the technique of the industry in which it operates is either fairly standardized or fairly simple, and consequently that innovations can be easily matched by other firms. If this were not so, we should expect a technical superiority to have been established by some other firm in the industry which would undermine the market position of the dominant firm. When the technology of a firm is standardized and fairly simple the productive services available within the firm are unlikely to generate many opportunities for expansion into areas where superior or unusual technical capacity is required. In other words, the existing resources of such a firm are not favourable for the development of a specialized technological superiority in the use of raw materials, special skills, or processes in substantially different areas of operation. Similarly, the firm will be less able to acquire other firms with a substantially different technology partly because the management of the firm is unlikely to feel great confidence in its ability to operate in fields entirely alien to its own experience, and partly because it will in general be more difficult for a firm with no special advantage in a new field to acquire firms with the special technical qualifications at a profitable price.[1]

Many firms in the United States have expanded rapidly, largely through acquisition, in fields where they have had no apparent technological superiority—for example, firms in the dairy industry—and have succeeded in establishing strong market positions on a national scale. Such positions facilitated diversification into complementary markets, which was often effected through the acquisition of other firms with prominent brand names or other selling advantages. As long as the expanding firms remain in their original market areas, their dominant market position may protect them for a considerable period. But the 'carry-over' of this position into other areas becomes weaker as they go farther afield, and the necessity of developing a technological as well as a marketing advantage becomes increasingly pressing. Hence one finds firms such as National Dairy, whose chief method of growth was originally the acquisition of local dairy concerns, placing great emphasis on research as they moved into other food products where technological innovation was an important competitive requirement.

Diversification and expansion based primarily on a high degree of competence and technical knowledge in specialized areas of manufacture are characteristic of many of the largest firms in the economy. This type of competence together with the market position it ensures is the strongest and most enduring position a firm can develop. It incidentally, of course, gives considerable scope for the exploitation of opportunities for the monopolistic control of markets and for the use of restrictive monopolistic practices, but extensive and indefinite expansion is by no means dependent on the direct exercise of monopolistic power in any restrictive sense. Diversification through both internal and external expansion is

[1] See Chapter VIII for a discussion of this point.

likely to be extensive because of the wide variety of productive services generated within such firms and because the especially powerful competitive advantages they possess are conducive to acquisition. Opportunities for expansion both within existing bases and through the establishment of new bases are likely to be so prevalent that the firm has carefully to choose between many different possibilities of action.

Some Examples

One of the more prominent of the corporations in the United States to-day is the General Motors Corporation, in 1956 the second largest industrial corporation in the country. It is primarily known as an automobile producer but it also produces a wide variety of other products—durable consumer goods of many kinds, locomotives, and airplane engines, to name a few of the more important types. The history of the company is well known: the original product was automobiles; the basic area of specialization, engineering for mass production. The broad lines of diversification are easily traced and are logically related to the original areas, growing out of them but also growing up and away from them as new production bases were established.

To avoid being tedious, I shall mention here only those diversifying activities of General Motors which are not within the general area of automobile production. One of the earliest of its acquisitions outside the automobile field was the Guardian Frigerator Corporation acquired in 1919. In a sense, the acquisition of this concern by the company was an accident: it had been bought in 1918 with his own funds by W. C. Durant, the founder of General Motors, when it was a moribund and virtually bankrupt firm, and he suggested General Motors take it over. A programme of research and development was launched and the name ' Frigidaire ' adopted. By 1925 the company said of the product:

> ' This apparatus lends itself both from the standpoint of type of manufacture as well as market possibilities to quantity production. The Corporation believes that through its broad experience in quantity manufacture, its research activities and through its purchasing ability on account of the large volume of its operations, it can more than maintain the dominating position that Frigidaire now enjoys. It is believed further that market possibilities largely parallel those of the motor car.' (*Annual Report*, 1925).

In other words, the company believed that the general type of productive services already existing within the firm provided a basis for the development and extension of the production of refrigerators. In the next few years Frigidaire production was set up in a separate operating division in line with General Motors' ' belief, based upon the former experience of the Corporation, that the decentralization of these activities into separate and distinct responsible managements will mean increased effectiveness from every standpoint.' (*Annual Report*, 1928). The broad base which led the company to develop the product was competence in engineering for quantity production, but further diversification arose as the new subsidiary went ahead to develop its own products. By 1933 the Frigidaire division was well on the way to further diversification:

> 'As part of its engineering program, Frigidaire has developed a line of air conditioning units covering virtually every field of application; the home, the office, the hotel, the hospital, the railroad car and other industrial fields.' (*Annual Report*, 1934).

During 1936 General Motors further

> ' broadened its position . . . by adding a line of electric ranges and other household accessories and equipment. The objective was not primarily that of expansion but rather that of protecting, from the commercial standpoint, the already existing lines by the development of a complete General Motors line of electric household utility devices.' (*Annual Report*, 1937).

As early as 1927 diversification had gone so far that the company reported

> ' . . . that the total earnings of the Corporation must not be taken as a measure of its earnings from motor car divisions. Notwithstanding the fact that the Corporation's motor car operations are equally if not more completely, self-contained than those of competitors, yet the motor car operations contribute only about one-half of the Corporation's total profits.' (*Annual Report*, 1928).

The next major diversification steps are reported in 1928 when General Motors acquired a 40 per cent interest in the Fokker Aircraft Corporation of America.

> ' General Motors, in forming this association, felt that, in view of the more or less close relationship in an engineering way between the airplane and the motor car, its operating organization, technical and otherwise, should be placed in a position where it would havn an opportunity to contact with the specific problems involved in transportation by air. What the future of the airplane may be no one can positively state at this time. Through this association General

Motors will be able to evaluate the development of the industry and determine its future policies with a more definite knowledge of the facts.' (*Annual Report*, 1929).

In 1929 the Allison Aircraft Company was acquired and by 1938 the Allison Division, which manufactured airplane engines, had ' attained a position of importance in the development and manufacture of high-powered aviation engines. In view of the substantial increase in orders, the manufacturing facilities of this activity are being materially enlarged by the addition of an entirely new plant.' (*Annual Report* 1939).

The war, of course, hastened the exploitation of this base of operations, and airplane engines and hundreds of minor products related thereto are now a substantial part of the company's activities.

In the same year that General Motors went into the airplane industry, it entered the radio industry.

' General Motors Corporation became interested in the radio industry through a study made in connection with the application of the radio to its motor cars. As a result of this study and recognizing that General Motors already had technical ability, manufacturing capacity and opportunities for distribution, it was deemed advisable to capitalize these advantages and diversify still further the Corporation's operations by entering this particular field in which a constructive opportunity existed.' (*Annual Report*, 1929).

The company's entry into the diesel engine field also stemmed from its automobile manufacturing activities:

' General Motors Research Laboratories started development work on the two-cycle, light-weight Diesel as early as 1928, two years before either Winton or Electro-Motive was acquired. Our primary objective was to develop a practical Diesel truck engine that would result in important operating economies.'[1]

In 1930 the engine manufacturing activities of the corporation were extended when it acquired a firm that manufactured power plants with engines employing both the Otto and Diesel cycles:

' In view of the developments taking place in the general direction of the Diesel type of construction it was thought desirable for the Corporation to deal in a practical way with the problem. Furthermore, it was felt that the Corporation's engineering and research staffs could contribute to progress in that direction.' (*Annual Report*, 1929).

[1] ' The Development and Growth of General Motors,' statement by Harlow H. Curtice, President, General Motors Corporation, before the Sub-committee on Antitrust and Monopoly of the United States Senate, Committee of the Judiciary, Dec. 2, 1955.

In 1933 improvements of Diesel engines were made:

'For the purpose of aggressively exploiting the possibilities of this new development, the Corporation has recently authorized the building of a Diesel electric locomotive plant, which will make possible complete Diesel electric locomotives engineered and assembled within the Corporation's activities.' (*Annual Report*, 1934).

The general diversification policy of the General Motors Corporation was summed up in the *Annual Report* of 1937:

' The policy of the Corporation is to maintain as broad a coverage as is practicable in the various fields in which it is engaged, giving consideration, of course, to the market possibilities for such products. The scope of its activities has broadened continually over the years, not so much as the result of a definite policy, but rather from the fact that through the evolution of its primary products in an engineering way there frequently arise opportunities to engage in the manufacture of additional components. This results in expanding the possibilities of profits and at the same time provides a more reliable, more efficient and more aggressive source of supply than is usually available in the outside market. Equally important is the fact that out of the Corporation's research and engineering activities there frequently arise opportunities for profitable expansion in the manufacture of new technical developments, more or less independent of the Corporation's scheme of things, but generally allied thereto in technical characteristics. Further, ways and means are frequently evolved whereby the exploitation of already existing products may be accelerated and markets expanded through the application of advanced engineering and research.'

The strength of the type of ' basic position ' developed by General Motors was strikingly demonstrated by the rapidity with which extensive adaptation could be made to the exigencies of war production.

' One of the most important long-range policies of General Motors has been concerned with the promotion of technical progress throughout its research, engineering and production activities, which has resulted in steady, evolutionary advancements in the Corporation's products. Today, the experience thus gained, the adaptability to change and the technique of applying mass production principles have become of inestimable value in dealing with the technical problems presented by the production of intricate machines of war.' (*Annual Report*, 1941).

The principle applies equally to the ' technical problems presented ' by the adaptations required to maintain and extend a firm's activities in peacetime.

A very different type of company, much smaller than General

Motors, but also illustrating some of the principles of diversification, is General Mills Incorporated. General Mills was founded in 1928 as a consolidation of five milling companies; some other companies were added in 1929 and a research laboratory established. The original products were flour, commercial feeds, and allied grain products. In 1937 these were still the only products mentioned in the company's annual report. But research activities were stressed from the beginning, both in the chemistry of the basic food products and in the mechanical problems of handling them. And by 1938 the company's subsequent extensive diversification was foreshadowed in its report to stockholders, which, though not mentioning the restricted possibilities for expansion in flour production, made clear in the language appropriate for public relations that the company believed its future lay in diversification:

> ' Increasingly it is apparent that progress, both for society as a whole and for the individual productive units within it, depends above all on the opening of new frontiers for useful and profitable effort through the development of new products and services. Such development can be accomplished only through ably directed and adequately financed research, in close association with the realities of manufacturing, merchandising and consumer needs. . . .
> ' General Mills, Inc., has definitely committed itself to a policy of expanding research activities. . . . Of equal significance is the Mechanical Development department. . . . The problems of converting the cereal grains into acceptable food products are primarily physical, and the Mechanical Development department has already developed notable and profitable improvements in machinery and methods used by the Company. Here, as in the Research Laboratory, the progress already made is doubly significant because of the promise it holds out for the future. . . . The Company is engaged in the experimental development and testing of additional products, in the firm belief that its future progress depends not only on doing the same things better, but on doing new things which will widen the scope of public acceptance of the Company's products.' (11th Annual Report, 1939).

Subsequent reports trace a progressive extension of the company's product line—numerous nutritional items, vitamin products and vitamin enrichment of old products, dietary food supplements, and non-food uses of agricultural products; in addition, an extensive mechanical department producing food processing machinery was developed. New raw materials became important, such as soya beans, and led to the production of oil and polyamide resins. Once research into food chemistry became significant, the company had prospective opportunities for new products continually ' under review ', but its major activity remained the processing of cereal grains into flour, package foods, and animal feeds.

Another field of production in which General Mills became engaged is of particular interest because it illustrates the effect of war on the productive services available to firms and also the effect of competition on attempts at diversification. Anything that significantly alters the selling relationships of the individual firm or the character of its productive activities will substantially alter its opportunities for producing new products. The mobilization of industry for war production brought innumerable firms into the production of products for which they had little, and sometimes, no, skill. When the same firms began once more devoting their attention to peacetime production, they found that they had developed extensive productive services suitable for products far removed from their pre-war products, services which would clearly remain unused in the absence of diversification. These included not only knowledge and skills of management, but also plant and equipment and the skilled services of workers, to say nothing of an abnormally large amount of liquid assets. Clearly an increased interest in the possibilities of using such services for appropriate peacetime products was to be expected, and some of the eager postwar search for new products can be thus explained.

The mechanical development department of General Mills was made into a division in 1940 and the division turned over to the production of war materials. The tools and equipment that had been used for engineering research and for the development of packaging and milling machinery were converted to the production of gunnery fire control equipment and instruments and other precision instruments. The company noted that the food production aspects of its wartime production

' were natural outgrowths of our customary business, but our present large operation in the manufacture of precision instruments for the United States Navy has taken us far afield. Our interesting but complicated experience with close tolerance production points the way to future opportunities in the field of mechanical products.' (*Annual Report*, 1943).

In 1946 with the termination of the war contracts, an electric iron, the first of a new line of home appliances, was put in production by the Mechanical Division. It was later followed by pressure cookers, toasters, food mixers, coffee makers, and other items. Eight years later the new line was abandoned, the home appliance business sold, and the mechanical division returned to its older specialities—the production of various lines of industrial equipment and precision equipment for the Armed Forces.[1] The fate of this attempt illustrates one of the restrictions that competition puts on efforts of firms to diversify; competition forces a certain measure of specialization, as we shall see a little later, because it forces firms to continue extensive investment in any new field they enter if they are to remain in it successfully.

The diversification of General Mills is extensive and continuing. At first sight it also seems to encompass a variety of unrelated products ' ranging from fine foods to electronic machines '.[2] Yet if the process of diversification is examined in detail the progressive movement into different products has clearly been based in the firm's existing areas of specialization, whether they be food or cellulose chemistry, the household markets for cereal products, or mechanical equipment.

Not only did mobilization of industry for war production significantly change the character of the production base of many firms, it also changed selling opportunities through the impetus it gave to the practice of sub-contracting. Connections were made which persisted in other forms after the war production programme was over, and postwar discussions of the possibilities of diversification, especially for small and ' ailing ' firms, stressed the opportunities that could be found in contracting to produce part of the requirements of larger firms.[3]

[1] ' In May, 1954, General Mills sold its home appliance business to the Illinois McGraw Electric Company. Under terms of the sale, the purchaser received capital equipment, tooling and inventories and agreed to service appliances now in use.

' The home appliance business accounted for only a small proportion of the Mechanical Division's sales, employees and facilities, which have always been devoted largely to industrial and defense efforts. To develop the home appliance further would have required a greater investment than its future prospects appeared to justify. Sale of the operation will now make possible more effective specialization in the development and production of precision electro-mechanical instruments.' Annual Report, 1953–54.

For further discussion of this kind of problem see the section on the ' Purchase and Sale of Businesses that are Not Firms ', in Chapter VIII.

[2] In the 1955–56 Annual Report, the firm listed 28 ' new products of the year.'

[3] See, for example, the recommendations in the report by Arthur D. Little, Inc., Diversification: An Opportunity for the New England Textile Industry (Federal Reserve Bank of Boston, 1955).

A rather surprising diversification achieved through wartime sub-contracting is described in this report: ' The Rock of Ages Granite Company, one of the oldest and most renowned monument manufacturers in the United States, diversified into the electronics industry via the subcontracting method. The company established itself

So much for our general discussion of the origin of opportunities for diversification. We have not included two considerations which are often put forward as incentives to, or ' causes ' of, diversification —the possession by a firm of extensive cash reserves and the existence of favourable opportunities to acquire other going concerns. The first is not specifically an incentive to diversify; it may provide an incentive, or even pressure, to expand but in itself does not affect whether expansion takes place in existing or new products. The second is more complicated and a separate discussion is required. There can be no question that much diversification which would not otherwise have occurred takes place through acquisition; on the other hand, diversification in any given direction will not ' normally ' occur through acquisition unless the firm has reasons for diversifying in that direction other than the mere possibility of acquiring another firm on favorable terms.

THE ROLE OF ACQUISITION

Acquisition plays such an important part in the diversification activities of firms that many writers purporting to discuss diversification in fact discuss only acquisition.[1] Our analysis of the effect of the continual creation of new productive services and knowledge on the productive opportunity of a firm was developed with reference to internal expansion—expansion through acquisition was put off for another chapter. Some of that discussion must be anticipated here, however, for this method of expansion has peculiar advantages as a means of taking up the production of new products.

It is evident that the out-of-pocket costs and the managerial and technical difficulties of entering a new field can be substantially reduced if a firm can acquire another going concern. Plant can often be acquired at considerably less than its reproduction cost, a valuable market position can be obtained which might otherwise have taken years to build up, and immediate pressure from competition may be substantially reduced. Of especial importance is the fact that a firm can also acquire an experienced management ' team ' and an

as a subcontractor during the war by doing work on proximity fuses. In 1945 it moved into the manufacture of electronic components on a subcontracting basis for a large electronics manufacturer. The company trained available labor in this work. Technical assistance was provided by the prime contractor,' p. 18.

[1] See, for example, David S. Meiklejohn, ' Financial Aspects of Diversification ', in *Charting the Company's Future*, American Management Association, Financial Management Series, Number 108 (New York, 1954); and Roy Foulke, *Diversification in Business Activity* (New York: Dun and Bradstreet, 1956).

experienced technical and labour force. Hence acquisition can be used as a means of obtaining the productive services and knowledge that are necessary for a firm to establish itself in a new field, and the addition of new managerial and technical services to the firm's internal supply of productive services is often far more important than the elimination of competition and the reduction of the costs of entry. For this reason acquisition is often a peculiarly suitable means of becoming acquainted with the techniques and problems of a new field when a firm wants to decide whether expansion in that field is an appropriate use of its own resources. Furthermore, acquisition frequently requires no cash outlay, and for firms whose financial position is not strong and whose managerial and technical services are highly specific to existing products, acquisition may be virtually the only way of diversifying activities.

Nevertheless, in spite of all these advantages, acquisition is by no means a universally available panacea for the ailing firm, nor does it permit indiscriminate and unlimited diversification for the prosperous one; a firm attempting to diversify and grow through. acquisition does not entirely escape the limitations either on the rate or on the direction of expansion imposed on it by its existing resources. Even external growth presupposes the existence of certain types of entrepreneurial qualities in the firm, and the successful integration of the acquiring and acquired firms into a single firm in the sense used in this study requires the managerial services of the acquiring firm.

In consequence, there is a limit to the rate of expansion of a firm even if acquisition is the principal method of expansion, for the managerial problems of regulating the relation between the parent firm and its new acquisition cannot be avoided. Consistent general policies must be worked out, financial and accounting procedures co-ordinated, personnel policies and the numerous other problems handled by the ' staff service ' departments must be integrated.[1] When the acquisition takes the firm into new and relatively unfamiliar fields, the problems of integration are less in some directions but are

---

[1] One writer insists that ' there is a legitimate analogy between a corporation with a new company acquisition and a family with a new baby. The new company, like the new child, does not simply represent the addition of one more member to the corporate family; it changes the relationships between everyone concerned. This requires patient adjustment of the new relationships and readjustments of the old '. Rodney C. Gott, ' Integrating and Consolidating Company Acquisitions ', in *Long-Range Planning in an Expanding Economy*, American Management Association, General Management Series, Number 179 (New York, 1956), p. 48.

greater in others: more autonomy in its own area may be permitted the new acquisition without risking a conflict with the parent company's policies and activities; on the other hand, the difficulties of working out an appropriate relationship between the two companies may be intensified.[1]

This limit on the rate of expansion implies that no firm can acquire every likely firm in sight in any given period of time; it must choose, and since mistakes may be costly and not always reparable, it will choose those enterprises which seem most likely to complement or supplement its existing activities, partly because of the predilections and experience of its management, and partly because such enterprises will tend to seem the more profitable. The expected profitability of a contemplated acquisition depends on the price paid for the new concern compared with its expected contribution to the earnings of the parent. Since acquisition is a purchase in which the price must be agreeable to the seller as well as to the buyer, the acquired firm must be more valuable to the acquiring firm (or combined with it) than it is to itself (or by itself); for only under these conditions will the one be willing to sell and the other be willing to buy at the same price.[2] There may be special reasons in individual cases (tax motives, desire of owners to retire, etc.) giving rise to the required difference in valuation, but by far the most overwhelming general reason is that the acquired firm in some way so complements the position of the acquiring firm that a bargain expected to be profitable to both parties can be reached. As we shall see in the next chapter, expansion by acquisition does not necessarily, or perhaps even usually, mean that a firm is entering a field for which it would otherwise have had no qualifications. Acquisition is often a profitable process precisely *because* the firm has peculiar qualifications in the new field.[3]

Thus the existing resources of a firm will not only limit the extent to which successful expansion can be effected through acquisition, but will also influence the direction of external expansion. It is not

[1] ' If growth is the principal objective of the acquiring company, that implies the closest kind of control over the activities of the new subsidiary. On the other hand, ventures into hitherto foreign fields imply a dependence on the local management which has been operating as an independent company in those fields. Too much control by the parent company would threaten the initiative and imagination of the business manager. Too little might threaten the growth of the two enterprises in their new combination.' Ibid., p. 40.

[2] We are not at present concerned with the conditions under which such ' willingness ' to sell may be forced on the seller.

[3] The argument summarized above is fully developed in the next chapter.

surprising, therefore, that investigations of merger and diversification show only a minority of firms moving into completely unrelated fields; and even then there is often more connection between the various activities of the merging firms than is immediately evident.[1] Where diversification involves not only entry into new markets but also the establishment of a new production base, the competitive advantage in the new field can often be traced to the fact that the firm has developed productive services in its existing productive activities which are especially valuable in the new activity. These services may arise from the high development of a particular type of engineering skill, or a particular kind of chemical process, or from an extensive knowledge of some material or waste product that the firm has discovered can be profitably used. Of hundreds of examples of diversification examined in the course of this study only a handful could be found where there appeared to be no technological link whatsoever between the new production base and the old, and this held true even though a large proportion of diversification was effected through the acquisition of other firms.[2]

The fact that firms are by and large specialized in a relatively few broad areas of activity, even when opportunities to diversify more extensively through acquisition have been open to them, is not entirely explained by the tendency of firms to restrict their attempts

[1] It should be noted that the ' conglomerate ' category used by the United States Federal Trade Commission in classifying mergers is not wholly applicable for the study of acquisition in unrelated fields in the sense used here. The Commission's application of the definition includes many mergers that we would not consider unrelated. Conglomerate acquisitions were defined by the Commission as ' . . . those in which there is little or no discernible relation between the business of the purchasing and the acquiring firms '. Presumably using this definition, the Commission found that slightly over 20 per cent of the total acquisitions in the period 1940–47 were conglomerate acquisitions. Apparently, however, all mergers that were not horizontal or vertical were classed as conglomerate. For example, new food products acquired by General Foods and Standard Brands (two speciality food concerns), the acquisition of other food products by dairy firms, the addition of new drug products to the line of drug firms, acquisition to manufacture chemical sprays by petroleum corporations, the entry into radio and agricultural equipment manufacture by aircraft concerns, were all treated as conglomerate acquisitions. Some of these would be treated here as diversification within an existing production base, while most of them would be considered to be diversification into new areas related to the old. See: *Report of the Federal Trade Commission on the Merger Movement* (Wash. D.C., 1948), pp. 59–63.

[2] Similarly, in the United States Temporary National Economic Committee survey referred to above, only 95 of 2,051 ' complex central office ' firms (i.e., firms with a number of establishments controlled from one central office and operating in more than one census industry) were found to have no ' functional relationship ' between the establishments, and it was noted that ' . . . a more intensive analysis of these 95 central offices might have revealed certain relationships among the plants which could not be ascertained in this study '. Temporary National Economic Committee, *The Structure of Industry*, Monograph No. 27, op. cit., p. 206.

to diversify to areas in which they already have some qualifications. After all, there are examples of truly ' conglomerate ' acquisitions and of firms which have clearly made no effort to establish themselves in any particular field, who have moved from product to product in a rather heterogeneous, free-swinging, and essentially unco-ordinated manner. For considerable periods the productive activities of some firms have been scattered and unconnected, there being no discernible ' sense ' in their selection of products. We have pre-viously noted, but left for later discussion, the fact that extensive and rapid acquisition can create ' firms ' which in certain stages of their growth have such an anomalous and amorphous organiza-tional structure that it is hard to see in what sense they can be called industrial firms. The process also often results in a similar dispersion of the productive activities of a firm and can create an extremely messy ' product structure '.

The profitability and even survival of a firm which fails to concentrate on the intensive development of any of its existing fields, and instead jumps from one type of production to another in response to changes in external conditions, depends entirely on the ability of its entrepreneurs to make shrewd financial deals, to judge correctly market changes, and to move rapidly from one product to another in response thereto. Individual fortunes have been made in this manner, but no enduring industrial organization is ever *main-tained* by this type of adaptation or growth, although it may have been a characteristic of the early years of some firms. Sooner or later such ' firms ' either break up or settle down to the exploitation of selected fields. The force responsible is that of competition. Although opportunities to enter into the production of new products may be a strong incentive for the firm to diversify its productive activities, and the prospects of acquiring profitable firms in unre-lated fields may be extensive, actual and expected external competitive pressures have to be reckoned with.

THE ROLE OF COMPETITION

Neither the attainment of a monopolistic market position nor technological progressiveness—the two ways in which a firm specializing in given products can meet the threat to its existence from competitors producing the same products—reduces the vulner-ability of the firm to adverse changes in total demand for the products it produces. It might seem, therefore, that a firm could best protect itself from both types of vulnerability by trying to produce as wide a variety of products as possible, thus reducing the impact on the firm as a whole not only of changes in total demand for individual products, but also of changes in its competitive position with respect to individual products. The notion that the production of many products is the most effective ' hedge ' against all kinds of adverse changes, and therefore the most appropriate method of offsetting the vulnerability of the firm to such changes, is extremely widespread.[1] It has, of course, a significant element of validity, but at the same time carries with it significant dangers, for the completely non-specialized firm is almost as vulnerable as the completely specialized one in the face of intense competition, especially when this competition is associated with rapid innovation.

The Necessity of Continued Investment in Existing Fields

In a competitive and technologically progressive industry a firm specializing in given products can maintain its position with respect to those products only if it is able to develop an expertise in technology and marketing sufficient to enable it to keep up with and to participate in the introduction of innovations affecting its products. If this proposition is valid for firms specializing in given products, then it is equally valid regardless of the number of products a firm produces. Thus if a firm chooses to produce a large number of products not closely related in technology and marketing, it must be in a position to devote sufficient resources to the development of each type of product to maintain its competitive position in the market for that type of product. In other words it must continue to invest in each of the several fields or be prepared to withdraw.

Withdrawal is often costly in the sense that the sale or scrap value of existing resources, or their value in some alternative use, may be considerably less than their value in their existing uses. Hence if their earning power is only maintained by additional new investment the return on that increment of investment may be high indeed, for all

---

[1] One investigator, for example, sent letters to some 200 businessmen and executives asking a variety of questions related to the problem of ' regularizing business investment '. He reported that ' The idea of developing supplementary product lines that either are more or less depression-proof or have a different cycle was endorsed more frequently by the respondents than any other single idea. . . . There is considerable experience, as well as statistical evidence, to show that new products and diversification provide some insurance against a general market decline '. See Emerson P. Schmidt, ' Promoting Steadier Output and Sales ', *Regularization of Business Investment*, report on a conference of the Universities-National Bureau Committee for Economic Research. (Princeton: Princeton Univ. Press, 1954), p. 343.

income over direct expenses obtained from the use of existing resources in existing uses may be attributed to the new investment.[1] Firms have therefore a strong incentive to continue investment in their existing fields so long as the gross profit earned exceeds the gross profit that could be obtained from alternative uses of the new investment funds together with whatever the firm could realize from the sale of the resources or from their adaptation to other uses. This does not mean that a firm will try to maintain the profitability of every product it produces for every market. Many resources may be fairly easily shifted from one use to another within any given production base and between groups of closely related bases, and within the limits of the mobility of resources a firm may add or drop product lines at little cost.[2] But this, too, requires investment in experimentation, research, and innovation.

Not only is new investment in existing fields likely to be required if cost and quality improvements of competitors are to be met, but expansion is also often necessary in a growing market because a firm's ' share in the market ' is sometimes itself an important

[1] Assume, for example, that the committed resources of a firm can be used only to produce existing products and that in this use the firm earns $1,000,000 over its direct costs. Assume now that an investment of $100,000 is required next year to effect a change in the major product in order to match innovations of competitors and that without this investment the firm could expect to lose virtually its entire market. The investment of $100,000 may raise net earnings by only $100 (or not at all) and yet the entire $1,000,000 is properly classed as a return on the $100,000. Of course, wherever committed resources have some alternative use, or can be sold, the relevant comparison is with their alternative earning power.

[2] The fact that several products can be and in fact are produced with the same general collection of productive resources is surely one of the primary reasons for the widespread use of ' full-cost pricing '. Under such conditions it would be thoroughly inappropriate for a firm to use variable direct cost (sometimes erroneously assumed to reflect marginal cost) for the calculation of the profitability of a given product. Direct costs do not correctly reflect marginal cost because they do not include the ' internal ' opportunity cost of the fixed resources used for the product, and it is of course well recognized that ' cost ' from an economic point of view must include opportunity cost. As the production of a particular product increases, more of the firm's fixed resources are absorbed by it and this should be taken into account in calculating the marginal cost of that product. In other words, what is fixed cost for the firm as a whole becomes variable cost for each product. In so far as a firm's calculation of the average cost of a product reflects the variation in the use of fixed resources at different levels of output, it becomes an approximation of the correct marginal cost. In other words, ' full-cost pricing ' (or the ' cost-plus ' principle) is appropriate policy if it means that the firm compares average profit margins in order to decide whether to make changes in the prices and output of its several products. Thus if several firms are producing roughly the same products in the same markets under similar cost conditions and the products are ' substitutable in production ', the price of each product will tend to stay considerably above direct costs; the competitive emphasis may be on market strategy, with price competition avoided, because each firm may in fact lose money if the profit margin on any product falls below that on the other products. See also the comment of D. H. Robertson, *Economic Commentaries* (London: Staples Press, 1956), p. 39.

competitive consideration. In some industries, for example in the production of certain types of durable consumer goods, consumer acceptance of the product is influenced by whether the producer can reasonably claim to be one of the ' leading ' producers. It is under these conditions that growth is often said, and with good reason, to be a necessary condition of survival.

A firm may go into many fields, but to maintain itself against competitive pressures it must be prepared to continue putting new funds into each field. This need for continuous new investment will restrict the number of fields a firm can support at any given time. The further from its existing areas of specialization it goes, the greater the effort required of the firm to attain the necessary competence not only in dealing with present production and market conditions, but also in making the adaptations and innovations necessary to keep up with competition.[1] After extensive periods of growth through acquisition, a reappraisal of product-lines is often called for, and considerable pruning and retrenchment may be required in order to maintain the profitability of each line the firm chooses to stay in.

Full-Line Diversification

Considerable diversification is often virtually forced on a firm as it tries to maintain its position in a given field. We have seen that much of the research responsible for the development of opportunities for the production of new products is itself a response to the exigencies of competition. The same competition will force a firm to take advantage of many of the opportunities thus created, not only to reduce costs and improve quality, but also to add new products. Whenever a firm has an opportunity to add new products which, together with existing products, would enable it to serve a wider variety of needs of its customers, it will have an incentive to add them because the convenience to consumers may well give it an advantage over competitors and enable it to attract new custom apart from any inherent advantages of the product itself. Thus the prospective profitability of a headstart, together with the expectation that the innovation might well be undertaken by some

[1] For an example of an extensive diversification programme that failed primarily because the programme was too extensive and too diverse for the company's existing experience and because preparations for the new activities were inadequate, see H. F. Williamson, *Winchester: The Gun that Won the West* (Wash. D.C.: Combat Forces Press, 1952), especially Chapters 7 and 8.

other firm at some other time, will encourage the firm to go ahead. If the new ' line ' is successful, other firms will be forced to follow suit; the necessity of carrying a ' full line ' then becomes an important reason for diversification.[1]

When customers expect to obtain a group of commodities from the same producer it becomes extremely difficult for a firm to maintain a position in the market unless it, too, carries the expected collection of products, and for an undiversified firm to break into any part of it. It was once reasonable in the United States for a firm to specialize in the production of washing machines; to-day few housewives would be willing to buy their automatic washing machine and their dryer from different companies. Matching models are required. Thus the combination of opportunities resulting from technological research and market standing may lead to diversification which is in the first instance a voluntary response to opportunities for the use of productive services and knowledge to better advantage. Such a diversification, once established, may create a customary and accepted relationship of complementarity in marketing which forces all other firms regardless of their particular productive abilities to conform. The basic areas of production in which a single firm must be competent widens in industries where this process is significant, and difficulties in the way of new firms desiring to enter the industry increase.

Much of the diversification of firms can be traced to this process, which varies in importance from industry to industry. It seems to be especially important in industries where there are a few large competing firms and also in industries producing durable consumers' goods. Diversification to meet innovations of competitors does not necessarily give rise to the kind of complementarity discussed above, for firms may introduce substitutes for their own

---

[1] Sometimes a firm is required to produce a ' full line ', not so much because of consumer convenience, but because of the technological relationship between the various ' products '; this also promotes vertical integration. Of integration and diversification in the early electrical companies, for example, Passer writes: ' Electrical products had to be part of a system—a lighting system, a power system, or a transportation system. To ensure that the component parts would operate together in a satisfactory manner, manufacturers found it advantageous to produce all, or nearly all, of the components of any system they chose to market. They also found it advantageous to sell and install the complete system. It was primarily the system characteristics of electrical products, therefore, that led an electrical firm to manufacture a full line of products and to assume the responsibility of placing them, in operating condition, in the hands of users.' Harold C. Passer, ' Development of Large-Scale Organization: Electrical Manufacturing around 1900 ', *Journal of Economic History*, Vol. 12, No. 4 (Fall, 1952), p. 390.

products in order to attract the customers of other firms. For example, the introduction by a firm of a new form of cigarette—'king size' or 'filter tip'—may cause consumers to switch their allegiance from competitive brands, and all producers may have to follow the innovator in order to keep their own customers. Nevertheless, the firm first to innovate may obtain a lead which permanently attracts a number of new customers to its products.[1]

Competition and Diversification into New Areas.

Although it may be profitable for a firm to continue to invest, and even to expand in its existing fields in order to ensure that its committed resources earn as large a return as possible, it does not follow from this that it will be profitable for the firm to attempt any significant improvement of its position when the improvement entails a significant additional commitment of resources. Having attained a satisfactory and reasonably secure position in its areas of specialization, a firm with resources available for expansion over and above those required to maintain its position in those areas may well find that opportunities for expansion into new areas look more promising than further expansion in its existing areas. Provided that the firm's position is sufficient to ensure it the important economies of production and marketing as well as the advantages of widespread consumer acceptance and confidence, the incremental investment required to obtain a larger output of existing products may be considered relatively unprofitable when new and attractive opportunities for the use of its funds are available.

In entering any new field, a firm must consider not only the rate of return it might expect on its new investment but also whether or not its resources are likely to be sufficient for the maintenance of the rate of investment that will be required to keep up with competitors' innovations and expansion in its existing fields as well as in the new one. Even when a firm enters a new field armed with a revolutionary innovation and is able to ward off competition with

---

[1] In a recent survey of 500 firms in four industries in four geographical areas, it was found that ' one of the more important effects of competition among manufacturers is that it induces " product dynamics ". Because of the appearance of a competitive product, new products were introduced by 36 per cent of the food firms surveyed, 42 per cent of the textile and apparel firms, 51 per cent of the electricity and electronics firms, and 31 per cent of the metal fabricating and light manufacturing firms.' Herner, Meyer and Co., *Research and Development and the Use of Technical Information in Small and Medium Sized Manufacturing Firms*: (A Report to the Office of Technical Services, U.S. Department of Commerce, 1956), pp. 22–23

patent protection or other restrictive devices, it must expect that in time it will be overtaken if it fails to continue to develop its advantage.

If entry is effected through internal expansion, more of the existing managerial and technical resources of the firm will be required to establish and maintain the firm's position in the new area than will be required if entry is effected through the acquisition of a profitable and well-managed concern already in the field. In the latter case the firm may frequently expect that the new acquisition will sustain itself, in the sense that any new investment required will be generated by its own successful operations. But to discover, acquire, and subsequently to effect the necessary administrative integration of other firms, calls on the services of existing resources in the various ways we have already mentioned. The limit thereby set to the rate of expansion through acquisition, together with the fact that the firm must expect to meet competition in each of its basic areas, tends to encourage a considerable measure of specialization in broadly defined areas of operation.

Firms, for the most part, do ' specialize ', but in a much wider sense than the ' logic ' of industrial efficiency would suggest, for the kind of ' specialization ' they seek is the development of a particular ability and strength in widely defined areas which will give them a special position *vis-à-vis* existing and potential competitors. In the long run the profitability, survival, and growth of a firm does not depend so much on the efficiency with which it is able to organize the production of even a widely diversified range of products as it does on the ability of the firm to establish one or more wide and relatively impregnable ' bases ' from which it can adapt and extend its operations in an uncertain, changing, and competitive world. It is not the scale of production nor even, within limits, the size of the firm, that are the important considerations, but rather the nature of the basic position that it is able to establish for itself.

A superficial look at the collection of products produced by many large corporations to-day might appear to contradict this analysis. Yet if one examines closely the established firms with a long history of successful growth, and in particular, the genesis of their product diversification, one will find that their strength lies in the fact that they have established and maintained a basic position with respect to the use of certain types of resources and technology and the exploitation of certain types of market.[1] Although they have rarely confined themselves to a narrow range of products, they have exploited the economies of production, organization, and growth, and have taken advantage of monopolistic and quasi-monopolistic market positions, in a small number of fairly well defined areas. The characteristic strength of the large, well-established firm does *not* derive from a miscellaneous collection of resources in many fields, but from the fact that it has 'defences in depth', as it were, in a few special fields. Nevertheless, just as there is a limit to the rate of growth of firms but not to their absolute size, so there is a limit to the rate at which they can enter new fields of production but not to the number of fields they can enter given only time. After all, the process of corporate growth and diversification has only in the past few decades become well developed; although extreme diversification is characteristic of some firms, specialization broadly defined is more the rule than the exception.

DIVERSIFICATION AS A SOLUTION TO SPECIFIC PROBLEMS

Even in a growing economy where major recessions in general economic activity are prevented, demand for particular products may be unstable, may grow at a very slow rate, or may even decline. In addition, the demand for the products of particular firms may be seriously depressed by the successful inroads of competitors. Diversification is widely seen as a solution to some of the problems that may be created for the individual firm by unfavourable movements in demand conditions.

Temporary Fluctuations in Demand

Seasonal and cyclical fluctuations in demand, the typical ' bunching ' of demand for many types of durable goods, fluctuations due to the temporary popularity of new products, etc., give rise to

---

[1] The analysis above has been the analysis of a process leading to a particular result, that is, to the development of a certain type of ' situation ' or ' state '. Wherever the process in reality is a continuing one (and few results or situations are final), there is a serious difficulty inherent in any attempt to demonstrate or illustrate theoretical conclusions with reference to observed facts. This difficulty is particularly evident in statements like the one in the text; for a firm may be ' long-established ' and ' successful ', but this fact alone does not guarantee its future, especially since its own actions and policies may at any time depart radically from those of the past. For example, such a firm may become so impressed by the vogue for ' diversification as such ' that the policies and actions to which we have traced its strength in the past no longer characterize its present, and statements treating its present position as a ' result ' of its past history must take such changes into account when recent history is substantially different in kind from earlier history.

periodic under-utilization of resources and to extreme fluctuations in earnings for firms producing products subject to such influences. These conditions stimulate firms to search for new products which will permit a fuller utilization of their resources and reduce the fluctuations in their profits. But if we assume that firms are primarily interested in total profits, neither the full use of resources nor the stabilization of earnings is sufficient to justify diversification unless total expected profits are increased thereby.[1]

There is no question about the profitability of diversification if a firm is able to find products which it can produce in those periods when demand for its major product is low and which do not conflict with its ability to take full advantage of its opportunities when demand is high. Firms whose products are subject to seasonal fluctuations, for example, can sometimes find other products that they can produce in the ' off season ', using some of their existing resources, and which they can abandon in the peak season in favour of their major product.[2] Demand for the new product may fluctuate inversely to that of the existing products, the market may be easy to enter and leave, or the firm may be able to produce for inventory in the slack period. Under these conditions the new product will not conflict with the maximum exploitation of the old and will be a clear gain.

The problem becomes more complicated when the output of the new product cannot be appreciably varied over short periods but must be maintained and perhaps expanded even when demand for the basic product is high; the firm, for example, may not be able to neglect its new customers, even for short periods, without running the risk of losing them entirely. If the new product uses some of the resources required for the old—as it must do if part of the purpose of the diversification is to permit a fuller utilization of the firm's fixed resources and help meet overhead costs—then the production of the new product may conflict with the desired production of the old when the demand for the old product is high; and the firm, in filling up the valleys, will have to shave off the peaks. To the extent that a firm can predict with reasonable accuracy the magnitude of the fluctuations and can compare the profit gained in the valleys

---

[1] On the other hand, the firm may be concerned about the continuing availability of resources, especially labour, if its activities fluctuate severely. It may also feel some responsibility to its work force, and for this reason attempt to stabilize its production.

[2] The traditional coal-ice diversification was surely prompted as much by the similarity of resources and markets as by the complementary fluctuations of demand.

with the cost of giving up gains at the peaks, its plans to even out fluctuations in the use of resources and in earnings can take explicitly into account the effect on total earnings. If they are not increased, the carefully calculating firm would forgo the diversification, for fluctuations in earnings are not particularly significant as such, except perhaps over fairly long periods, if both the timing and extent of the fluctuations are sufficiently predictable to enable the firm to calculate its total earnings over a period. Unless there are special circumstances (for example, tax issues, community responsibility), a firm should not sacrifice higher earnings for lower earnings merely because the latter are more evenly distributed in time.

The real difficulties arise when fluctuations in demand are not easily predictable; in this case not only are the problems of financial management intensified, but the unknown profitability of the peak periods and the unknown duration of the lean periods, forces the firm to calculate earnings over a ' cycle ' with a heavy discount for uncertainty. Other things being equal, it is reasonable for a firm to choose a more certain over a less certain income. There is a presumption that earnings from products in steady demand are likely to be easier to forecast than earnings from products the demand for which fluctuates unpredictably. Uncertainty alone, therefore, will bias a firm in favour of producing products that will yield a more stable income, a bias that will be overcome only if the most confidently expected earnings from the products in unstable demand are sufficiently high to offset the necessary discount for the uncertainty with which the expectation is held.

Except for seasonal variations, it is rarely possible accurately to predict fluctuations in demand. The less accurate the firm feels its predictions are, the more uncertain are profit expectations; consequently the firm will give more weight to the possibilities of obtaining a more complete utilization of its resources and a more stable income stream and less weight to the possible restriction on its ability to meet fully the peak demand for its existing product.

Firms whose products are particularly susceptible to cyclical movements are in this category. The timing and extent of cyclical fluctuations are not reasonably predictable, yet past experience lends force to the expectation that recessions are likely to occur. Firms producing durable goods, and especially durable producer goods, can confidently expect severe fluctuations in demand even in the absence of any severe fluctuations in the general level of activity. They are unable to predict these movements with any precision and they often attempt to diversify into the production of products the demand for which is influenced by circumstances different from those influencing their existing markets. Thus manufacturers of durable goods try to take on less durable products, manufacturers of producer goods try to reach forward towards the final consumer, or producers of 'luxury' goods search for products less sensitive to changes in consumers' incomes.[1]

Diversification to deal with temporary fluctuations in demand that are definitely expected but that cannot be estimated with sufficient accuracy to make profit calculations more than informed guesses comes very close to diversification as a device for coping with a generalized uncertainty. The larger and more pervasive effects of uncertainty—which give rise to a feeling that it is somehow safer to maintain a diversified portfolio, and to a general distrust of putting all eggs in one basket, even if that basket is closely watched—are not overcome simply by adjusting net revenue calculations. Many a firm has proclaimed the philosophy that its security is greater if it produces a wide range of products instead of concentrating on those products which, even after all practical allowances for risk have been made, seem to be the most profitable. In other words, diversification becomes a hedge, not against those changes that are definitely expected (although it fulfils that function too) but against changes of any sort which the 'luck of the game' may bring. In practice, however, firms recognize that different kinds of products are subject to different types of risk and, within the limits permitted by their productive resources, choose a range of products designed to give the greatest protection against the various definable types of risk.

Permanent Adverse Changes in Demand

When a firm's chief motive for diversification is to ensure an overall stability of earnings in the face of a generalized uncertainty, it is concerned as much with possible long-run adverse changes in the demand for any of its products as it is with possible fluctuations. Indeed the expectation that demand for major products will eventually slacken is a major reason for firms searching for new products. Here the firm that diversifies because it expects the demand for its

---

[1] For discussion and examples of this see the Universities-National Bureau Conference volume, *Regularization of Business Investment*. (Princeton: Princeton Univ. Press, 1954). Especially the paper by Emerson P. Schmidt, pp. 319–368

existing products to decline should be distinguished from the firm that finds the demand for its existing products growing too slowly to satisfy its desire to expand. There is no substantial difference between the actions of the two firms except, perhaps, that the former may be willing to act on less attractive opportunities than the latter for which diversification may be not only a condition of continued growth but even of survival.

Sometimes the necessity of searching for new products is pressed upon a firm faced with an unexpected and unprepared-for decline in the demand for its basic product which appears permanent. Firms in such circumstances have the greatest need for diversification and often the least ability to effect it. Fundamental changes in demand such as those arising from changes in technology or in consumers' tastes are rarely so sudden and unheralded that the enterprising firm could not have prepared for them while its position was still strong enough to give it the advantages it needed to enter successfully some new field. The absence of such preparation is prima facie evidence that the resources of the firm are extremely specialized or that entrepreneurial ability is not of a very high order.

The Direction of Diversification

Diversification—the production of new products—is the obvious course of action for firms in any of the circumstances outlined above. The one common characteristic of such firms is a motive for diversification which arises neither from the perception of specific opportunities to take on the production of particular new products nor from the pressures of competitive innovation. In other words, for them the desire to diversify precedes the perception of any special opportunities for diversification, and the problem is to find suitable products for the purpose. Once again, however, the search is necessarily circumscribed by the existing productive services available to the firm, of which the so-called ' intangible ' services of managerial and technical skill may be far the most important. Bold ventures require entrepreneurial imagination, large ventures require managerial talent, entry into highly specialized fields requires some specialized ability, acquisition requires cash or at least sufficient standing in the capital market, or general reputation, to make it profitable for another firm to accept an exchange of shares. For firms with none of these, diversification into products which provide promising scope for the future will be difficult indeed.

Where firms have no special advantages which will ease their entry into new fields and are not in a position to acquire well-established and successful firms already in the field, they must, like any new and not particularly well-endowed entrepreneur, look for fields where entry is easy and no special skills are required. Given sufficient flexibility of outlook there is nothing to prevent their entry into such fields, even when the technology and markets are completely unrelated to their existing activities, but the attempted diversification may be short-lived, for it is in precisely this kind of field where competition is likely to be intense and disappearance rates high for the existing population of firms, and where few firms without special advantages will succeed in maintaining their footing for long.

In considering the role of existing resources in determining the direction of diversification that is sought for its own sake, we must make a distinction between the kind of productive services required for internal expansion and the kind required for acquisition. For the former, existing plant, equipment, types of raw materials, skills, knowledge, and original ideas will be much more important forces than they will be for the latter. The task of entry and the task of maintaining the new field against competition is easier if other advantages in addition to entrepreneurial and managerial capacity are available. When it is possible to expand and diversify by buying other firms, the only restriction on the direction or scope of the expansion is that set by the entrepreneurial ability to discover an appropriate firm and to negotiate the acquisition, and by the managerial resources required to effect the necessary integration. The selection of firms to be acquired can be made with little reference to the other productive services available in the acquiring firm but rather with reference to the way in which the new product will supplement seasonally, cyclically, geographically, in market relationships, or in any other relevant way the firm's existing productive activities. In spite of this relative freedom of choice, however, the truly conglomerate diversification is relatively rare, as was pointed out above, because wherever the firm has other advantages, especially technological and marketing links with the new products, its competitive position is thereby strengthened. For this reason we find that company after company looking for new products stresses its own peculiar productive specialities, although particularly for the large corporation, successful diversification is possible even in fields completely unrelated to existing activities.

DIVERSIFICATION AS A GENERAL POLICY FOR GROWTH

There are fine distinctions between diversification in response to specific opportunities, diversification to solve specific problems of demand, and diversification as a general policy for growth. In practice they are inextricably intertwined, and often the same act of diversification can be explained with reference to any one of these motives, or to all three together. Many firms proclaim diversification to be the appropriate ' policy ' for a growing firm—' policy ' in the sense that the firm should plan to be constantly looking for profitable fields in which to enter. It was suggested above that diversification is one means of protecting the firm as a whole against foreseen and unforeseen changes which might adversely affect individual products— in other words, a means of providing a kind of insurance against otherwise uninsurable risk and uncertainty. Firms that diversify primarily for this reason are presumably acting on the conviction that profitable growth over the long haul can be better secured through diversification; but this is not the chief reason why diversification as a policy for growth is so important. There are even more powerful reasons why the enterprising firm may diversify in the interests of growth.[1]

In earlier chapters the nature of the internal restrictions on the rate of growth of firms was analysed as well as the nature of the internal inducements to expansion. Among these inducements are to be counted not only the specific opportunities presented by a firm's resources, but also the unused services of management. If firms are not concerned to ' maximize ' the rate of return on a given amount of capital, but rather to increase their total profits by increasing their total investment, then clearly whenever a firm's management feels that the firm's capacity for growth is greater than that permitted by existing markets and existing products, it will have an incentive to diversify.[2] The possibility of producing new products

[1] As was pointed out in Chapter II, a preoccupation with growth does not necessarily conflict with an equal preoccupation with profits. We have assumed that firms are concerned with increasing their total profits over the long period from their own operations. They therefore will invest as much as they profitably can in these operations, for all profitable investment in the firm will increase total profits. Hence behind the notion that diversification as a general policy is conducive to growth lies the notion that it will turn out to be more profitable than specialization.

[2] See the motion filed in the Federal courts by the Cudahy Packing Company requesting that it be freed from the restrictions imposed on its diversification by a consent decree following an antitrust action in 1920. The Company complained that its opportunities for profit were limited because its diversification outside the meat-packing industry was prevented, that it was unable to compete with other similar companies because it could not take advantage of the changed conditions of distribution, and that

and acquiring new markets frees the firm from the restrictions on its expansion imposed by the demand for its existing products, although not from the restrictions imposed by its existing resources.

The extensive development in modern times of efficient techniques for decentralized administration as well as the extensive opportunities for expansion through acquisition make possible an extremely rapid rate of growth of firms, at least up to a point. It seems likely that few individual markets can grow as fast as many firms in the middle-size range can grow. It is therefore to be expected that ' diversification ' will become the slogan of firms that are reasonably well established, possess efficient managerial resources operating in a reasonably well worked-out administrative structure and want to increase their profits at a more rapid rate than their existing products permit. Existing markets may be profitable and growing, but all that is required to induce diversification is that they do not grow fast enough to use fully the productive services available to the individual firm.

VERTICAL INTEGRATION

A special form of diversification, which in many cases is of great significance for the growth of the firm, involves an increase in the number of intermediate products that a firm produces for its own use. A firm may integrate ' backward ', and start producing products it previously bought from others. It may integrate ' forward ', and start producing new products (including distribution services) which are closer in the chain of production to the final consumer. In this process some of its existing final products may become intermediate products. Both of these processes are methods of growth. I do not want to enter into an extensive and exhaustive analysis of vertical integration here, but merely to discuss some of the important factors affecting a firm's decision to put its available resources into this type of productive activity rather than into a further expansion of its existing products or into some other products.

Much of the foregoing discussion of diversification into new final products is equally applicable to vertical diversification; opportunities arising from the nature of the productive resources of the firm giving the firm an advantage in the production of some of its

' instead of promoting free competition, the application of the provisions of the decree to Cudahy restricts competition '. *Wall Street Journal*, Feb. 2, 1956.

own requirements, market opportunities in the case of forward integration, competitive pressures of various kinds, special problems arising from the existence of uncertainty, all play a similar role.

We start with the same basic assumption that firms will in general devote their resources to those areas of productive activity which they believe will be most profitable when due allowance is made for risk and uncertainty. In a purely formal sense it follows from this that backward integration will take place only if it is expected to reduce costs, for the decision to integrate backwards is a decision to make instead of buy materials or processes which enter into the costs of production of existing products; in the last analysis, the profitability of backward integration is measured by its effect on the net revenue of the firm. Hence the opportunity to increase profits by integrating backwards is to be treated in the same way as other productive opportunities of the firm—the additional profit expected must be compared with the expected profit from alternative uses of the resources required.[1] Consequently, even though firms may well be able to produce more cheaply than they can buy many of the products they use, the diversion of resources to this purpose may be far less profitable than their use in other ways.

The relevant savings in production that backward integration may bring can be divided into two categories: those relating to the efficiency with which the production of the firm's existing products can be organized, and those relating to the price that must be paid for supplies. In the first category come all of the problems in obtaining supplies of the required kind, of adequate quality, in adequate

---

[1] In other words, the estimates of the cost savings traceable to backward integration, like the profit estimates with respect to other possible avenues of expansion, do not include the opportunity cost of resources, for these can only be discovered after the alternative calculations are made. Hence, the carefully calculating firm will not integrate backwards merely because a comparison of the costs of production with the cost of buying outside the firm shows a decisive saving. It could not, from this information alone, decide whether integration would be the most profitable use of the resources that would be absorbed by it. A reduction in cost is therefore a necessary, but not a sufficient, condition for profitable integration. That many firms have an insufficient appreciation of this fact can perhaps be inferred from the numerous strictures of accountants and management experts directed to the alleged propensity of firms to ignore, not only the fact that resources will be absorbed which can be used elsewhere, but also the increase in fixed cost which the taking on of new activities will eventually, if not immediately, cause. Robert L. Dixon has called the ' piecemeal attachment of relatively minor activities of service and supply ' by the name of ' creep ', because a firm may start out with a small activity which seems to have cost-saving opportunities without considering whether or not the increment of new investment which will be required if the integration is successful will be the best use of its resources. See his ' Creep ', *Journal of Accountancy*, Vol. 96, No. 1 (July 1953), pp. 48–55.

amounts, at the required times. Difficulties in obtaining supplies may be particularly apparent when tools and materials must conform to rigid specifications in quality and design, in rapidly growing industries where the different ' levels ' of the industry do not expand simultaneously,[1] where there are close technological links between the various stages of production, where monopolistic squeezes by suppliers take place, or where there are periodical difficulties in obtaining the required materials due to intense supply or demand fluctuations.[2] Finally backward integration, like other forms of diversification, is promoted by a desire to avoid the risk of fluctuations and to enhance the security of the firm in the face of a generalized uncertainty. In this latter case, the statement that a reduction in cost is a condition of profitable backward integration is a purely formal one, for ' cost ' is reduced only because of an arbitrary, non-calculable, and essentially psychological element attributed to the firm's attitude towards uncertainty.

The foregoing dicussion of conditions conducive to backward integration relates primarily to integration as a method of ensuring the firm's sources of supply. But it is not necessary that gross difficulties in obtaining supplies occur or are feared; even minor irregularities in the flow of operations, particularly if they are uncertain in their incidence, intensify the managerial problem of organizing efficiently the production of a firm's existing products.

---

[1] Firms producing products the demand for which has been growing rapidly may be faced with difficulties in obtaining semi-manufactured items needed in their production process because of lags in the development of the supplying industries. This may be particularly important for mass-production firms in a relatively new industry which require large supplies of fairly specialized products, and is one of the reasons for some of the integration of the faster growing firms in the less industrialized countries. Or uneven growth at different levels of an industry may result from differences in technological developments and rates of investment. McLean and Haigh in their intensive study of integration in the oil industry, discovered that integration patterns were affected by the unequal growth of different sectors in the industry; for example differential technological developments between crude oil field and refinery, between refinery and marketing, and between wholesale and retail operations: ' Technological developments often prompted alterations in integration patterns . . . the most dramatic example may be found in the technological development of the products pipe line ' after which a ' broad movement toward integration into products transportation activities was launched '. See John G. McLean and Robert W. Haigh, *The Growth of Integrated Oil Companies* (Boston: Harvard, 1954), p. 513.

[2] In periods when supplies are exceptionally scarce relative to demand, individual firms are often unable to obtain all of their requirements without delay from their customary suppliers and they find that other suppliers are reluctant to disappoint their own regular customers for the sake of an occasional stranger. The importance attached by firms to the maintenance of their existing business relationships tends to modify their willingness to let prices be the sole, or even the primary, guide in their selection of customers, especially when periods of high prices are only temporary.

Hence where efficient management is a scarce resource, there will be a strong tendency to integrate in order to reduce the managerial difficulties not only of planning and controlling existing operations but also, and sometimes especially, of planning future investment. Any cost-savings may be extremely difficult to estimate since the type and amount of managerial service which may be freed for other uses may be virtually impossible to identify, and integration may occur less in response to economic calculations than to engineering calculations of efficiency. Furthermore, since management is itself frequently specialized, a company may well find that opportunities for using their specialized services are greatest in some form of backward integration.[1]

In addition, backward integration may appear profitable because the firm believes it can produce some of its requirements so much more cheaply than it can obtain them in the market that the reduction in costs adds more to total profits than any alternative use of resources. The suppliers of an important product to a firm may be organized in a close monopoly which restricts output and raises prices to an extent that makes integration profitable for their customers. Or a firm may have special productive advantages which enable it to produce at exceptionably low cost. In this case, the firm may even produce for sale outside the firm as well as to meet its own requirements.

Forward integration, *mutatis mutandis*, is subject to much the same kind of influences, but unlike backward integration, it may draw the firm into new markets as well as into new types of production. As we have seen, breaking into new markets requires the diversion of resources to selling. In so far as the new products can be sold by the same organization that had been selling the firm's products before the integration occurred, no new resources may be required. But if substantially new selling techniques must be developed and new channels of distribution created, the tasks of the firm are not essentially different from those discussed with respect to other forms of diversification into new markets.

Vertical integration is one method by which a firm attempts to maintain its competitive position and to improve the profitability of its existing products. Much integration is directly traceable to

---

[1] McLean and Haigh found that ' In nearly all cases, the shifts in the prime field of managerial competence were accompanied sooner or later by corresponding shifts in a company's integration pattern.' *Op. cit.*, p. 512.

the technical efficiency of conducting a sequence of operations in close proximity, and to the maintenance of a smooth flow of supplies and more stable markets; some of it is profitable because of the superior ability of a firm to produce at least some of its own requirements. As is true for other forms of diversification, however, once a firm has resources committed to any type of productive activity, it is often profitable to continue the activity even after the conditions have passed which made the original decision to integrate appear profitable. Occasionally, a firm makes special efforts to promote the development of other firms capable of supplying its needs because it realizes that it can make better use of its resources in other directions. Or when technological advance is rapid in the production of some of the firm's intermediate products, and technical skills are required which are not closely related to those in which the firm is especially proficient, the firm may well find it not worth while to continue the investment necessary to keep up with the rest of the industry. It is not uncommon, either, for firms to find that an act of integration was originally a mistake, to acknowledge their error and withdraw. This seems the fairly frequent fate of integration that involves a movement from manufacturing to retailing, or from retailing to manufacturing. On the other hand, the managerial economies in the control of operations and the planning of capital investment, even if not important original causes of integration, are sometimes an important reason for maintaining it once it has been effectively organized.[1]

THE FIRM AS A POOL OF RESOURCES

The discussion of the role of diversification in the process of growth perhaps brings out more clearly than would anything else the significance of the statement made in an earlier chapter that a firm is essentially a pool of resources the utilization of which is organized in an administrative framework. In a sense, the final products being produced by a firm at any given time merely repre-

[1] Cf. the following appraisal of this aspect of integration in the oil industry: 'It appears therefore that the managerial and operating gains permitted by vertical integration were rarely an important motivation for integration and were generally unanticipated at the time the moves were made. Ultimately, however, these gains may transcend in importance the specific forces and circumstances which have thus far prompted integration decisions . . . . The managerial and operating gains realized from vertical integration . . . have grown steadily in importance throughout the entire history of the industry, and there is considerable reason to believe that their full potentialities have by no means yet been realized.' John G. McLean and Robert W. Haigh, op. cit., p. 302.

sent one of several ways in which the firm could be using its resources, an incident in the development of its basic potentialities. Over the years the products change, and there are numerous firms to-day which produce few or none of the products on which their early reputation and success were based. Their basic strength has been developed above or below the end-product level as it were—in technology of specialized kinds and in market positions. Within the limits set by the rate at which the administrative structure of the firm can be adapted and adjusted to larger and larger scales of operation, there is nothing inherent in the nature of the firm or of its economic function to prevent the indefinite expansion of its activities.

The continual change in the productive services and knowledge within a firm along with the continual change in external circumstances present the firm with a continually changing productive opportunity. Not all firms, to be sure, possess the qualifications which will permit them to take advantage of such opportunities, but it is sufficient for our purposes to have outlined the qualifications, to. have analyzed the factors determining the direction of expansion of those firms possessing the requisite qualifications, and to have shown that there is no necessary limit to growth as time passes.

The adaptations and adjustments that are required of the firm as it expands are directly influenced by the external resistance to its expansion. We have shown how the necessity of maintaining a competitive position in its basic fields restricts the rate of diversification of a firm, and how the innovating activities of competitors restrict and sometimes shape the pattern of diversification, although we have touched only lightly on other considerations affecting the rate of growth of firms.

In spite of the opportunities and pressures which lead firms into the production of a wider range of products, it seems likely that most firms still derive the bulk of their income from a relatively few closely related products. That this should be true of the small and medium-sized firms is not surprising in view of the difficulties attendant upon extensive diversification, but it seems also true of many of the larger firms.[1] No comprehensive and detailed empirical

[1] The T.N.E.C. investigation of the product structure of 50 large manufacturing companies found that the ' major portion of their total revenue tended in most cases to be derived from relatively few products '. Monograph No. 27, op. cit., p. 629. But for reasons pointed out above little can be concluded from the T.N.E.C. study. Not only is the sample small, but the ambiguity in the definition of ' product ' and the fact that

study of all aspects of the diversification of firms has ever been made; the information is not available from published figures and individual firms are reluctant to provide the quantitative and qualitative information required, even if they have it, which most of them probably do not for earlier periods.[1] We know that diversification is widespread to-day[2]; we do not know how widespread it was earlier in the century. We know from the annual reports of corporations that most of the large firms lay great emphasis on the possibilities of diversification, and we know that the speeches and writings of management experts, business executives, and 'informed commentators' extol its virtues.[3] It may be that diversification as a method of growth is becoming increasingly important; it seems likely, but the impression may be wholly false. In any event, it follows from our analysis that any change in circumstances that widens the productive opportunity of firms or increases their managerial capacity for growth in relation to the growth of demand for their existing products will tend to increase diversification.

It is perhaps reasonable, therefore, to assume that the development and dissemination of the techniques of decentralized managerial organization, the rise of a professional management class, government actions (especially tax policy) which create favourable

we do not know what kind of firms were included in the sample makes interpretation difficult.

The Federal Trade Commission study of diversification does not give information about the revenue of firms, but does show that 'a company's 5 principal product classes constituted over 80 per cent of the total shipments in the case of every 1 of the 50 smallest firms among the 1,000 companies, in the case of 48 of the 50 median companies and in the case of 30 of the 50 largest companies'. And, furthermore, 'that generally companies were much more dependent on a few industries than on an equal number of product classes', op. cit., p. 39.

[1] The only usable published material is to be found in the annual reports of corporations which until the last ten to twenty years were remarkably uninformative. Such reports, together with discussions with businessmen, have provided much of the empirical material from which the analytical framework of this study sprang. No attempt was made, however, to collect and to analyze systematically the wealth of information available. The 'testing' in this manner of the propositions put forward here remains to be done.

[2] The Federal Trade Commission report to which we have referred above provides extensive statistical information by size-groups of firms for one year and is sufficient to establish the proposition that diversification is extremely widespread to-day. It also provides considerable information on the 'extent' of diversification so far as census product-classes and census industries are concerned.

[3] The remarks of C. W. Walton, General Manager, Adhesives and Coatings Division, Minnesota Mining and Manufacturing Company are typical: 'Corporate growth possibilities can be unlimited for you if you will employ to-day's modern methods of diversification research and new product commercialization in the conduct of your business.' From 'Corporate Growth Through Diversification Research and New Products Commercialization', in *Michigan Business Papers*, No. 28. *Conference on Sales Management*, March 12, 1954. (Ann. Arbor, Univ. of Michigan, 1954), p. 15.

conditions for acquisition, the extensive development of industrial research and the consequent widening range of knowledge of chemistry, mechanics, electronics, and other fundamental aspects of industrial science which create within the individual firm an industrial technology suitable for a broad range of products, will all tend to raise the rate of growth of firms. We have yet to discuss the factors influencing changes in the rate of growth; before doing so we must analyse, more systematically than has so far been possible, the process of acquisition and merger.

CHAPTER VIII

Expansion Through Acquisition and Merger

The corporation and merger. The economic basis of acquisition. *Personal considerations and special situations. Critical points in the process of expansion. The competitive expansion of Alpha. Where Beta blocks the expansion of Alpha. Combination.* The purchase and sale of ' businesses ' that are not firms. *Economic basis for the sale of a ' business '. Effect on the process of growth. The appropriateness of diversification.* The role of entrepreneurial services. *Entrepreneurial temperament and the profit motive. Empire-building and merger.* The role of managerial services. *The necessity of administrative integration.* Merger and the dominant firm.

Until recent times the rise and eventual decline of individual business firms in a competitive economy was often treated as almost a law of nature.[1] So long as the fortunes of firms depended on the fortunes of individuals or families on whom rested a personal responsibility for their firms' operations, both the rate of growth and the size of individual firms were severely restricted. The widespread adoption of the legal device of incorporation substantially affected not only the possible size of firms and their rate of growth, but also the process of growth.

There can be no question that the corporation has many advantages over the unincorporated individual proprietorship or partnership in raising capital, but this alone would not have changed the nature of the expansion process. The more important consequence of the introduction of the corporate form of enterprise for the process of expansion was the easy legal transfer of the ownership of firms which in fact accompanied it, in particular the ease with which one incorporated firm was permitted to acquire or merge with another.[2] The absorption of other firms, though possible, is

---

[1] Some contemporary observers take the same view, however. See, for example, Kenneth Boulding, *Reconstruction of Economics* (New York: Wiley, 1950), p. 34.

[2] This point has also been stressed by George Stigler: ' The only persuasive reason I have found for their [mergers] late occurrence is the development of the modern corporation and the modern capital market. In a regime of individual proprietorships and partnerships, the capital requirements were a major obstacle to buying up the firms in an industry, and unlimited liability was a major obstacle to the formation of partnerships.' George J. Stigler, ' Monopoly and Oligopoly by Merger ', *American Economic Review*, Vol. XL, No. 2, *Proceedings* (May 1950), p. 28.

more difficult, at least on a large scale, for the unincorporated firm, and new methods of expansion spread rapidly as more and more firms adopted the corporate form. In addition, opportunities in the industrial field for the activities of ' promoters ' and ' captains of finance ' were widened.

This last consequence has been partly responsible for a distinct tendency in the literature to treat merger and combination as almost a study in economic pathology. Haunted by the ghosts of financiers and hard-hitting industrialists like Morgan, Gary and the elder Rockefeller, inextricably associated in the public mind with the more mysterious machinations of high finance, and surrounded by an aura of monopoly, collusion, and exploitation, corporate merger, combination, and acquisition have seldom been given a respectable place in the economists' models of economic activity.[1] The rudimentary biological theories of the growth of firms break down over merger: life-cycle analogies make no provision for abrupt discontinuities and changed identity in individual development; ecological analogies have trouble with sudden unpredictable changes in the very nature of individual organisms and the consequent changes in their relation to their environment. But the inadequate theoretical attention to the processes of merger and combination is only another aspect of the lack of any developed theory of the process of the growth of firms. In the traditional ' theory of the firm ' it is only the competitive or market position of the firm that is relevant, not how or why the firm came into that position— indeed, as has been pointed out, the economists' formal models of firm behaviour are not often concerned with a firm's position as a whole but only with price and output policy regarding particular products. Thus, in the literature of economics the question of merger is treated most extensively in connection with studies of monopoly and competition, market structures, the degree of concentration, etc., although recently the relation between merger and size has received considerable attention.

In spite of the anomalous position of merger and acquisition in the theoretical literature of economics, however, economists have

[1] Jesse Markham suggests that ' mergers have been associated so closely with the monopoly problem ' largely because ' the paths of economic theory and merger literature have rarely crossed. . . . Accordingly, the vast body of merger literature shows the lack of cohesive purpose that may have followed from empirical testings of merger theory '. Jesse W. Markham, ' Survey of the Evidence and Findings on Mergers ' in *Business Concentration and Price Policy* (Princeton: Princeton Univ. Press for National Bureau of Economic Research, 1955), p. 143.

not denied that these processes are normal and natural consequences of profit-seeking in a competitive economy in which the corporation is the dominant form of business organization and the law permits one corporation to acquire another. They are thoroughly consistent with the nature of the actors and the possibilities for action existing in such an economy. The fact that fixed capital, ' market position', or even 'good will', once created, persist in time means that there is always a choice between recombining the old and building anew. If legal institutions permit one going concern to purchase or merge with another, then, whether expansion takes place through the building of new plant or through the acquisition of another firm will, in any particular case, depend on which appears to be the more profitable course of action.[1] Whenever merger is considered to be the most profitable way to expand, there will surely be a tendency for merger to occur. Economic analysis that treats it only as a means of reducing competition, or establishing monopolistic dominance, is placing the wrong emphasis on one of the most significant characteristics of the firm in the modern economy.

In this study the term ' merger ' is used to denote any method of combining existing firms, whether it be the acquisition of one firm by another, the combination of two firms on equal terms, or the reorganization of an entire industry through a consolidation of its component firms. Merger as a method of expansion of an individual firm is of the first type only, and when it is useful to identity it specifically I shall speak of acquisition. The other two forms of merger involve more than simple expansion and I shall call them combination and consolidation respectively. Sometimes the second is almost indistinguishable from the first, the difference being largely one of name; and sometimes through a successive series of simple acquisitions the same result—a reorganization of an entire industry—is obtained by the first type of merger as by the third. But this absence in practice of a clear separation of the three types of merger need not worry us at this point.

Finally, we shall deal with a still different form of acquisition which has become of increasing importance in recent years, but is still largely neglected in the literature—the acquisition of one of the ' businesses ' of another firm (for example, the purchase by Illinois

---

[1] This statement is a simplified first approach. It ignores the problems raised by what I have called ' empire-building ' desires of entrepreneurs. But it will do for the moment.

McGraw Electric of the home appliance 'business' of General Mills mentioned in the preceding chapter). Often the large firms organize their various types of business in separate divisions or subsidiaries, and in many ways the purchase of such a business is little different from the purchase of an independent firm.

The same general procedure will be followed in this analysis of growth by merger as was followed in the analysis of the process of growth without merger. Except for illustrative purposes, no attempt will be made to describe particular mergers, or to discuss in detail the course of merger in any country or at any period. There is a large body of literature on this and related subjects, including statistical studies of the occurrence of merger in the economy as a whole as well as studies of the merger activities of particular firms. From these studies have emerged lists of the incentives for merger, about which there is little disagreement, and of the consequence and significance of merger, about which there is considerable disagreement. I do not intend to review this literature in whole or in part, for in this chapter I am concerned not with the detailed problem of interpreting a particular series of events in history, but rather to present a general analysis of the relation of merger to the process of expansion of the firm.

THE ECONOMIC BASIS OF ACQUISITION

In principle there are two methods of expansion open to the individual firm: it can build new plant and create new markets for itself, or it can acquire the plant and markets of already existing firms. If a planned expansion is considered profitable regardless of any change in the existing position of other producers or in the distribution of the ownership of existing industrial assets, then the firm will choose to expand through acquisition only if acquisition is considered cheaper than internal expansion.[1] If, on the other hand, a change in the position of existing producers is sought (for example, a reduction of competition) or a change in the distribution of control over existing industrial assets (for example, over patent

---

[1] One must be careful not to confuse the motives for expansion with motives for choosing the merger method of expansion. For example, among the motives for merger, one sometimes sees listed the desire to achieve economies of large-scale production, distribution or advertising economies, or the financial advantages of large size. These are motives for expansion but not necessarily for the merger method of expansion. Cf., however, J. Fred Weston, *The Role of Mergers in the Growth of Large Firms* (Berkeley: Univ. of California Press, 1954), p. 86.

rights or monopolized supplies of raw materials), acquisition may be the only way of achieving these objectives. In either case, acquisition will occur only if there are firms who are willing to part with their assets, including their ' good-will ', at a price equal to or less than their value to potential buyers. For acquisition to occur there must be a seller as well as a buyer both of whom expect to gain by the transaction.[1]

Regardless of the type of merger, however, the first and fundamental question to begin with is the question why acquisition should be a ' cheap ' method of expansion. The mere fact that one firm wants to acquire another in order to limit competition, to facilitate entry into a new field, or for any other reason, does not yet explain why acquisition should be 'cheap ', that is, why the price at which the other firm can be acquired is less than the value of that firm to the acquirer. What is it that depresses the value of some firms to themselves below their value to another firm, or raises their value to another firm above their value to themselves? In the general case, that is to say, in the absence of special *individual* circumstances, should we not expect the price of existing firms (i.e., their value to themselves) to be, if anything, above their value to other firms?

The economic value of any firm can be looked upon as the present value of the stream of gross profits expected over the period relevant to the calculation.[2] Hence no firm would, in the absence of special circumstances, set a price on itself less than the present value of this expected stream of profits. Clearly, unless the firm has made mistakes and expanded productive capacity so far that prices no longer cover average costs (i.e., the firm is ' unprofitable ') capitalized expected profits will not be lower than the initial investment outlay required to earn them.[3] If existing firms in an industry have some advantage over outsiders, profits will be increased by the costs of entry, and the value of the firm will be correspondingly higher. On the other hand, whenever the purchase of another firm is considered the cheaper method of expansion, it follows that the price of this other firm is less than the investment outlay (including the opportunity cost of all resources) required for the expanding firm to build the

[1] This statement is misleading, though perhaps literally true, if the seller is under pressure from the buyer.
[2] The term ' gross profits ' is used here for profits after taxes but before the deduction of depreciation and interest charges.
[3] The initial investment outlay includes, of course, all expenditures required to build up a market as well as to produce the product.

necessary plant, markets, and trade connections. An economic analysis of acquisition requires, therefore, an analysis of the causes of this divergence, and the interesting question is whether the prevalance of growth by merger can be explained only by special individual considerations in each case, or whether there are important general considerations, in particular, considerations relating to the expansion of firms of different sizes.

In the following discussion the acquiring firm will be called Alpha; the firm to be acquired, Beta. We shall now consider the several kinds of circumstances which will cause the price of Beta to be less than its value to Alpha, beginning with particular personal considerations, on which we need spend little time, and proceeding to the more general considerations related to the growth of Alpha and Beta.

Personal Considerations and Special Situations

At all times there are firms ' on the market '—firms whose owners want to sell out—where the initiative for merger comes from the seller.[1] One does not have to seek far to discover why this would always be so, even if one were to assume that costs and demand conditions were the same for all sizes of firm. There is nothing in the basic propositions of economics that asserts or implies that all men view the future with the same degree of optimism, or that the value of a given cash payment is the same to both parties to a transaction, or that the same income will call forth the same effort from all men and regardless of the time of life. On the contrary, it is well recognized that some men are more optimistic and more willing to take risks than others, in which case the expected net income from operating a given firm will be greater for the more optimistic and less discounted for the risk of not getting it. Or the worth of a present cash payment may be greater to the recipient

---

[1] In one survey of mergers, it was reported that ' . . . there were about three and a half times as many instances in which the seller clearly took the initiative or was known to be " on the market " as instances in which the purchasing company took the initiative in bringing about a merger with a company not already " for sale ". . . .' J. K. Butters, J. Lintner, and W. Cary, *The Effect of Taxation on Corporate Merger*. (Harvard Univ. 1951), p. 309. On the other hand, the Federal Trade Commission in its *Report on Corporate Mergers and Acquisitions* of May 1955 stated: ' On the basis of available materials, it appears that by far the most important type of promotion [of merger] is that which is carried on by the acquiring company ' (p. 73). But ' Initial promotion by the acquired company appears to be a rather common procedure in merger or acquisition development ' (p. 75). The Commission gave illustrations but no statistics to support its contention that promotion by the seller is more important than initiation by the buyer.

than to the giver, the former placing a relatively lower value on future income.

In small firms where the owner and manager are one, the income from the firm may no longer be sufficient to call forth the effort required to run it—the owner may want to retire from business and there may be no adequate successor in his firm or family; or he may want to acquire cash or easily marketable securities to increase the liquidity of his estate in preparation for his final retirement from the world. In these and similar circumstances owners may be willing to take less than the capitalized value of the profits they could be expected to earn.[1] In other cases a firm's existing management may be simply inefficient and the firm doing badly for that reason. Here the profits anticipated by the firm's present managers will be less than those anticipated by other and better managers appraising the value of the firm. Thus the very existence of firms that are not very successful or of firms owned by people who want to leave the business is in itself conducive to merger.[2]

In addition to this kind of personal element reducing the value of a firm to its existing owners are a variety of special institutional considerations. Of these, the role of taxation is particularly significant. Taxation may affect the decisions of businessmen with respect to the form in which income is best received or wealth best held; it may limit the extent to which firms can without penalty retain earnings; may in some circumstances put a penalty on the distribution of earnings; and may even convert the losses of some firms into assets for others who can acquire title to the right to deduct these losses from taxable income.

To illustrate, the closely held small firm may be sold to increase the liquidity of the owner's estate and thus enable heirs to meet the estate tax on the owner's death; if capital gains are taxed at a lower rate than income, the relative worth of cash (or securities) received through a sale now and of profits to be received in the future is

---

[1] But it should be noted that a willingness, or even a desire to sell is not necessarily the same as a willingness to sell cheaply; it may merely indicate that the firm is willing to accept a reasonable offer—a willingness not always apparent among independent small businessmen. In one of the examples cited by Butters, Lintner and Cary of an owner-manager desiring to sell because he thought his estate would thereby be left in a better condition, it is clear that the price of sale was based on capitalized future earnings, Op. cit., p. 91.

[2] Butters, Lintner and Cary have an excellent description and discussion, based on their empirical investigations, of the 'non-tax motivations for sale of business enterprises', to which the reader is referred for further examples. See especially, pp. 213–222 of the book cited.

accordingly affected; the retained earnings of a firm may be considered excessive and subject to a tax which can be avoided if the firm is sold to another for which the earnings would not be considered excessive;[1] sometimes mergers can be effected by tax-free exchanges of stock; and finally, provisions in the tax law which permit losses to be offset against profits enable a profitable firm acquiring an unprofitable one to reduce its taxable profits to the extent of the losses taken over, and this in effect converts the losses into assets for the acquiring firm. Tax considerations of these kinds were found to be a major reason for the sale of medium-sized firms in the only extensive study of the problem that has been made in the United States.[2]

An undervaluation by the market of the shares of a firm may be another reason why a particular firm may be acquired relatively cheaply. There may be a variety of special conditions at any given time which lead to undervaluation of the publicly traded stock of a firm, but probably the most important general conditions are a lack of knowledge on the part of the investing public of the value of the firm, a lack of confidence in its management, or a discounting of the less marketable stocks for lack of liquidity. The undervaluation of stock is apparently still of some importance as a factor promoting mergers in the United States,[3] although probably not so significant as has been the case in the past, and is of considerable importance in some countries where capital markets are less developed. In Australia, for example, there have been waves of acquisition through what are called ' take-over ' bids, by which outsiders desiring to gain control of a particular firm buy its stock in the market at prices which, though above current market prices, still substantially undervalue the firm relative to its earnings prospects. One of the chief reasons advanced for the successful use of this technique of acquiring firms relates to the lack of information provided to investors by Australian firms. When annual reports, balance sheets, and operating statements are designed as much to

---

[1] Section 102 of the United States Revenue Act of 1950 imposes penalty taxes on retained earnings beyond the reasonable needs of business.

[2] The study by Butters, Lintner and Cary cited above is almost the only systematic analysis and presentation of information regarding the effect of taxes on merger.

[3] Butters, Lintner and Cary report: ' One of the reasons for the acquisitions of other companies during the recent merger movement was the fact that the market prices of the stock of so many companies were substantially below their book values, and even more so below the replacement values of the underlying assets. It was therefore often much cheaper to acquire desired items—facilities, products, market outlets—by buying another company rather than by building or developing them directly.' Op. cit., p. 312.

conceal as to reveal the true condition of the firm, outside investors have less ability to judge the value of their stock and may be easily induced to sell out when an offer significantly higher than the ruling market prices is made for it. A thin market reducing the market-ability and consequent liquidity of stock is, of course, a contributing factor.

Special considerations, whether relating to the personal characteristics of the owners and managers of firms, to the impact of a particular system of taxation, to the nature of the market for securities, or to other similar things, are always present and account for a fair proportion of the small and medium-sized firms on the market at any given time. They are not, however, particularly related to the processes of growth nor to any general relationship between the positions of the acquired and acquiring firms, although their importance is different for different sizes of firm. The question to which I now want to turn is whether there is a more or less systematic tendency towards merger and acquisition in an economy characterized by growing firms of different sizes, apart from any power of the larger firms to put monopolistic pressure on the smaller ones.

Critical Points in the Process of Expansion

When a firm is relatively small the division of managerial labour will not be extensive (indeed it cannot be) and the most important decisions are sometimes made by only one man. As the firm grows it reaches a point where a change in its managerial structure must take place because of the necessity, if growth is to continue, of subdividing the managerial task, and especially of decentralizing managerial 'decision-making'. As we have seen, growth is not for long, if ever, simply a question of producing more of the same product on a larger scale; it involves innovation, changing techniques of distribution, and changing organization of production and management. Accounting control and budget-making and fore-casting techniques must be refined and adapted to replace many of the quasi-instinctive judgments of one or two individuals that may predominate in the simpler form of organization suitable for small-scale operations. Tax calculations become more complicated and tax experts may have to be hired; if invention and innovation are important, patent problems arise and a special staff of patent experts may be called for; labour and personnel relations may require the creation of a specialized personnel section. There is no need to elaborate the details: the growing small firm inevitably reaches a critical point where the managerial services appropriate for the efficient organization of production and distribution on a small scale are no longer sufficient.[1] A thorough knowledge of the problems of production, a keen understanding of market forces, an ability to make shrewd business decisions always remain important, but much more is needed. The additional managerial resources required to set up and control a more complicated administrative organization can of course be hired, but for the transformation in the structure of the firm to take place an understanding of what is happening and what is needed, and a willingness to accept substantial changes in the old ways of doing things are required of the original management.[2]

In some concerns management is not only willing but eager to delegate decisions and functions, to hire the requisite new services, perhaps first on a consultant and then on a permanent basis, and thus gradually to adapt the structure of the firm to the requirements of growth. In such cases the ' critical ' point may pass unnoticed and it becomes virtually impossible even to identify the period of transition. But for others, the pressures build up to a point where ' a man is willing to give in '[3] and to face the necessity of adapting or getting out.[4] We do not at present have enough information to

[1] For an excellent discussion of some of these problems see C. Roland Christensen, *Management Succession in Small and Growing Enterprises* (Cambridge: Harvard Univ. Press, 1953), where the same point is made: ' Top management's job in the small but growing enterprise is a changing one . . . growth calls for the development of new administrative and leadership skills . . . at this stage the advantage shifts away from the manager who is able to do every job or watch over every detailed operation ' (p. 158).

[2] That some of the greatest managerial difficulties arise in the act of changing the managerial structure has often been stressed by theorists of management. See, for example, the various discussions in H. J. Kruisinga (ed.), *The Balance Between Centralization and Decentralization in Managerial Central* (Leiden: Stenfert Kroese, 1954), especially the papers by E. F. L. Brech and H. W. Ouweleen.

[3] The words of an owner-manager quoted by Butters, Lintner and Cary, who sold out in order to ' get out from under the terrific pressure and burden of running what was essentially a one-man business. . . .' He had competent technical assistance but he ' had not been able to delegate responsibility for the top-management decisions in either the technical or general administrative phases of the enterprise ', op. cit., p. 75.

[4] For example, C. R. Christensen reported: ' Finally, and most important, in small companies growth is severely restricted because management is incapable of building and using a supporting organization. Enterprises, like individuals, pass through various critical stages in their development. One such stage . . . occurs when the incumbent president steps down and a new manager is put in his place. Another takes place when the enterprise grows to a certain size, where effective performance and growth are impeded if the manager continues to run his firm on a one-man basis. If at that juncture the chief executive is able to bring along other men to take over some of his management responsibility, we have the beginnings of an executive organization

say for what size of firm these problems become of crucial importance. An executive of one large United States concern that had
just completed a series of acquisitions pursuant to an expansion
programme, wrote in a discussion of the characteristics which had
induced the acquired firms to sell out that

> because of the complexity of doing business today, with our many
> government regulations, taxes, unions, etc., a small, growing business
> finally reaches a point where life is just too complicated for the
> original management. At this point the best solution to the problem
> is to sell out to a large corporation which has the necessary financial
> resources and all of the legal and accounting experts and industrial
> consulting facilities that a small company cannot afford. A company
> seems to reach this point when sales pass the ten million [dollar]
> mark.[1]

In addition to the management problem is the financial one. It
is often difficult for a small company to generate sufficient internal
funds to finance even those amounts of expansion of which it is
otherwise capable, partly because of the tax laws and partly because
of competitive pressures and restricted markets; its lines of external
credit are often limited and equity capital is often difficult to attract
unless the firm possesses unusual entrepreneurial ingenuity in
raising capital.[2] But perhaps more important than the difficulty of
raising equity capital is the fact that owner-managers of small firms,
if faced with the choice of losing control through dilution of their
equity or of losing control through sale to a larger firm, may well
find substantial advantages in the latter course, especially if the
large firm is willing to take over their services. Not only may they
feel a prestige associated with being a ' vice-president in charge of
. . .' in a large firm, but if they are going to lose sole control and
thus lose the status of ' independent ' businessmen, they may well
prefer to rid themselves of the types of strain which go with the
continuance of the sole responsibility of management.

Whether these managerial and financial considerations can be
looked on as inducing a systematic tendency for small firms to sell
out when they reach the point where substantial changes in the

and increased chances for growth and survival. In many small companies, however,
management does not have the skills needed to develop an organization '. C. Roland
Christensen, op. cit., p. 150.
[1] In a private letter to the author.
[2] Here again we meet the problem discussed in Chapter III, of the relation between
entrepreneurial ability and the availability of capital. The two are so closely related that
it is extremely difficult to isolate one or the other as the fundamental problem of the
small firm.

managerial and financial structure of the firm are required depends on whether it can reasonably be assumed that a significant number of small firms are started by people who are capable of efficiently running a small concern but incapable of the adaptations required when the firm begins to leave the ' small ' category. If this were so, if, say, even 30–40 per cent of small firms had such management, then clearly we would be entitled to state that such a tendency existed. There are only three alternatives for such firms: to sell out, to stop growing significantly, or gradually to become more inefficient and fail. Many firms follow the last two courses, and the first and third from some points of view come to the same thing. We have no statistical evidence on any of these questions. Few studies have been made of merger from the point of view of the acquired firm and I know of no extensive statistical analysis of the history of a significant sample of small firms. Hence we are forced back on the general impression to be gained from ' business biographies ' (which in general deal with the successful firms) and from the fairly large number of acquisitions which have been described in the literature. From both of these sources one can fairly conclude that it is highly probable that small growing firms very often find in merger the solution to problems they are otherwise unable satisfactorily to meet.

The Competitive Expansion of Alpha

Let us now turn to those aspects of acquisition that are especially related to the relative size of the acquiring firm and to its expansion processes. It has been shown that to explain acquisition one must explain why Beta (the acquired firm) is worth more to Alpha (the acquiring firm) than it is to itself. An analysis of acquisition with reference to the size and expansion of Alpha, therefore, can be expected to centre on the question how these factors alone can be expected to influence the price of Beta in relation to its value to Alpha. We shall not consider those situations in which Alpha is in a position to exert pressure on Beta through the use of various types of ' unfair ' competitive practices. There is little doubt that small firms have on occasion been forced to sell out on unfavourable terms to large firms because of the predatory activities of the latter. Although in most, if not all such cases, unfair competitive pressure is possible only because Alpha is substantially larger than Beta, discussion of such mergers is omitted here because no further analysis is necessary to understand them. They have at times been important but their importance seems to have substantially declined under the influence of law and custom.

Assume that Alpha plans an expansion which it considers profitable regardless of the possibility of acquiring another firm in the relevant field. It is reasonable to suppose that if a firm plans to expand in markets already occupied by other firms (whether it be further expansion in its present markets or expansion into new markets), it does so because it believes that it has some competitive advantage which will ensure the profitability of the investment that will be tied up in the expansion. The advantage may be based on a technological superiority of some kind, on marketing strength, on access to larger supplies of funds, on the prospects of obtaining operational economies of scale not available to existing firms in the market (who may, for example, be too small to undertake an amount of expansion large enough to achieve the significant economies), and on other economies of growth of the kind discussed earlier.

If an existing firm plans an expansion of output which is large relative to the size of the market for the products in question, the increased output can be expected to affect adversely the sales of other producers. Hence if other producers know of the planned expansion and believe that the expanding firm has genuine advantages in costs or in marketing ability, or merely that it has sufficient financial power to withstand losses during the initial period when it competes for a larger share of the market, the mere expectation that their markets will be affected will reduce their expected profits and hence their present value.

If the competitive power of the expanding firm is believed to be very great, each of the other firms in the market becomes a potential Beta. On the one hand, the larger the expansion in relation to the size of the market, the greater will be the reduction in the present value of existing firms; on the other hand, the larger the expansion and the greater the total investment outlay required for it, the higher the price that the expanding firm would be willing to pay for suitable Betas permitting the same amount of expansion. This can be clearly seen if we consider the case of a firm planning entry into a new field where the outlay required to enter the field is high.

This outlay may include not only the costs of building and equipping new plant but also the cost of acquiring new customers and new channels of distribution and of building up trade connections in order to ensure a smooth flow of supplies and favourable conditions for obtaining them. We are assuming that after due consideration of cost and revenue possibilities, Alpha has decided that expansion into the new field is profitable even if it cannot acquire other suitable firms. Nevertheless, if such firms are available, Alpha may, through acquisition, obtain at one stroke not only existing plant and equipment, perhaps the least item in the outlay required for expansion, but also customers, good-will, sales channels, connections with suppliers, sometimes accepted brand names and peculiarly qualified and experienced personnel. Not only may the cost of developing these from the beginning be considerable, but the process takes time and adds to the uncertainty of the venture. In circumstances where demand is unusually high, speed of expansion may be unusually important, and the cost of delay proportionately greater. In some lines of activity there are genuine economies of large-scale production to be obtained and a new venture must start on a large scale. Yet if a market has to be built up, the firm may have to count on making losses for a long period. The firm, therefore, may be willing to pay handsomely for existing firms with the characteristics it requires.

But the very fact that such outlays would be required of any firm wanting to enter the industry would normally raise the gross profits of the firms already in the industry and therefore the price at which they would be willing to sell out. These are outlays that any firm considering entry would know it had to make, and to the extent that they are sufficient to deter potential entrants, the level of demand and of prices will be correspondingly raised for existing firms.[1] But can we conclude from this that if Alpha plans to enter the industry it will have to pay a correspondingly higher price for a Beta—quite apart from any personal or special considerations inducing Beta to sell out?

Clearly we cannot, for if Alpha intends to enter the market and is merely deciding whether to ' build or buy ' its way in, then the

[1] These outlays are of a kind that might result in what Joe S. Bain has called ' shake-down losses ' for new entrants—losses that a new entrant to an industry may have to incur for a period while it is getting established. In his empirical study of barriers to new competition he found that ' shake-down losses of entrants . . . in some cases may be large and prolonged ', and if the capital requirements of entry are taken into consideration, ' there is probably *some* progression of the entrants' disadvantage and the height of the resultant barrier to entry with the increase in capital requirements '. Joe S. Bain, *Barriers to New Competition* (Cambridge: Harvard Univ. Press, 1956), pp. 156–165.

prospective profitability of each existing firm (potential Betas) is immediately adversely affected provided that it views the competitive threat seriously. In the extreme case in which Beta believes that Alpha could capture the entire market in a relatively short period, the value of Beta would rapidly sink to the present value of whatever margin over direct costs it could expect to make until Alpha became established, plus the scrap value of its assets. This figure will be far below the present value of the firm before the threat of Alpha's competition and may be far below the outlay required of Alpha in entering the industry; clearly a merger will then be profitable for both firms.

When high investment outlays are required to start production in a field, competitors whose financial strength is small will be deterred. Hence new entrants will have to be financially powerful and will be able to operate on a large scale. Unless the market is growing so rapidly that there is ' room for all ', existing firms may become very worried for their future profits. Since Alpha can afford to pay large sums for suitable Betas, there will often be a large margin for negotiation, depending on Beta's estimate of the alternative investment outlay required of Alpha and of the effects of Alpha's competition upon its own worth. A weak Beta might feel happy to sell out for anything above the scrap value of its assets, even though it had been very profitable before the threat of new competition arose from Alpha. The greater the anticipated investment outlays of Alpha, the greater must be the revision of the expectations of existing firms if Alpha decides to enter the market. At the same time, the greater these outlays, the more Alpha can afford to pay to acquire existing firms.[1] Clearly merger may be profitable for both Alpha and Beta.[2]

---

[1] Furthermore, since the foregone earnings on the capital funds tied up in an expansion programme must be counted as part of the cost of the expansion, the longer the time required for a given internal expansion, the greater the cost saving if acquisition of already going concerns can be effected, and the higher the price Alpha would find it worthwhile to pay for Beta.

It has often been pointed out that entry into an industry where the optimum plant is very large may be impeded by the large investment outlays required. It follows from the above, however, that the entry of a new firm into such an industry through acquisition may actually be facilitated by this fact in those cases where the new firm has a significant competitive advantage, because of the effect of the threatened entry on the capital values of existing firms.

[2] If Alpha is in a strategic position *vis-à-vis* Beta by virtue of a monopolistic control over such things as raw materials and distribution channels, or is able to indulge in an ' unfair ' competitive use of financial strength, this alone will force Beta to write down heavily its prospects of future income. The potential power of Alpha to compete so successfully with existing firms in the market that the latter's profits will be substantially

There are, in addition, a variety of situations in which the expansion of Alpha may have especially adverse effects on the future of smaller firms with which Alpha has commercial relationships. For example, expansion which involves the vertical integration of Alpha may leave smaller suppliers without adequate alternative outlets and such suppliers will, in turn, often find it more profitable to sell out than try to remain in business.[1]

Where Beta Blocks the Expansion of Alpha

In the above analysis it was assumed that existing firms had assets, tangible or intangible, which were of value to Alpha but which were not indispensable for its profitable expansion. Under such circumstances Alpha's expansion became a threat to the value of existing firms. But if existing firms possess assets which are indispensable for Alpha's plans, the competitive power of Alpha is no longer a factor reducing the value of existing firms. On the contrary, presumably firms controlling such assets could expect to obtain from a potential Alpha their full monopoly value and thus wipe out the profitability of acquisition for Alpha.

There are a variety of productive assets which, when under the control of existing firms, can effectively prevent the profitable expansion of existing competitors and the entry of new competitors. They include, for example, strong patent protection of products,

reduced should not, however, be treated as a similar form of pressure. But even if Alpha actually uses ' unfair ' tactics, such as selling below cost to eliminate competitors or to force them to terms, it cannot be inferred that Alpha's expansion would not have been profitable without such tactics. Their use may be merely one way of ensuring that an expansion considered profitable in any circumstances is effected as cheaply as possible. This, of course, does not justify social approval of ' unfair ' competition, but if ' fair ' competition can do the job, the fact that ' unfair ' competition is used may not only reduce the cost of expansion for the large firms, but may also reduce the total losses of small firms in those cases where the large firms would enter and ' out-compete ' them anyway. On the other hand, consumers may gain less than they would have from a prolonged depression of prices.

[1] This is the basis of much of the United States Federal Trade Commission's opposition to extensive vertical integration. It is the common situation where large firms supply most, but not all, of their own requirements of certain parts or materials, relying on small independent producers for their marginal requirements. ' This shifts to the independent parts manufacturer the risk of changes in volume of production which arise from changes in demand for products at the consumer level. Loss of a large contract by such an independent parts manufacturer may mean the difference between profitable and unprofitable operation or even may lead to bankruptcy. . . . In case of loss of an important customer, the facilities of an independent parts manufacturer may become available for purchase in the open market. The result is that when either a raw material producer or a consumer goods manufacturer finds it desirable to expand his production of component parts, he frequently finds some facility already in operation available for purchase.' Federal Trade Commission, *Report on Corporate Mergers and Acquisitions*, 1955, op. cit., p. 116.

equipment or productive processes; trade names, brands, and other protected methods of differentiating otherwise similar products and thus of holding consumers' loyalty; private control of non-reproducible factors of production such as particular sites of land and certain mineral deposits; knowledge of processes which can be kept secret; occasionally even possession of the services of especially gifted, trained, or experienced individuals. A great deal of the so-called monopolistic protection against competition may involve the possession by entrenched firms of ' assets ' of this kind, and the consequent restrictions on new entry are as much a cause as they are an effect of merger.

Let us now assume that a given firm, Alpha, has decided that expansion in a particular direction would be the most profitable step for it to take provided it can acquire one or more of the types of ' assets ' just mentioned which are under the control of existing firms. The incentive of the existing firms to sell is obviously different when they can prevent the expansion of a large competitor from what it is if they are faced with the prospect of new competition in any circumstances. Except for firms that are poorly managed or whose owners want to sell out for personal reasons, we must assume that existing firms would be unwilling to sell at a price below the discounted value of an expected profit that will continue to reflect the particular advantages the assets in question confer upon them. We shall assume, too, that these assets are so important that it is not worth while for a Beta to sell them without selling out entirely.

If existing owners of Beta know the full value of their firm, apart from any relation it may have to the activities of a potential Alpha, they would not in general be willing to sell at a price below this value. Hence, Alpha must consider Beta, or more accurately the acquisition of Beta's assets, to be worth more than the full value of Beta to its existing owners. How much more than this full value Alpha would have to pay would depend on Beta's estimate of Alpha's maximum price. But when would Alpha believe it profitable to pay more than the full present value to Beta of Beta's monopoly rights? Under what circumstances would an economic basis for acquisition exist?

Inability to obtain the required assets and thus effect the desired expansion may prejudice the existing position of Alpha or it may merely prejudice the prospects for profitable expansion in the desired direction. For example, in the first case, patent-protected new technology which reduces production costs or improves the quality of products may present a serious threat to a firm's existing products; or the ability to sell existing products may be hindered by an inability to sell at the same time certain complementary products. In the second case, Alpha may be prevented from using some of its own productive services in directions that would, but for the barred access to a specific technology or the necessity of incurring heavy initial market-creating expenses, be extremely profitable. In either case, a basis for acquisition exists whenever Alpha stands to lose a great deal more by not effecting the acquisition than Beta could expect to make in profits from its own operations. If Beta were in a position to make as much of its monopoly rights as Alpha could, then Beta would not sell at a price Alpha could afford. In the example above, if Beta expected to gain as much as Alpha lost from the impaired competitive position of Alpha's existing products, the prospective value of Beta would be correspondingly raised. Hence if all Alpha wanted to do was to put itself in Beta's position, the acquisition of Beta would be profitable only if Beta did not realize the full value of its position, or were, for some other reason, unable or unwilling to hold out for the full price. If, however, Beta cannot with equal advantage undertake the full expansion programme that Alpha could undertake once it had acquired Beta, then, although Beta may be in a strong bargaining position, it will often pay both firms to come to terms. If Alpha is substantially larger than Beta, or operates with a substantially different composition of resources and produces a different collection of products, it may be profitable for Alpha to acquire Beta at a price higher than that representing the present value of Beta's expected profits.

If a particular expansion programme contemplated by Alpha is frustrated by barriers that could be overcome only by the acquisition of Beta, the cost to Alpha of failing to acquire Beta is equal to the discounted net revenue expected from the new investment over the relevant period less the result of a similar calculation for the next most profitable use of the resources involved in the projected investment programme. The total net revenue expected from any given expansion programme will be larger, the larger the size of the programme (or otherwise a smaller expansion would have been planned). A firm's expansion programme may, of course, involve fairly long-run plans for a series of outlays over a period of time, and the relevant amount of investment to be considered from this point of view is the total investment actually planned for the entire programme at the time the acquisition of Beta is being considered. The larger the total programme in relation to the size of Beta, the more important becomes the 'loss' if Beta is not acquired, and the less becomes the significance of the price of acquiring Beta. In other words, Alpha does not merely want to put itself in Beta's position, but rather it needs Beta only as a component of a larger programme. At the same time, if Beta is very small in relation to Alpha, it cannot expect to undertake an equal expansion in the same period of time. And even if the managers of Beta hold the theory of growth set forth in this study, and thus believe that over the course of time Beta could reach Alpha's position, the mere fact that a longer period would be required to make the same total profits reduces their present value. Hence if Beta is motivated by a rational calculation of financial losses and gains, it will be willing to come to an agreement with Alpha.[1]

Similarly, if Alpha and Beta have been operating with a different collection of resources or producing a different collection of products (though they may be in competition in some product markets), the internal potentialities of expansion for the two firms will be different, and this will be true even if there is no great difference in their sizes. If they have been producing roughly comparable products, Alpha may, for example, have concentrated on the development of a sales organization, while Beta paid more attention to research in and development of production techniques and product quality. Or the composition of their product line may be different but be based, for example, on the same general assortment of raw materials. In both cases, the productive services within each firm, which provide the internal incentives for expansion or determine the response of the firm to external incentives, will differ. Hence it may fall out again that Alpha can plan, not necessarily a more extensive, but perhaps a more profitable expansion programme than Beta can plan, and again there will be a margin for negotiation within which acquisition will be profitable for both firms. If the two firms are roughly the same size, the merger may be effected on roughly equal terms and be

---

[1] Although I have assumed that firms are primarily interested in the profits they can make from their own operations rather than from outside investments, it does not follow from this that firms are in general unwilling to sell out entirely for a satisfactory price, even if they should use the funds to set up again in business. Furthermore, a distinction between the attitudes of owners and of managers is often significant. Where owners and management are the same, or where management reluctance has a significant influence on owners, the terms of sale often will include the provision of satisfactory positions in the acquiring firm for the managers of the acquired firm.

more properly classed as a combination of two firms into a new firm than as an acquisition by one firm of the other.

Combination

Where two (or more) firms combine on equal terms thus forming a new firm, the process of expansion conceived of as the growth of a single firm comes to an end; in effect, both firms go out of existence and another firm is created with administrative structure, personnel, product-mix, markets, productive facilities, and financial resources different from those of its progenitors. But although this type of merger creates difficulties for those who like to treat firms as organisms and construct growth curves instead of family trees, it makes only a formal, not a substantive difference to the economics of the problem. After all, any substantial acquisition changes these characteristics of firms in much the same way, and often it is merely a matter of convenience, or personal prestige or manoeuvering, or of the respective reputations of the two firms, that determines whether a given merger will be technically an acquisition of one of them by the other or a merger on equal terms. But if neither firm does in fact ' buy out ' the other, then we cannot explain the process, as we have in the preceding discussion, by examining the considerations which cause a difference between Alpha's and Beta's estimates of the value of Beta. Nevertheless, most of the preceding analysis of the process of acquisition could have centered around the same question posed in a different way: what are the considerations that make two firms more valuable when they are combined than when they are separate? Clearly these are, for the most part, precisely the considerations that make it profitable for Alpha to pay for Beta the price that Beta demands. Put in this way, it can be readily seen that the economic basis for the combination of two firms is much the same as it is for simple acquisition: we need merely omit some of the personal considerations and some of the considerations which arise directly from differences in size or from monopolistic advantages possessed by one of the firms over the other.

No two firms can ever be exactly alike or develop in exactly the same way. Differences may, of course, be negligible in many important respects, and the economist may be justified in treating some firms as ' identical ' for special purposes. On the other hand—and it would seem more commonly, taking each firm as a whole— differences may be considerable. Even if Alpha and Beta should be in the same general industry, and have started out with the same general structure, productive resources, and products, their processes of growth are apt, by the very nature of the productive services generated within the firm and of competition itself, to lead to differences in quality and type of product, to an emphasis on different classes of consumers and different markets, to the introduction of different processes of production, or to a relative specialization on different stages in the production of the same type of product. These factors, as was pointed out above, are among the reasons why one firm would find it profitable to acquire another, but equally they may provide a basis for a combination of the two firms.

Under these circumstances, there are many reasons unrelated to an extension of monopoly power, why combination may seem an efficient use of resources for both firms. Expansion into the same area—e.g., into the same type of new product-line, or forward for Alpha and backward for Beta—may appear to each firm independently as the most effective way of using its existing productive services. But if both undertook the same expansion, competition between them would be intensified, and this would reduce, or perhaps even eliminate, the profitability of the expansion for each. Expansion into the new area on a combined basis is obviously less wasteful from the point of view of both, and if the proposed expansion bulks large in the total activity of both firms, combination may seem desirable. Such a combination need not be undertaken to protect the combining firms against competition from others but may, in effect, be a merger to overcome the barrier to entry that each presents for the other. A similar basis for combination exists when the two firms possess complementary productive services in the use of the same type of raw material—for example, if they have specialized in different varieties of product or at different stages in the production process. Again, merger may be primarily an economical way for both firms together to embark on a new programme of activity, but the merger need not be so much a method of avoiding a potential competitive struggle between the two firms as they expand as it is a way of obtaining the collection of productive services without which neither firm could enter the new field in any significant way.

THE PURCHASE AND SALE OF 'BUSINESSES' THAT ARE NOT FIRMS

From the point of view of the economics of acquisition in relation to the growth of firms, the acquisition of a ' going concern ' which is not a legally independent firm, but merely part of a larger firm, may have much the same significance in many respects as other types of acquisition. It makes little, if any difference to the acquiring firm whether the particular productive organization or new ' business' that it purchases is technically a subsidiary, a division or merely a ' product-line ' of another corporation or an independent firm. Nevertheless, the fact that it is possible, and indeed easy, for a firm to sell part of its own organization makes a considerable difference for the behaviour of firms in the process of growth. Of course, a firm has always been able to sell particular individual assets, both tangible and intangible, without disrupting its own operations and organization, but this is not quite the same as being able to sell a piece of itself as a going concern without seriously disrupting either the organization and operation of the going business sold or of the rest of the firm as a whole; the difference between selling individual assets and selling a ' business ' is important, for, as is well known, the whole is in most cases, though not always, worth more than the sum of its parts.

There is some evidence that acquisitions of whole divisions or subsidiaries of other corporations instead of independent firms are becoming an increasing proportion of the total number of acquisitions.[1] The Federal Trade Commission suggests that the increased importance may be due to changes in the tax laws (presumably the introduction of loss carry-over provisions). Why tax laws would encourage this type of acquisition at the expense of others is not clear, but one does not have to fall back on taxation as the explanation, for extensive diversification plus decentralized organization would surely lead to a relatively high number of acquisitions that involve parts of firms.

If in fact there has been an increase in the kind of diversification which leads the large corporations into new basic areas of specialization, we should expect, quite apart from any changes in tax laws, an increase in the purchase and sale of the relatively specialized parts of business firms. Diversification of this kind leads firms into

---

[1] The T.N.E.C. Monograph (No. 27, op. cit.) in 1941 did not mention this type of acquisition at all and it appeared in the Federal Trade Commission statistics for the first time in 1955. In the report of that year the Commission stated: ' Such acquisitions during 1940–47 appear to have been rare. However, owing perhaps to recent changes in tax laws, this type of action has become increasingly important, accounting for about 9 per cent of the total number of mergers and acquisitions reported during the 1948–54 period.' The Commission now includes these in the statistics of acquisition and merger that it reports. *Report on Corporate Mergers and Acquisitions* (May 1955), op. cit., p. 18.

relatively unfamiliar areas of activity by definition. Some mistakes will be made and some expectations disappointed. The obvious way to rectify mistakes is to sell out. It is perhaps reasonable to assume that the more significant the fundamental diversification of large firms, the larger will be the number of 'mistakes' and the greater the number of such businesses that will be sold in order to correct mistakes. And the larger the percentage of the total number of firms that are significantly diversified, the greater will be the proportion of such sales in the total number of firms and businesses that are sold.[1]

Furthermore, the adoption of a decentralized type of organization is characteristic of firms as they grow larger; this type of organization not only makes possible efficient specialization in more than one basic area of production, but also permits the separately organized 'businesses' to act in many respects like independent specialized firms[2] and often to be bought and sold without disrupting the organization of the parent firm nor significantly altering the self-contained organization of the division. Some reorganization both by the acquiring and selling firms will be necessary, as we have pointed out, but it is likely to be on a scale considerably smaller than would have been involved if the acquiring firm had had to build up the business from within, or if the selling firm had had a thoroughly centralized organization.

The fact that firms can and do sell specialized parts of their activities bears on our analysis in three ways. In the first place, the factors creating an economic basis for merger are somewhat different for this type of sale than for the sale of independent firms; secondly, the process of growth of firms is affected; and finally, a more efficient pattern of diversification may be promoted over the long run.

[1] The impossibility of measuring the 'extent' of diversification has been discussed in the preceding chapter, and there are no statistics which classify mergers in a manner relevant to the above analysis. Hence the argument cannot be statistically supported.

[2] The decentralized system of General Motors, for example, 'contemplates that the responsibility of each individual unit in the system is complete. The objective is to make each separate unit self-contained, complete with all the functions essential to its full development. Its chief executive is charged with the responsibility for its success or failure'. *Annual Report*, 1942. And of Proctor and Gamble Company, the American Institute of Management noted with respect to its three major products divisions: 'Each of these three divisions is a separate business with its own operating departments; and each in effect has its own general management with its separate recruitment and training programs'. American Institute of Management, *Management Audit*, Special Audit No. 148, Vol. VI, No. 14 (Feb. 1957), p. 5.

Economic Basis for the Sale of a 'Business'

Many of the considerations causing small firms to sell out are clearly not relevant to the decision of a large firm to sell one of its ' businesses '. Personal positions of owners, tax considerations relating to liquidity of personal estates, financial and managerial handicaps traceable to small size, and similar considerations are rarely significant motives for the sale of a business by a large firm. The small firm, in selling out, obtains cash or securities for its owners. Only where the sale is effected because the owners see better productive uses of their entrepreneurial and productive abilities (rather than merely better ' placements ' for their funds) are the economic considerations of the sale similar to those surrounding the sale by a large firm of one of its businesses. For, in general, such a sale by a large firm depends on whether there are better alternative uses in production of the productive services available to the firm.

We have seen that the productive opportunity of a firm (and its competitive advantage) is largely determined by the productive services it has at its disposal, and that the internal resources of different firms are not equally suited to all fields of activity. Since the true profit on any particular activity is governed by the opportunity cost of the resources absorbed in it, fields that are highly profitable for one firm will not necessarily be equally profitable for another. The resources absorbed include not only labour, materials, and other purchased inputs, but also part of the permanent resources of the firm, particularly management and engineering staff. Whenever a firm believes that it could put the resources currently absorbed by one of its specialized product-lines to better use in some other field, it may desire to sell the ' line ', for clearly the firm will be losing money in that business, even if its accounts (which ordinarily do not take into consideration alternative opportunities for the profitable use of resources) show a positive profit. Although assets which have already been acquired and are specific to a particular line of activity have no opportunity cost inside the firm since they cannot be used for other purposes (this may be the case, for example, for trade-marks, patents, licence agreements, specialized equipment, and occasionally even whole factories), they do have an opportunity cost when some other firm would be willing to buy them. In calculating the profitability of a specialized field of production the firm ought, therefore, to take account of the use it could make of the proceeds it might receive if it sold out. Furthermore, it ought also to take account of the alternative return on any additional funds it expects to have to invest if it stays in the field at all.

When the organization of a firm is such that the profitability of its various specialized lines of activity can be appraised separately, that is to say, when an estimate can be made of the resources of the firm absorbed by each activity as well as of the new investment required over time, then a rate of return can be calculated which can be compared with rates of return on other activities open to the firm for the use of the resources and of the finance which would be freed if the firm sold out. Clearly, when such a comparison shows that the firm could make better use of its resources, it would pay the firm to sell. Hence the various businesses of a firm may be evaluated in much the same way as individual products are evaluated, being added or dropped according to their performance, with the difference that in general a larger collection of assets is involved in the decision to add or drop a specialized activity than in a similar decision for an individual product, and more of the resources are likely to be more completely specialized.

If, however, a field of investment can be considered unprofitable when opportunity costs of the resources used in it are counted, and profitable only when they are not counted, it is implicitly assumed that there is a limit on the expansion of the firm—that the firm is unable to take full advantage of other opportunities for the use of its resources unless it contracts their use in the activity in question. Since both funds and managerial services become available when a business is sold, the significance of the price that could be obtained from a business depends on the relative importance of capital and management as a restriction on the firm's ability to expand.

If both capital and management are in abundant supply, that is to say, if the firm has unused managerial services available of the same kind as are absorbed in the business in question, and if it can easily obtain all the capital funds it needs for expansion, it will not be willing to sell any of its businesses except at a price above the present value of the expected gross profits, for here the opportunity cost of the resources employed in the business approximates their market price, that of management being zero.

If, on the other hand, management is fully absorbed in existing operations and would have a high opportunity cost, either in expansion of some of the businesses in which the firm is engaged or in new businesses that look especially attractive, the firm may find it profitable to sell an existing business which absorbs important managerial services and yields only a relatively low profit net of the high opportunity cost of managerial services. This would be true also if capital funds within the firm were so abundant that the funds obtained from selling out would be of little significance.

If capital funds are not abundant in the firm but have a high opportunity cost, while management services are in abundant supply, the firm may find it profitable to sell out one of its businesses for the sake of the funds received and released. In this case, however, the business most profitably sold will, *ceteris paribus*, be one from which the firm can obtain the largest supplies of capital: hence the price at which it can sell will have a greater influence on the profitability of selling out than in the case where the supply of management was the more significant factor.

If both capital funds and management are scarce and the firm would have profitable uses for both liquid funds and released managerial services, it would pay to sell one of its businesses even at a relatively low price, the lowest price at which it would sell being determined by the relative opportunity cost of managerial services and free capital funds.

This brings us back to the factors discussed in the preceding chapter which force a firm to specialize in a few broad areas. It was argued there that diversification is promoted when firms have the ability to expand faster than the markets for their existing products, and that the direction of diversification will to a large extent be determined by the existing resources of the firm. These resources may be of many types, and many different opportunities may appear to promise success. But ' success ' is not simply a question of making an accounting profit; to be deemed successful a new activity must turn out to have been a better use of the resources of the firm than any alternative use; and it remains successful only so long as it continues to be the most profitable use, not only of whatever new funds are required to maintain the competitive position of the new business, but also of the managerial and other resources absorbed by it. Clearly, with limited managerial services and with incompletely versatile resources, the number of things a firm can profitably get into is much more limited if it counts the opportunity costs of its resources in any one use than if it merely considers whether it can successfully compete with other firms in particular markets.

When firms are engaged in a number of different lines of business but are actively attempting to use their resources in the most profitable manner, they will be continually reappraising the profitability of their different activities as changes occur in external conditions and in the quality and quantity of the productive services internally available. Furthermore, to the extent that diversification is promoted because firms are actively seeking new fields in which to expand, and hence pursuing ' diversification for growth ', a great deal of their diversification will be experimental in nature. Thus there are always likely to be firms who want to withdraw from given lines of activity: expectations of profit may have been too optimistic and the actual results disappointing; or new opportunities may have arisen as a result of developments within the firm or in the outside world. On the other hand, we cannot assume that businesses unprofitable for their existing owners will also be unprofitable acquisitions for others. Under these conditions, we should expect the rise of a ' market ' for those separable activities of firms that are no longer desired by their existing owners, the market being governed on the supply side by the factors outlined above, and on the demand side by the same factors that influence the acquisition of independent firms.

Effect on the Process of Growth

The existence of this kind of market has an important effect on the process of growth of firms: it both promotes and helps to eliminate ' excessive ' diversification. It facilitates the correction of ' mistakes ' and thereby reduces the risk of loss when a firm experiments with new lines of activity, thus encouraging such experimentation.

In the absence of such a market less fundamental diversification would undoubtedly take place. It is difficult to imagine how such a market could be eliminated under modern conditions, for it is difficult to see how a prohibition on firms selling out entirely or in part could be effectively enforced without an inconceivably drastic alteration in the size and structure of firms which would virtually push them back to extremely small and specialized entities. But be that as it may, if one can imagine the kind of economy we have to-day without such a market, it is clear that the rate at which firms could enter new fields would be reduced substantially. Internal expansion (which is the alternative to acquisition) takes longer and is often more expensive; and the penalty for mistakes would be higher since firms could only liquidate their mistakes by selling off individual assets piecemeal rather than as part of a going concern. In such circumstances firms would have to be more careful in planning expansion programmes than they now have to be, for now they can dispose of their mistakes at relatively little loss and sometimes at a profit. Consequently the premium on conservative attitudes is reduced under the present system, and experimentation, not only with new products but with whole new lines of business and even with expansion into new geographical areas, is encouraged.

It is not surprising that at times some firms appear to be going somewhat wild in attempting diversification of all kinds. There have, of course, always been firms whose grandiose plans have led them into trouble, and there is no implication in the present analysis that the excessively optimistic and careless firms will always be able to pull through simply by taking advantage of the opportunities to sell a business injudiciously acquired, especially if their expansion is essentially of the empire-building type. But it does imply that the relatively conservative well-established firms can afford to take more chances, and the less conservative and aggressive newer firms can grow very fast and successfully establish themselves in spite of serious failures of some parts of their total business.

The Appropriateness of Diversification

Finally, the growing importance of the sale and purchase of businesses that are not firms affects the economic appraisal of merger activity in the economy. To the extent that the rate of merger is raised by the purchase and sale among the larger firms of parts of their business, this clearly does not in itself indicate a further concentration of economic activity in the hands of the large firms at the expense of small firms, although it may, and very likely will, be accompanied by an increase in the concentration of particular types of activity in the hands of fewer firms.[1] Industry or product concentration will increase if a few firms already established in particular types of activity have a competitive advantage in the production of related products and, in the process of swapping, end up with the bulk of the businesses sold in that type of activity.

In spite of this consequence the swapping process may well

---

[1] This is an increase that statistics of concentration not separating the activities of a diversified firm into the several appropriate industries will be too crude to pick up.

promote an appropriate pattern of diversification among firms, that is, an efficient use of resources from each firm's point of view. For if the ease of selling out encourages experimentation, some of which turns out to be inefficient, it provides at the same time a method by which mistakes can be corrected. For so long as sales are not fully matched by inappropriate acquisitions, a more efficient distribution of productive activities from the point of view of the use of resources of individual firms will be brought about. At least this will be the result unless it is assumed that entrepreneurs are so stupid or so unlucky that when they enter new fields or acquire new businesses they take action which turns out to have been a mistake from their own point of view more than half of the time—an assumption that would leave a great deal of economic analysis of the behaviour of firms and of the processes of resource allocation in the economy in a rather regrettable quandary. If at least half of the total sales and half of the total acquisitions are appropriately made, the tendency over the long haul will be towards a progressive redistribution of productive activities between firms which, on balance, would lead to an appropriate pattern of diversification from the point of view of the use of resources of individual firms, even though any given firm at any given time may have been led into excessive or inappropriate diversification.

If we could assume that the private gain which is associated for a particular firm with a competitive advantage in any line of activity was also a social gain, we could identify an ' appropriate pattern of diversification ' from the point of view of the firm with a more efficient use of resources from the point of view of society as a whole. This assumption is clearly warranted in some cases (for example, where the competitive advantage flows from a superior technical competence in a competitive market, or from the availability of particular productive services which would otherwise be unused); clearly unwarranted in other cases (for example, where the competitive advantage flows from a monopoly of some scarce natural resource or from power to apply financial or other pressure on suppliers or competitors); and uncertain in still others (for example, where the advantage rests on a patent or on a well-cultivated reputation with consumers). Hence we cannot in general say what net effect the ' swapping ' process has on the efficiency of the economy as a whole.

It has generally been recognized that an acquisition which

involves an improvement in the efficiency with which a business is managed, or avoids capital losses resulting from an unnecessary breaking up of a going concern, is on balance a benefit to the economy if it does not reduce the competitive performance of the economy. Similarly, the reshuffling of particular types of businesses among existing firms can be presumed to improve efficiency so long as the competitive performance of industry is unimpaired. But this statement does not take us very far, partly because it is difficult to define what is meant by an 'impairment' of competition when 'competition' includes not only price competition but also product improvement and fertility in innovation, and partly because it is possible that impairment of competition in whatever sense it is defined may under some conditions be quite consistent with an improvement in economic efficiency, that is, with an increase in economic product in a given period greater than would have occurred under more competitive conditions. But further discussion of questions of this kind is reserved for our final chapter.

THE ROLE OF ENTREPRENEURIAL SERVICES

Since entrepreneurial services are among the productive services available in firms, an analysis of the economic basis of acquisition and merger which starts from an examination of the significance of differences in the productive services firms possess must pay special attention to the nature of entrepreneurial activity. After all, when I say 'Alpha can plan a larger or more profitable expansion than Beta can plan', I really mean to say that the entrepreneurs of Alpha believe they can do certain things that the entrepreneurs of Beta either do not believe they can do or perhaps never even thought of. Beta may be efficiently operated under existing management in the sense that Alpha would not expect to perform the managerial functions better than Beta, but at the same time Alpha may see opportunities for innovation or expansion that Beta does not see. In other words, among the productive services available to Alpha must be counted a type of entrepreneurial service not possessed by Beta. Whether the actual ability of Alpha turns out to have been overestimated is irrelevant to what Alpha attempts, but the reasons for this difference in appraisal do not all fit comfortably within the framework of an analysis based upon relatively simple psychological assumptions regarding the economic behaviour of human beings.

Entrepreneurial Temperament and the Profit Motive

A distinction was drawn earlier between entrepreneurial and managerial services, managerial services including the services required to operate a concern and to draw up and execute plans for expansion, and entrepreneurial services including those required for the creation or acceptance of proposals for innovation and for initiating and making decisions on proposals for expansion. The desire to create a dominant firm is a product of entrepreneurial energies and ambition. Such energies and ambition are as much productive services from the firm's point of view as are entrepreneurial abilities which are devoted to improving and extending the efficient use of the internal resources of the firm. Both types of ability may be combined in the same man; such men are indeed hard to ' hold down ', and much extensive merger activity can only be understood in the light of an entrepreneurial drive spurred by the vision of organizing and controlling the use of economic resources on a grand scale. For such a task the industrial corporation is only one means to the end; it has proved to be the most effective one, partly for legal reasons, but probably also because of the reduced scope for unauthorized action by the constituent parts.

With respect to this question, I have so far done little more than note that a distinction must be made between growth which proceeds in accordance with sober calculations and comparisons of the more profitable ways of using resources, and growth which is stimulated largely by the desire of entrepreneurs to build widespread industrial ' empires ', or to use the corporate device as a means of extending financial power. There can be little doubt that such a distinction can be found in reality. Business history, and in particular the early history of many of the large successful firms in the economy to-day, is dramatically punctuated by the activities of men with grandiose visions of what they wanted to do, although the less obtrusive and more sober contribution of entrepreneurs whose style was workmanlike, but perhaps lacking in excitement, is ' probably more important for the interpretation of the meaning of the historical record.[1]

---

[1] Many of the earlier studies of entrepreneurial activity gave sensational emphasis to empire-builders, and were often concerned largely with either attacking or glorifying the leading figures. There may have been some justification for this in earlier times, but certainly to-day the role of the empire-builder is of marginal importance for the understanding of business growth. There is now a respectable body of serious literature on the nature of entrepreneurs. One of the leading studies is by R. A. Gordon, *Business*

Nevertheless the explanations I have advanced with respect to the origins of entrepreneurial ideas or the limits to the expansion planned by entrepreneurs do not account fully for the direction, method, or extent of the expansion of firms in instances in which the entrepreneurs are in search of power and of a widespread area over which to exercise it—when careful economic calculations are subservient to an abnormally enterprising and expansive ' temperament '. I have placed emphasis on considerations such as the ' inherited ' resources of firms, the way in which new internal productive services develop, and the emergence of certain types of market opportunity, all of which are more amenable to economic analysis than is ' temperament '. To be sure, I have assumed that entrepreneurs of successful firms are ambitious and enterprising, and that they will try to make as much profit as seems feasible— that given a choice of actions and making due allowance for un-certainty they will not choose those courses of action they think will be the less profitable.

No doubt sociological research can and does throw some light on the environmental factors determining the kind of thing entre-preneurs consider appropriate in a given environment, on the conditions under which they will be shamelessly aggressive in search of profits, and on the influence of custom and tradition on their view of the external world and thus on the kind of productive opportunity they perceive; but economic analysis is not equipped to analyze these non-economic determinants of entrepreneurial ideas and behaviour.[1] Consequently, we make the simple assumption that firms are in search of profits. This assumption has always created difficulty for many, partly because in an uncertain world there is no single objectively identifiable road to the greatest profit and different entrepreneurs with different temperaments choose different roads, and partly because money profits do not encompass the whole of entrepreneurial ambition. These two difficulties reinforce each

Leadership in the Large Corporation (Washington: Brookings, 1945). See also, Mabel Newcomer, *The Big Business Executive* (New York: Columbia Univ. Press, 1955) and the works cited by her.
    [1] There is an extensive literature dealing with these and similar problems, to which economists as well as sociologists, political scientists, historians, and even philoso-phers have contributed, and which is far too diverse to cite. One of the leading research groups is the Harvard Research Centre in Entrepreneurial History, the studies of which should be consulted by the student. The subject has received renewed attention since the resurgence of interest in the problems of underdeveloped countries, and in almost every applied analysis in this area some discussion of the availability, attitudes, and abilities of entrepreneurs is required.

other. For example, the entrepreneur who desires above all to build an industrial empire can at the same time insist that he has chosen the best way to make the most money; and who is to gainsay him before the event?

In an analysis of the expansion of the individual firm the profit-seeking assumption is useful so long as it is possible to set forth in reasonably objective economic terms the considerations that will determine the probability that certain specified directions of expansion will be more profitable than others. But as soon as such factors as the ' temperament ' of the entrepreneur—the strictly personal characteristics affecting his judgment—are admitted into the picture it makes little difference whether we assume that he is in search of profits or has a multiplicity of motives for action; in both cases economics must give way to psychology.[1] All we can do is to note that there are apparently far-reaching differences in entrepreneurial ambitions and to enquire into their significance for the process of growth of firms.

In a purely formal sense it seems more satisfactory in the framework of this study to treat abnormally expansive behaviour as a personal interpretation of the ' best ' way to make money rather than to try to substitute for the profit motive a striving for power, prestige, or the mere enjoyment of the game. After all, even though many such entrepreneurs may set little store on the increase of an already adequate personal income and may frankly be in business for the fun, influence, or prestige obtained from it, profits remain the condition of survival, a social (as well as an economic) test of success and of influence, and a means to even more extensive accomplishments.[2] To the extent that entrepreneurs believe this to be true they are unlikely to pursue those courses of action which they think will be less profitable than others, and the assumption is a plausible one, although it is untestable and affords no basis for prediction.

[1] And in my view economists should frankly recognize this. Attempts to reduce all behaviour to mathematical utility functions are surely as unenlightening as they are complicated and add little to the solution of our problems. I have no objection to economists putting on other hats to handle such non-economic questions provided they look in the mirror occasionally to see which hat they have on.

[2] William Lever, the founder of Unilever, for example, stated frankly: ' . . . I don't work at business only for the sake of money. . . . I work at business because business is life. It enables me to do things.' Charles Wilson, *The History of Unilever* (London: Cassell, 1954), p. 187. But, in general, this merely meant that Lever was more ruthless and imaginative in taking chances than a man more preoccupied with pecuniary calculations might have been; it does not mean that he took action that he believed, at the time when he took it, would turn out to be unprofitable.

Empire-Building and Merger

In any event, I want now to consider the effect of 'abnormally' expansive behaviour on the growth of firms, a behaviour which I shall loosely characterize as 'empire-building' behaviour. Since we are interested in the growth of industrial firms, we shall consider only that type of empire-building which is ostensibly the expansion of a non-financial corporate firm. Men who acquire sufficient stock in numerous corporations to obtain control or to get themselves elected to the boards of directors may be building personal financial empires for themselves, but they can hardly be considered as growing 'firms' in our sense; corporations set up by one or more financiers operating to obtain control of other corporations may be nothing but financial holding companies created largely for the purpose of 'milking' a diverse group of businesses, and should be treated as such. On the other hand, where the facts suggest that empire building activity is motivated largely by the desire to obtain monopoly or to create an extensive and powerful firm, it comes within our purview even though the corporate structure may be largely that of a holding company with operating subsidiaries and could not, in the early stages at least, be properly considered an industrial firm.

In a sense there are two types of empire-building activity here which have different results from the point of view of the economy as a whole. An aggressive entrepreneur may reach for monopoly profits through the establishment of a near-monopoly in a particular market by extensive acquisition of existing firms, or he may be interested in creating a large and powerful firm the success of which does not depend upon the destruction of competition in particular markets but on profits derived from operations in many markets. There may be little connection between either the production or the distribution facilities of the acquiring and acquired firms, especially if the acquiring firm does not intend to change the management of the firms it acquires. Growth of this sort is characteristic of non-operating companies who do not seek monopoly profits particularly (except in so far as the individual firms acquired have monopolies) but who find widespread direct investment a profitable use of funds and of a particular type of venturesome entrepreneurial ability. Such firms grow in response to incentives and require services which are similar to those of investment firms and certain other types of financial institutions. Hence probably most of them are outside the scope of this study, but some of them succeed in establishing extensive, diversified, but adequately controlled industrial empires operating within a co-ordinated administrative framework. Moreover, firms may at different times emphasize one type of empire-building activity or the other and may finally emerge as a cross between the two 'types', possessing both strong monopolistic positions and extensive diversification.[1]

From the point of view of the process of growth, the significance of industrial empire-building is greatest for two problems: the role of acquisition and merger, and the nature of the administrative organization of the rapidly growing firm. The reason for this special significance is found in the speed with which growth by merger can proceed. It should be clear from the analysis of earlier chapters that neither extensive acquisition of existing firms, nor entrepreneurs bent on achieving monopoly and dominance are necessary for the explanation of the emergence of large and dominant firms. Even in the absence of much acquisition the more favourably endowed firms possessing the more able and enterprising managers and entrepreneurs can, in time, be expected to grow very large. Furthermore, the well-established and moderately large firms in an economy which are able to maintain their managerial and entrepreneurial competence through successive generations of men have a decided advantage over very young and new firms, and may for long periods grow at a relatively faster rate, thus obtaining dominant positions in the economy without having had any specific policy of so doing.[2]

Nevertheless, internal expansion takes more time than does external expansion, and any entrepreneur who is ambitious to create an extensive firm in his own lifetime will find his opportunity to do so in the acquisition of already existing firms. Hence, in addition to the fact that acquisition may in particular circumstances be the most efficient way for a given firm to expand, it is also the way for the entrepreneur with extensive ambition to achieve impressive results in a relatively short space of time. In other words, if 'empire-building' entrepreneurs 'in a hurry'[3] are active in the

---

[1] Such a crossbreed is perhaps found in Unilever, the story of which provides an excellent example of 'empire-building', which was none the less largely based on industrial operations.

[2] This point is discussed more fully in the last chapter which deals with concentration and the rate of growth of firms.

[3] The vice-president of a relatively new firm, but one which had recently been growing extremely fast through acquisition, was complaining to me about the difficulty of maintaining a satisfactory administrative organization of such a rapidly growing firm, He asked how the conflict between speed of expansion and adequate organization could be resolved. I told him I thought it could not be resolved except by reducing speed to

business world, we may expect the history of the firms with which they are connected to show an abnormally large incidence of merger and acquisition.

There is no need here to recapitulate the various methods by which the aggressive entrepreneur can, through extensive acquisition, establish a dominant firm or even a ' monopoly ' in a short time. The details are limited only by the law or, more accurately perhaps, by the extent to which it is deemed practicable to evade the law, and by the scruples and imagination of the entrepreneur. The oft-told histories of the formation of the great ' trusts ' around the turn of this century in the United States are outstanding examples of the process. It can hardly be questioned that the purpose of these mergers was to obtain strong monopolistic market control. To be sure, some of the participants at least were undoubtedly firmly convinced that such action was consistent with, or indeed even necessary for, a sound economic organization of productive resources. Whether it was or not is another question; the point at issue is that merger was the method chosen and was clearly the only method of achieving the result in a short space of time—in particular, within the lifetime of the men behind the movement.

To be successful in the sense that the firms sought are actually acquired, an acquisition programme need not involve any serious attempt to integrate the operations of the acquired firms with the operations of the acquiring firm; the result is that many combines in their formative stage hardly fit the definition of a firm set forth in this study. The immediate purpose—the concentration of legal control under one ownership of a very large amount of productive assets—may be accomplished without any of the important characteristics or economic functions of the single firm, as distinct from cartels and pooling arrangements, attaching to the combine. It is for this reason that entrepreneurial services alone are sufficient for an acquisition programme. They are not sufficient for the ultimate successful establishment of a firm, but they are sufficient for the expansion process itself.

Herein lies one of the really significant differences between internal and external growth. Not only can external difficulties of

---

managerial capacities. ' But,' I asked him, ' what is the hurry? ' He replied that Mr. X, the head of the firm, ' is trying to build one of the biggest in the field before he dies. He has to be in a hurry, and he intends to acquire more and more firms, expecting me to solve the problems.' This is, I think, a not unusual attitude to be found among able but impatient businessmen.

expansion (costs of and barriers to entry, competitors' advantages, etc.) be reduced by merger, but internal difficulties as well—at least for an initial period. Successful acquisition of another firm may require no more than financial ability, bargaining skill, aggressive initiative, and a sense of strategy. Such are the entrepreneurial qualities required for an effective programme of acquisition aimed at achieving ' monopoly ' or at building up a ' dominant firm '. This stands in sharp contrast to the requirements of a programme of internal expansion where managerial planning and execution cannot be avoided in the very process of expansion and other internal bases for expansion are also usually necessary.

Thus the significance of entrepreneurial ' empire-building ' does not lie only in its contribution to the creation of large and dominant firms whose history is inevitably marked by extensive acquisition. It lies also in the way in which entrepreneurs using the industrial corporation as a means of extending their power and the scope of their operations, and relying largely on their financial acumen and their skill or ruthlessness in negotiating with suppliers, customers, or competitors, resolve one of the most important conflicts facing firms with extensive opportunities for growth—the conflict between speed of expansion and the maintenance of efficient managerial co-ordination. The ' empire-builder ' tends to sacrifice co-ordination and consolidation to the pace of expansion. It is this that brings his activities closer to those of the ' financier ' than to those of the ' industrialist ' and that creates special difficulties for the unambiguous definition of an industrial firm.

ROLE OF MANAGERIAL SERVICES

For the purposes of this study it was necessary to distinguish the industrial firm from financial power groups, combines and holding companies, cartels, pools, and similar loose but in certain respects powerfully centralized, groups. In doing so we examined the function of industrial firms and concluded that the organized administration of productive activities was the distinguishing function of an industrial firm and the chief reason for analyzing it as an economic entity. Hence some standards of co-ordinated administration must be met before we are justified in treating a given collection of economic activities as an industrial firm. The mere fact that ownership or financial control has become centralized is not enough.

Some of the conceptual and practical difficulties involved in identifying the boundaries of a firm were discussed in Chapter II. One of these difficulties arises from the fact that an industrial empire built up by acquisition and merger, and carried out with little regard for administrative organization is not an industrial firm in our sense until a certain minimum of integration has been achieved. Furthermore, as an industrial firm grows it may reach a point where it has become so large, the decentralization of its activities so great, and the independence of some of its parts so complete, that we must at once seriously question whether the whole should be treated as a single firm. Thus we may be in the anomalous position of treating a particular ' firm ' as properly a firm in the economic sense only in the middle of its life—in the beginning it may have been only an amorphous combine, and in the later part of its life it may again become a somewhat shapeless organization receiving payments and disbursing funds to numerous virtually independent operating organizations but hardly fulfilling any administrative function as an industrial firm.[1] Strange as it may seem, however, this may be a useful way of looking at the matter, especially from the point of view of public policy towards acquisition and size.

The Necessity of Administrative Integration

A combine that is formed in one year only to crash in the next year or two cannot be considered to have been successfully established. The question how long a firm must survive and how extensive must be the co-ordination of its administration before it is successfully established is subject to no precise answer. In general, if the disorganization accompanying very rapid growth has been

---

[1] None of the old established industrial firms in the United States, large as they are, seems as yet to have approached this ' final stage ' in its life as an industrial firm. The organization of DuPont, for example, is largely governed by what has been called the ' DuPont investment formula ': ' This formula, as is well known, is based upon the idea that management, through its financial officer, acts as a kind of holding company for its several operating divisions. It furnishes the most capital to those divisions which promise the greatest rate of return '. (Alfred N. Watson, ' Operations Research and Financial Planning ', pp. 5–6 in ' Techniques and Data for Planning Financial Policy ', *Financial Management Series*, No. 102, American Management Association, 1953). Nevertheless, the degree of financial control and its pervasive influence on operating policy and practice seems to be such that the DuPont organization as a whole can properly be classed as an industrial firm in our sense. There seemed to have been no such control exercised by DuPont over General Motors in which it had a controlling interest until the Supreme Court required it to dispose of its General Motors stock. The absence of pervasive administrative control is sufficient reason to refuse to treat the two firms as one firm in spite of the fact that DuPont apparently could, through its influence on General Motors, ensure for itself a preferential position as a supplier.

eliminated, and the firm is operating as a profitable well-organized institution whose securities are no longer looked upon as highly speculative in the long run by conservative investors, it is reasonable to conclude that it has been successfully established. Similarly, if an already established firm embarks on an extensive programme of acquisition it may pass through a stage of extreme disorganization, but so long as serious attempts at managerial co-ordination are being made, the process is properly considered an expansion of the firm rather than merely an increase in its investment portfolio.

It follows, as we noted in the previous chapter, that much more than entrepreneurial and financial services are required for the successful establishment or expansion of a firm through acquisition. After, or accompanying, the initial entrepreneurial ventures, there is still the managerial task of organization to be completed.[1] If adequate management is lacking and cannot be obtained through reorganization or otherwise, the firm will break up, through bankruptcy or sale, disintegrating into its constituent parts. Hence if the ruling spirits of the firm do not possess the required managerial talents or have not the ability (including the good sense) to place others who do in responsible managerial positions, they will have to be displaced if the firm is to become solidly established as more than a financial holding company.[2] Clearly a firm created largely

[1] Again the history of Unilever provides an excellent example. Asa Briggs in reviewing Charles Wilson's book summarized this aspect of the firm's history as follows: 'Bold enterprise and wide-ranging imagination made Lever successful in the long run: the continued success of Lever Brothers and ultimately of Unilever demanded more specialized and more orthodox qualities of management and control. . . . The qualities which made Lever great could not necessarily keep Unilever strong.' Lever's successor, d'Arcy Cooper, took up the task of creating an integrated administrative organization and ' . . . this was the beginning of a new phase, in which first Lever Brothers and then Unilever passed into the hands of new men and became increasingly " institutionalized ".' Asa Briggs, 'Essays in Bibliography and Criticism: XXXV. Business History ', The Economic History Review, Second Series, Vol. IX, No. 3 (April 1957), pp. 490–491.

[2] Consider, for example, the following description of the early years of General Motors, which was the result of a consolidation promoted in 1908 by William Durant in association with Buick. 'Buick, Oldsmobile, and Oakland—three of the largest plants and three of the " best names " in the industry—had been brought together in less than three months '. Subsequently ' in what must be reckoned a terrific outburst of corporate energy ' the company proceeded to acquire other companies: ' By the end of 1909 General Motors had acquired or substantially controlled more than twenty automobile and accessory companies. Two other prospective purchases narrowly missed fire—Thomas and Ford '. 'Acute indigestion followed.' Control was poor, accounting not organized, and the exact amount of liabilities was uncertain. Finally reorganization and consolidation were required; the bankers took over and a ' general plan ' was worked out in 1913 by ' ultra-conservative men ', which ' still stands ' though still subject to revision as circumstances dictate '. Arthur Pound, The Turning Wheel: The Story of General Motors (New York: Doubleday, 1934), pp. 119 ff.

through consolidation or extensive acquisition may fail disastrously from the point of view of its promoters and its backers, yet still emerge as a successfully established industrial firm in the sense that it remains relatively intact as an industrial organization. It may earn relatively low profits or perhaps go through an extensive reorganization, but neither of these conditions necessarily prevents the firm from remaining large nor necessarily precludes a successful future.

The 'success or failure of industrial mergers' has often been analysed in the light of several different criteria of success. From our point of view a merger is 'successful' if it creates a larger industrial organization than before and one that survives and provides a basis for future growth. But even on this criterion there have been many failures. Apart from initial entrepreneurial misjudgment regarding the possibilities of achieving particular ends in a given environment (for example, a failure to appraise correctly the basic possibilities of obtaining a monopoly where the success of the merger is known to depend upon the achievement of monopoly market control), it seems clear that financial mismanagement, financial ineptitude, administrative incompetence, or administrative inability to handle the organization problems have been the most important factors in these failures.[1] And so it has often happened that a combine, promoted from within or without, survived only after a managerial reorganization which forced a breathing spell or after the administration of artificial respiration through financial reorganization, often under the aegis of bankers.[2]

Financial problems can, of course, bring an empire-building expansion programme to grief long before it runs into problems of administrative organization. But once the stage is reached where managerial problems become important it is difficult, if not impossi-

---

[1] A. S. Dewing in his study of corporate reorganizations found that ' every crisis studied was the result of financial embarrassment ' but pointed out that this in turn was the result of two other ' sets of causes ': one, ' the difficulties attending the administrative management of a large business. The other . . . the difficulties attending the creation of a business organization sufficiently powerful to dominate an industry in the presence of actual or potential competition '. A. S. Dewing, *Corporate Promotions and Reorganizations* (Cambridge: Harvard Univ. Press, 1914), p. 558.

[2] There is no need to review here the methods or results of the several empirical investigations into the success of mergers. In addition to the study by Dewing cited above is the same author's 'A Statistical Test of the Success of Consolidations', *Quarterly Journal of Economics*, XXXVI (Nov., 1921), pp. 84–101, and Shaw Livermore, ' The Success of Industrial Mergers ' also *Quarterly Journal of Economics*, Vol. L (Nov. 1935), pp. 68–93. J. Fred Weston has given a useful review and critique of these and other studies in Chapter V of his *Role of Mergers in the Growth of Large Firms*, op. cit.

ble, to separate financial from managerial failures: the success of operations affects the financial status of the company and the financial status affects operations. Recognizing that the managerial problem can be mitigated if acquisitions are confined to already well-managed companies, firms that cannot afford a drain on their own managerial resources often require that the firms they take over have a high standard of existing management. Though reduced, the managerial problem is by no means eliminated in such cases, for, as we have shown above, the integration of the acquiring and acquired firms still needs to be effected.

One type of expansion, however, which sometimes escapes the need for administrative co-ordination is expansion through the acquisition of subsidiaries in foreign countries. In the first instance the managerial resources of the parent firm are almost inevitably required, since it is only through the knowledge of existing management transplanted abroad that the firm can make use of the type of productive services from which its own peculiar competitive advantages are derived. But once established, the new subsidiary can, and sometimes does, operate virtually independently of the parent. Technical services may be drawn on, but if the market of the subsidiary is unconnected with the market of its parent, there may be little scope for, or purpose in, an attempt to co-ordinate the activities of the two firms or even to establish a close financial control. Such subsidiaries may occasionally be permitted to grow using their own retained earnings and to make their own managerial decisions. Except for the technical services required by the subsidiary, and for the payments required by the parent as dividends or for services rendered, there may be little relation between the two firms. These two exceptions are indeed important. The value to the receiving foreign country of the direct investment represented by the new subsidiary may depend almost entirely on the former, while the country may show considerable resentment against the latter. But neither of these relationships is sufficient to bring the parent and its subsidiary within the definition of an industrial firm that we have adopted. In some cases, though probably not in most, expansion that involves the acquisition of foreign subsidiaries should be treated as an expansion of economic influence or simply as an investment akin to other investments in financial assets.[1]

[1] See the discussion of some aspects of this question in my ' Foreign Investment and the Growth of the Firm ', *Economic Journal*, Vol. LXVI (June 1956). However, E. R.

Thus, as we have seen before, there are necessary limits to the rate of growth of a firm through merger as well as to the rate of growth through internal expansion, in both cases the ultimate limits being set by managerial capacity. The difference is in the shape and position of the growth curves, so to speak. In principle internal growth must be either a reasonably smooth curve or a step-like curve in which each step bears a close relation to the base from which it rises. Growth through acquisition, on the other hand, can proceed in very large steps relative to the base, but the ' plateaus ' after periods of extensive expansion will tend to be longer.[1] If, however, we accept the view that in both cases growth can continue indefinitely, although perhaps, after a point, at a slower rate as external resistance to expansion in a given line encourages diversification (where internal obstacles are greater), what significance should be given to acquisition and merger as a ' cause ' of established and continued dominance and of high industrial concentration?

MERGER AND THE DOMINANT FIRM

An analysis of the relationship between merger, the emergence and persistence of dominant firms, and the level of industrial concentration involves three different, though related, problems: (1) the role of acquisition in the process of growth and its contribution to the size of individual firms at any given time; (2) the significance of merger for the relative sizes (size distribution) of firms at any given time; and (3) the importance of merger as a means of maintaining

---

Barlow in his study, *Management of Foreign Manufacturing Subsidiaries* (Cambridge: Harvard, 1953), which was concerned with United States subsidiaries in Mexico, found that considerable co-ordination and control was exercised by the parent corporation. My impression of United States subsidiaries in Australia was that there was rather less control, but I did not make an extensive study of this particular problem. Distance and the supply of local entrepreneurial and managerial resources would, of course, account for some of the differences.

[1] For some time after the United States Steel Corporation was created, for example, it ran into extensive administrative problems, faced many difficulties, and its growth was slow. In consequence the company was frequently held up as an example of the diseconomies of size. Although it is apparently true that the fear of public opinion exercised a retarding influence on its expansion, there can be little question, it seems to me, that the basic difficulties could be traced to an excessive early rate of growth, that is to say, to a rate of growth in a short period exceeding the rate at which the organizational structure could be efficiently adapted; ' diseconomies of rapid growth ' would be a more accurate diagnosis than diseconomies of size. The absolute size of the firm would not, under present-day standards, be considered remarkable. To be sure, there have been fundamental innovations in administrative ' technology ' since 1901, but even to-day an equivalent administrative task could probably not be carried through without set-backs.

a dominant position once acquired. The preceding analysis is directly concerned only with the first of these three problems.

Empirical analysis will never be able to tell us the quantitative contribution of merger to the growth and size of firms. Even if one could measure accurately the exact proportion of total assets that a given firm had acquired by merger, the effect of the acquisitions on the present size of the firm must remain unknown. Not only does a firm inherit the potentialities for growth of the firms it acquires, but a merger tends also to leave pools of unused productive services available to the combined firm which would not have been available in the independent firms. These provide a basis for a further growth much of which might not have been possible for either firm before the merger. A particularly important source of such unused services is often found in the personnel who had to be taken over with the acquired firm but who could be efficiently used only in an expanded programme of operations. Furthermore, since external expansion draws on the existing productive services of the acquiring firm, the more extensive the external expansion in any given period of time the less can existing resources be used for internal expansion in the same period. Since an attempt to measure the effect of acquisition must relate to a particular period, one cannot assume that the growth of a particular firm in that period would have been reduced by an amount equal to the amount of acquisition.

Nevertheless, it follows from the comparison of the processes of internal and external growth that, except under special circumstances, a greater rate of expansion is made possible by merger. Hence so long as merger is a feasible and profitable method of expansion, we can safely assume that firms that have grown by merger will in general be larger than they otherwise would have been. Were merger prohibited, the size and scope of operations of the larger firms in the economy would almost certainly be less than they are to-day. There is, however, no conclusive reason for thinking that to-morrow they would not reach the position through internal growth that they have obtained to-day with the help of merger. The mere fact that a given firm chose the merger path does not mean that this was the only path open to it and leading to the same goal; but it is reasonable to presume that it was the shortest path.

The other two aspects of the relation between merger and dominance are concerned not with the growth processes of individual firms but with the relative position of firms in relation to the structure of the economy as a whole. The emphasis in this study so far has been on the individual firm; in the next three chapters we take up some aspects of the growth of firms as it relates to the economy as a whole. This involves us first in an examination of the factors that determine the relative rates of growth of different firms.

CHAPTER IX

The Rate of Growth of a Firm Through Time

Special assumptions. *Measurability. The fundamental ratio.* Managerial services available for expansion. *Increase in the administrative task with growth. Impact of changing environmental conditions.* Managerial services required for expansion. *Character of expansion. Relation to existing activities and market conditions. Method of expansion.* Changes in the rate of growth with increasing size. *The 'growth curve'.*

We are now in a position to examine the relation between the analysis so far developed and the purpose of studying the growth of firms as set forth in the opening pages of this book. The growth and size of firms is of significance for the economy as a whole largely because the organization of production within the administrative framework of the individual firm is substantially different from the organization of production brought about through the operations of the open market.[1]

Markets and firms are interacting institutions, each being necessary to the existence of the other. The function of both is ' resource allocation '—the portioning out of the resources of the economy among the various demands on them for production or consumption. But the way in which this function is fulfilled and the pattern of resource allocation in space and time depends very much upon the way in which market forces impinge on the firm, and this in turn depends not only upon the size of an individual firm's supply of (or demand for) a given product in relation to the total supply of (or demand for) that product in the market, but also on the kinds and amounts of productive services with which the firm is already operating. Most of the discussion so far has been directed to the latter point and we have paid but passing attention to the way in which the process of growth of individual firms and the movement through time of the economy as a whole affect the relative position of different firms *vis-à-vis* ' the market '.

[1] The distinction is valid in spite of the problems of identifying the ' boundaries ' of a firm and in spite of the existence of a ' grey ' area which obscures on the periphery any clear-cut line between ' administrative ' and ' market ' decisions.

In particular, does the proposition that there is a tendency, *ceteris paribus*, for individual firms possessing appropriate managerial services to expand continuously and without practical limits, imply the further proposition that older and larger firms will tend to absorb ever larger proportions of an economy's resources? Much of the significance of the first proposition for the working of the economy depends upon the answer to the second. If, in all stages of industrial development, each individual firm grew at much the same rate on the average as industry as a whole, thus leaving the relative position of all firms largely unchanged, many of the problems of economic policy which exercise the talents of economists to-day would not have arisen.

In this chapter we shall examine the factors causing changes in the rate of growth of firms as they get larger and larger. The chief purpose of this and the following chapter is to lay the foundation for the subsequent discussion in Chapter XI of the significance of our analysis of the growth of firms for some aspects of the performance and structure of the economy as a whole.

SPECIAL ASSUMPTIONS

The analysis of any general economic problem in which labour and real capital are important components suffers severely from the inability of economists (thus far at least) to invent a method of taking adequate account of the essential and significant heterogeneity of each of these factors of production while at the same time preserving a manageable analytical framework. Extreme simplification of concepts may be justified for carefully specified purposes, but it may also lead to an analysis which conceals more than it reveals of the essential characteristics of those aspects of the world that it is designed to explain; insufficient simplification, on the other hand, will prevent the development of any general analysis at all. To consider capital or labour as homogeneous factors is a severe abstraction which, nevertheless, has its uses for certain purposes; such concepts, for example, as the capital-labour ratio or the capital-output ratio are valuable tools of analysis in a rough-and-ready sort of way. I shall make use of a similar simplification and with a similar justification—that of enabling us to isolate and understand certain relationships fundamental for our problem.

Measurability

We shall be concerned with the productive services available to firms and the productive services required for expansion, specifically, unless otherwise stated, with entrepreneurial and managerial services. I have stressed over and over again that one of the most significant characteristics of such services is their heterogeneity, their uniqueness for every individual firm. The productive services that the entrepreneurs and managers of any given firm are capable of rendering to that firm are not reducible to any common denominator and are therefore incapable of quantitative treatment.[1] Yet, for the present analysis I shall assume for expository purposes that such services can be measured in comparable units, that qualitative differences can in some manner be expressed as quantitative differences, for I think that the relationships we will discover exist regardless of the statistical impossibility of accurately measuring them.

We are also concerned with increments to the size of firms—with amounts of expansion. Again, even apart from the practical accounting difficulties, there is no way of measuring an amount of expansion, or even the size of a firm, that is not open to serious conceptual objections.[2] Monetary measures of the capital investment involved cannot easily make allowance for differences in relative prices, for differences in the proportions of the various factors of production employed, or for technological differences which affect the capital-output ratio. Similarly, physical measures, for example workers employed, are distorted by differences in the proportion of factors used—an expansion involving a high proportion of machinery to workers would be underestimated relative to an expansion with a significantly lower proportion of machinery if workers employed were taken as the measure of the expansion. Total sales do not take sufficient account of the degree of integration, and ' value added ' is an income concept and not an asset or ' size ' concept. These are all familiar and serious difficulties, but each measure has

[1] Of those economists to whom this difficulty indicates that the analysis is meaningless, I would only ask that instead of throwing the book down at this point they would read on to see if their skill in quantifying the unquantifiable, which has already been so ingeniously demonstrated in other fields, has equal scope here.

[2] See the useful discussion of the accounting problems in the interpretation of the financial statements of firms in Edgar O. Edwards, ' Funds Statements for Short- and Long-Run Analyses ', *The Journal of Business of the University of Chicago*, Vol. XXV, No. 3 (July 1952), pp. 156–174. Also the discussion of various measures of the size of firms in Gertrude Schroeder, *The Growth of Major Steel Companies*, 1900–1950 (Baltimore: Johns Hopkins Press, 1952), pp. 24–35.

its own special significance. Nevertheless, for the purpose of this chapter I shall ignore these difficulties and assume that expansion can reasonably be measured in constant monetary units of investment.

The following analysis will proceed with reference to the entrepreneurial and managerial services available and required per dollar of expansion; of these, managerial services are in some ways the most important for the analysis, and to avoid the repetition of a long phrase I shall speak of ' managerial services ' to include both unless I indicate otherwise.

The Fundamental Ratio

Of the managerial services available to a firm, some will be required for current operations; the amount required will depend on the size of the firm and on external conditions. The rest will be available for use in an expansion programme; but the same amount of expansion may require different amounts of these services in different circumstances. Under given circumstances, therefore, the maximum amount of expansion will be determined by the relevant managerial services *available* for expansion in relation to the amount of these services *required* per dollar of expansion. The factors determining the availability of managerial services and the need for them in expansion will therefore determine the maximum rate of growth of the firm, where rate of growth is defined as the percentage rate at which the size of the firm increases per unit of time.

The larger the firm, the larger must be the absolute amount of expansion if any given rate of growth is to be maintained as the size of the firm increases. In Chapter IV it was shown how the productive services available to a firm increase as the firm grows. If we assume that a firm is fully using its capacity to grow, the maintenance of any given rate of growth over time requires that the supply of the managerial services available for expansion increase at a rate at least equal to the rate at which the managerial services required per dollar of expansion increase; an increased rate of growth can be achieved only if the former are increasing at a rate greater than the latter; a reduced rate of growth must follow if the relevant services become available for expansion at a slower rate than the requirement for those services per dollar of expansion is increasing.

For the purpose of examining the factors affecting the rate of growth of a firm as it grows larger we shall assume a simplified stylized model of a growing firm. By implication, therefore, our firm when it starts out must have a special productive opportunity which it can exploit and which enables it to establish a solid foundation from which further growth takes place; it neither finds itself in a position where it prefers to sell out, nor runs into competitive conditions which preclude further growth. Such a firm may not be characteristic or ' typical ' of firms in general; on the other hand, it is schematically characteristic of some; there do exist firms that have started out on a moderate scale and have grown into the large-firm class. Although for expository purposes I shall describe a firm that is very small in the beginning, the analysis is applicable regardless of the size at which the firm begins. A firm starting out fairly large as the result of a merger, or for any other reason, merely enters our picture in the middle, so to speak, and, with minor changes, the analysis will be equally applicable to it.

We have set out the hypothesis that the factors determining the rate of growth of firms can usefully be analyzed with reference to the ratio between the managerial services available for expansion and the managerial services required per dollar of expansion. We shall now enquire if any change in this ratio can reasonably be expected to take place as a firm grows. Of the relevant managerial services, those of particular interest for this analysis are the unique services that can be rendered by personnel already experienced in the firm. The following section deals with changes in the managerial services available for expansion, by far the most speculative aspect of the problem and the one about which least can confidently be said.

MANAGERIAL SERVICES AVAILABLE FOR EXPANSION

The services available for expansion are the difference between the total services available to the firm and those required to operate it at the level of activity appropriate to its existing circumstances. From the analysis in Chapter IV of the growth of managerial services in a growing firm, we may conclude that the total supply of managerial services will in general be growing at a rate somewhat faster than that of the firm. The fact that as a firm grows it gains new personnel, it adopts techniques for using personnel more efficiently, and at the same time its existing personnel gain new experience, means that the firm continually gains additional managerial services. It has been demonstrated that both the processes of normal operations and the process of growth create new services which can be fully used only in expansion, if at all. Except in the unlikely case where the *total* services needed to operate a firm *declines* as it grows larger, the capacity of the firm to grows depends upon a rate of growth of total services which is larger than the rate of growth of the firm, although there may at times be lags of considerable proportions.[1]

Of this growing total of managerial services, the amount required to operate the firm will be affected by changes in the nature and size of the administrative task as the firm grows larger and by changes in environmental conditions that the growth of the firm may itself bring about.

Increase in the Administrative Task with Growth

In the larger firm, there will be a greater number of administrative tasks, a larger number of different activities, and a larger number of people whose activities must be co-ordinated. Presumably, therefore, a larger supply of managerial services will be required for the larger job. Yet, of the total services available, the proportion absorbed by the administrative task need not rise for two reasons.

First, there is greater scope in the large firm for an increased division of managerial labour, making possible the more efficient use of the services available, as well as greater scope for the use of equipment which saves managerial time and reduces the input of managerial services relative to the size of the task to be accomplished.

Second, the administrative task need not always grow proportionately to the growth of the firm, particularly when the larger firm employs more capital-using methods of production. The use of machinery and large-scale mechanized plants results in a substitution of capital for labour in the productive processes. In these circumstances the managerial task is not likely to be increased proportionately; with everything else equal, the co-ordination of productive activities is in general a simpler process when large machines instead of many people do the work. The saving of managerial effort in this direction may, of course, be more than offset by an increase in the marketing and other managerial functions required to deal with the larger-scale of output, but it need not be so offset under all conditions.[2]

---

[1] With the exception noted, a rate of increase of total services slower than the rate of growth of the firm implies that a constantly increasing proportion of services would be absorbed in operations and eventually there would be no managerial capacity left for expansion.

[2] In a study of administrative overhead in United States manufacturing Seymour Melman found that worker productivity grew faster than administrative overhead (the

On the other hand, it seems reasonable to deduce from the mere fact that organization and co-ordination become such a central topic of discussion and concern for the larger firms that such a stage of increasing returns, if it exists, does not last very long; and that after a point the firm has constantly to be alert to prevent a strong rise in the proportion of managerial services required to conduct current operations efficiently. There seems no evidence that the problems of administration become progressively *easier* as a firm grows bigger and bigger. From this, however, we cannot conclude that the *ratio* between total available services and those required for operating purposes must rise at some point. For equally, there is no convincing evidence that firms using the best administrative techniques have found that they must devote an increasing *proportion* of their total managerial services to current operations merely because the administrative task has become more complex.[1]

Certainly there may be critical periods when administration is not well adjusted to the size of the tasks it must handle, and where the leaders of the firm begin to worry about whether it has become too big to be efficient, especially if the firm has been going through

ratio between administrative and production workers—A/P ratio) between 1899 and 1947. He also found that productivity increases were to a large extent a function of mechanization. It would seem from this that the A/P ratio should fall with increasing productivity, but he found no correlation between changes in the A/P ratio and changes in productivity when he examined 21 American industries for the period 1909–1937, nor when he examined this ratio for manufacturing industries as a whole in three different countries at the same time. He therefore concluded that there was no causal relation between changes in productivity and changes in the A/P ratio and ascribed the changes in the ratio to changes in the nature of the managerial function. That is to say, the effect of increasing mechanization was more than offset by an enlargement of the managerial tasks and by increases in managerial functions. Nevertheless, he did find that the larger firms tended to have lower A/P ratios than smaller firms. This could be explained partly by the considerations discussed above. Seymour Melman, ‘ The Rise of Administrative Overhead in the Manufacturing Industries of the United States, 1899–1947 ’, *Oxford Economic Papers* (New Series), Vol. III, No. 1 (Feb. 1951). Also his *Dynamic Factors in Industrial Productivity* (New York: Wiley, 1956), pp. 69 ff.

[1] In one empirical study dealing with the ratio of administrative expense to size of firm, it was found that this ratio was lower in the larger firms than in the smaller firms, but that as increasingly larger firms were examined the rate of fall of the ratio slowed up. It was suggested that there may be ‘ an exponential relation between administration expense as a percentage of net sales and the size of firms. Viewed in this manner, the ratio at first declines steeply with increasing size at the lower end of the asset size scale. As one moves to the larger size groups the rate of decrease in the ratio lessens, tapering off asymptotically for the largest size firms. In the absence of detailed studies of management practices by firms along the size range it is not possible to offer a more comprehensive statement of the administration expense-size relationship ’. Seymour Melman, ‘ Production and Administration Cost in Relation to Size of Firm ’, *Applied Statistics*, Vol. III No. 1 (March 1954), p. 8.

It should be pointed out, however, that managerial services in the sense used in this study cannot be accurately measured either by the number or the cost of managerial personnel a recent period of very rapid growth.[1] But the very purpose of the battery of modern techniques for decentralizing administration, for controlling operations through budgetary and accounting devices, and for the extensive introduction of ' managerial machinery ' is to ensure that administration is well adapted to the size of its task and that the managerial input does not rise disproportionately. It cannot be concluded, as yet at least, that these techniques have not successfully accomplished their purpose.[2] It has, for example, been argued that even though large firms can attract the ' abler ' men, they also need abler men to handle their administrative problems. Apart from the difficulty of finding a criterion for comparing ability ' in general ' when *different* abilities may be needed in the top executives of large firms (for example, ability to ' deal with people ') than are needed in those of small firms, it is unlikely that extremely rare personal ability is nearly as important for administrative efficiency as is the appropriate adjustment of the administrative framework or administrative organization. Once this adjustment has been effected, the problems of administration relative to the resources for dealing with them do not seem to lead to a general inefficiency in the organization of productive activity nor to the absorption of a significantly larger proportion of the growing total of managerial services.

Impact of Changing Environmental Conditions

A large firm necessarily faces an environment different from that of a small firm,[3] and the different environment of different sizes of

[1] I am, of course, ignoring the sharp rises in the difficulty of the managerial task that may occur after an expansion has taken place and before the new activities have become thoroughly familiar, the new staff (or the old staff in new jobs) working smoothly, and the various ' bugs ' ironed out in whatever administrative reorganization has been required. It is perhaps more appropriate to consider such increases in managerial requirements as requirements for expansion rather than as requirements for normal operations.

[2] I do not mean to imply, however, that all, or even any firms, do in fact adopt the optimum managerial techniques available at any time. The rate at which the best managerial practices are adopted may well fall far short of the optimum rate, especially when firms are to some extent protected against competitive pressures. This is just another example of the well-known fact that entrepreneurs, through ignorance or inertia, do not always adopt the lowest cost methods of production, even when it would be profitable to do so, unless forced to by competition. See, for example, the dicussion in *The Wall Street Journal*, Feb. 26, 1957, of the response of firms to the pressures created by the high levels of economic activity in the United States at that time to cut costs, particularly managerial and labour costs.

[3] I want here to make a distinction between those changes in environmental conditions which can reasonably be related to the fact that a firm has grown bigger and those changes which are unrelated to the increasing size of the firm. Only the first of these

firms has itself an impact on the nature and difficulty of a firm's operating problems. A new firm having to exert special efforts to keep its existing footing, let alone expand, may have to devote an extraordinarily high proportion of its existing managerial talent to current operations; once it succeeds in catching the public fancy, in obtaining the confidence of capital suppliers and of consumers, in solidly establishing its trade relations, the operating problems may diminish, growth becomes possible and if growth can take place in the firm's existing areas of operations, the proportion of total services that must be devoted to operations may remain relatively low. On the other hand, if competition is intense and supply and demand conditions require constant adaptations, the firm may not be able to do much more than keep on its feet and, if it expands at all, can expand only slowly.

There can be little question that in general the larger and older firm has certain advantages over the smaller and newer firm which ease its operating problems and reduce the managerial services required for operations.[1] Some of these advantages will be related to various kinds of market protection the older firm may have been able to erect, others merely to the removal of disadvantages attaching to the unknown and untried, for past success is a powerful aid to future progress. It does not follow, however, that the *largest* firms have the same types of advantages over *large* firms. In other words, while a case can be made for the proposition that the managerial services required for operations become proportionately less for the medium-size and moderately large firms than for the very small ones, it is more difficult to make a case for the proposition that the proportion continues to fall, or remains low, as the firm grows larger and larger.

If growth took place exclusively in fields already familiar to the firm and if the increasing size of the firm implied an increased protection from competition and a decreased compulsion to adapt, innovate, and manoeuvre in order to maintain the firm's competitive position, then the larger the firm the easier presumably would be the

changes is dealt with here. The second will be dealt with in our discussion of the relation between the growth of the firm and changes in the economy. In neither case, however, are we concerned with the kind of external change which might be called 'accidental' in that it affects a particular firm only; rather we are interested in those changes in external conditions which affect whole groups of firms and are significant because of their effect on the relationships between firms of different sizes.

[1] See the discussion in the next chapter of the relative position of small and large firms.

operating problems. But growth in the modern world of competitive capitalism does not very often proceed so simply. The large diversified firms, although undoubtedly wielding much power and occupying strong monopolistic positions in some areas, do not, so far as we can see, hold their position without the expenditure of extensive managerial effort. And it is quite possible that the proportion of total managerial services required to maintain the current operations of a firm will begin to rise when it becomes large enough to get caught up in the kind of competitive innovating struggle with other large firms that was described in Chapter VII; it seems most unlikely that this proportion would fall.

There is, of course, no way of separating in practice the effect that the increased difficulty of administrative co-ordination has on the managerial services required for operations from the effect of changes in the competitive position of the firm. Most of the discussions of the managerial problems of the large firms have centred on the increased co-ordination problem; a distinction is made here only for the purpose of bringing to the surface the significance of changed competitive relationships. Both changes could be expected to affect the managerial services required for current operations in much the same way, but little can be said with confidence about either. Further speculation would avail but little, and enough has been said, I think, to indicate the difficulties of supporting a presumption. It seems unlikely that the proportion of managerial services available for expansion would increase as firms become very large, more likely that it would decline, if only slightly. But if we had to rely exclusively on speculation about changes in the ratio of managerial services available for expansion to the total of such services we could say little about changes in rate of growth with increasing size of firm, except that we would not expect the availability of managerial services for expansion to increase at a greater rate than that at which total services increase, and thereby provide a pressure for an accelerating rate of growth of firms.

MANAGERIAL SERVICES REQUIRED FOR EXPANSION

The other term of the crucial ratio controlling the rate of expansion is the managerial services required per dollar of expansion. Many of the same circumstances that determine the amount of managerial service required to run a firm also determine the amount required to expand it, but their influence is more pronounced on the act of expansion than in the routine of current operations. Here we are not dealing with the size of a going operation, but with the planning and implementing of a change which includes the perfecting of the administrative framework in which current operations can subsequently be conducted.

The managerial requirements per dollar of expansion depend upon (a) the character of the expansion itself, (b) the relation between the type of expansion, the existing activities of the firm, and the complex of external circumstances that I shall simply call ' market conditions ', and (c) the method of expansion.

Character of Expansion

The more complex the character of an expansion in relation to its size and, with some exceptions, the larger an expansion, the more managerial services we should expect to be required per dollar of expansion. An expansion programme can be considered more complex the more varied the activities contained in it. Consequently, an expansion that involves the production of a variety of different products for different markets will, *ceteris paribus*, require a proportionately greater input of managerial services than one which involves the increased production of a single product for existing markets. An expansion that involves the establishment of several kinds of plant will be more ' complex ' in relation to the size of the expansion than one that requires only the duplication of similar plants. In the latter case, much of the basic planning for a single plant can be used, perhaps with small changes, for all the others, and the managerial requirements per unit of expansion will be low. Similarly, a large expansion programme that consists of the creation of a single new plant may require a smaller input of the services of management with experience within the firm than an equally large expansion that consists of the creation of a number of plants (although the total engineering services required may be greater in the former).

The larger demand for the services of experienced managerial personnel in a ' complex ' expansion programme arises not only because of the greater variety of managerial tasks to be performed, and the consequent greater variety of managerial experience required, but also because of the problem of co-ordination. ' Co-ordination ' includes not only capital budgeting and the working out of the relation of each of the different major activities involved in the expansion to the activities of the rest of the firm, but also the

necessary expansion and revision of the firm's administrative structure and the necessary decisions relating to the scope of responsibility and authority to be entrusted to those concerned with the
execution of the expansion and the operation of the expanded
activity. Hence, in addition to the administrative task of planning
the expansion itself, there is the task of maintaining the necessary
integration with the rest of the firm and, at the same time, working
out flexible administrative arrangements so that the execution of
the expanded programme will not be handicapped by bureaucratic
bottle-necks. We have seen that there are times when the difficulty
of making the necessary administrative adaptations may result in a
very critical period in a firm's growth during which its continued
existence hangs in the balance.

As the size of a planned expansion increases, whether there will
be a more than proportionate increase in the requirements for
managerial services or not will depend partly on the extent to which
the complexity of the expansion increases *pari passu*.[1] Complexity
of the kind that demands the services of the limited amount of
personnel with experience within the firm need not increase, as I
have indicated. A capital-extensive expansion, for example, presumably requires less co-ordinating services per dollar of capital
expenditure, and although the engineering aspects of the expansion
may be considerable, it seems unlikely that the managerial planning
and co-ordinating tasks are increased accordingly.[2] If this is the case,

[1] Referring to the rate of growth of firms, E. A. G. Robinson writes: 'As to what is
the maximum efficient rate, individuals in the same industry appear to hold widely
divergent views. A firm, it must be remembered, is an organism in itself. Its parts
depend upon each other. Smooth working arises, we have seen, from the most perfect
co-ordination of many individuals. A too rapid expansion will introduce so many
disharmonious elements that efficiency will be destroyed. . . . The most efficient rate of
growth would appear to be lower in those industries where a high degree of planning
and co-ordination is necessary, higher in those where the technical processes of production are fairly straightforward, and the different departments not closely inter-
dependent.' E. A. G. Robinson, *The Structure of Competitive Industry* (New York:
Harcourt Brace, 1932), p. 56.

[2] Richard B. Tennant, in his extensive study of the American cigarette industry,
provides an example of this. He writes: ' . . . if technological methods had remained
unchanged, it seems unlikely that cigarette firms as large as those we know to-day could
have grown up. . . . With the introduction of machinery, however, the problem of
supervising hand labour was removed, and the principal obstacle to continued industrial concentration disappeared. It was possible to increase the output of a firm simply
by adding more machines, and the firm was free to expand to the extent that its sales
would allow. There was no obvious limit to the number of machines which a firm
might operate without decline in efficiency. In this purely negative sense, the adoption
of machinery removed potential barriers to the scale of enterprise'. Richard B.
Tennant, *The American Cigarette Industry* (New Haven: Yale University Press, 1950),
p. 20.

we have here one, though by no means the only, explanation of why the large firms often prefer a single large, capital-using project to a number of smaller ones; it also throws light on the processes of industrial concentration in industries where the minimum size of a plant is large, for in this case the rate at which expansion can take place is increased, and a given firm in such industries can expand relatively faster than firms in industries where the minimum size of plant is small. But more of this in our discussion of the process of industrial concentration in the following chapter.

Relation to Existing Activities and Market Conditions

Where expansion takes place in fields that are closely related to the existing activities of the firm and to the types of knowledge and skills already possessed by the firm's management, we should expect the managerial effort required per dollar of expansion to be less than a similar amount of expansion into unknown fields; expansion in market areas where the firm is already known and established will require less effort than expansion into markets new to the firm. Here, of course, not only the total supply of managerial services available for expansion but also the particular kind of such services becomes important. But if we assume for present purposes that existing management can always learn new things given sufficient time (or take on people who do), then the fact that a type of service is called for which is not already possessed by the firm merely represents an increase in the total of the managerial services required to effect the expansion. There is little question, as we have shown before, that one of the reasons for the choice of acquisition as the method of expansion into fields new to a firm is precisely that the managerial effort required for the expansion is reduced.

Clearly the state of competition in both factor and product markets will powerfully influence the managerial services required per dollar of expansion. If a firm has to spend considerable effort attacking the positions of competitors, obtaining the skilled labour or other factors of production required, negotiating for capital supplies because money is ' tight ', planning and executing extensive advertising campaigns, or organizing unusual selling programmes, both the managerial services directly required for planning the expansion and those required for the administrative organization of it will be accordingly increased. This hardly needs elaboration.

The new and small firm starting out with the kind of business opportunity that gives it a genuine chance to establish an especially favourable position may, once it is solidly established, enjoy profitable and comfortable growth as a medium-size firm for a considerable period, demand for its product expanding with relatively little effort on its part, particularly if it does not compete directly with larger and financially more powerful firms. With continued expansion, however, the original opportunities may become 'exhausted', so to speak, or at least yield less richly, and the firm, though well established, may find that further growth must take place under less favourable market conditions.

The advantage of the established firms with some degree of ' market-control ', public acceptance, or, if you like, monopoly, can hardly be questioned, but it is again pertinent to ask whether these advantages reduce the task of expansion for those firms whose expansion must take place in competition with firms of similar strength, position, and size. Only rarely, it seems, does the large firm consider itself free from competitive pressures in those areas in which it produces or contemplates expansion. In fields where expansion depends largely on innovation and improvements which presuppose extensive ' research and development ' the managerial requirements per dollar of expansion are surely raised; for all of the managerial services required in the organization, co-ordination, and experimentation that are involved in the effort to innovate and in the process of diversification are properly classed as managerial inputs for expansion.

Method of Expansion

Finally, we must consider briefly the significance of acquisition and merger. We have already shown that the possibility of acquiring other firms raises enormously the maximum rate of expansion, primarily because it substantially reduces the managerial services required per unit of expansion. But acquisition is open to firms of all sizes, and the point we are interested in here is whether the significance of acquisition for the rate of growth of firms changes as the firm grows larger.

If we consider merely the managerial problem involved in acquiring other firms, it seems likely that the larger the acquiring firm in relation to the acquired firm, the less the managerial difficulties of integration. Hence for the acquisition of another firm of given size, the larger the size of the acquiring firm, the easier the managerial task of effecting and integrating the acquisition; consequently for a given amount of expansion through acquisition, the smaller the acquiring firm, the greater proportionately the managerial input required. On the other hand, the larger the *number* of firms acquired in a given period, the greater the average managerial effort necessary to discover and acquire appropriate firms and to incorporate them into the acquiring firm.

Again, therefore, if we consider the change in external circumstances as a firm grows larger, acquisition as a means of maintaining or increasing a firm's rate of growth becomes, after a point, less significant. Consider a firm growing entirely through acquisition. The larger the firm, the larger must be the amount of acquisition per unit of time if its rate of growth is not to decline. Therefore it must acquire larger and larger firms (or parts of firms) or more and more smaller firms. So long as larger firms are available, the number of firms acquired does not have to rise as the size of the expansion plans of the acquiring firm increases, and its rate of growth can remain very high. But when the firm reaches a size where few large acquisitions are possible in appropriate fields, then acquisition as a method of maintaining the firm's growth becomes more and more difficult and the managerial input for a given amount of expansion through acquisition rises sharply because of the increasingly larger numbers of firms that must be acquired to maintain a given rate of growth.[1]

Occasional mergers of 'giants with giants' may take place, but whereas the medium-sized firm may be able almost to double its size every year or so for several years through acquisition, this prospect is simply not open to the giants either through acquisition of other large firms or through the acquisition of larger and larger numbers of small firms. This is partly because of an increasing scarcity of large firms that can be acquired and the consequent difficulties of discovering suitable small firms in sufficient numbers and absorbing them at a rapid rate, which is a question of the size of the growing firm relative to others; and partly because

[1] This implies, of course, that so long as large firms are able to maintain their rate of growth through the acquisition of other firms there will be an increasing degree of concentration of assets in the hands of the large firms which must, by definition, eventually bring the process to an end. As we shall see in our analysis of concentration, it is only under the most peculiar set of assumptions that it is possible to imagine a situation where the rate of growth of individual firms remains unchanged throughout an indefinite lifetime while at the same time no change takes place in the concentration of industrial activity.

of the administrative difficulties of efficiently absorbing ever-larger additions to its size, which is a question of size alone.

I am not implying, however, that acquisition is unimportant to the very large firm as a means of breaking into new fields, of reducing annoying competition, or of preventing the rise of new competitors. Acquisition may indeed be almost necessary if the firm is not to suffer a sharp, rather than a gradual, decline in its rate of growth.[1] The sole issue here is whether acquisition can be expected to offset the tendencies for the managerial input per dollar of expansion to rise after a point. We can conclude that the prospects of expansion through acquisition may raise the maximum rate of growth for medium-sized and moderately large firms but will probably become less significant for the very large firms simply because acquisition becomes for several reasons quantitatively less significant in their expansion programmes.[2]

For the larger firms in competition with each other, therefore, it seems that all of the factors which tend to increase the managerial services required per dollar of expansion are present in an increasing degree; the only significant offsetting factor in the very large firm arises from the possibility of increasing the capital intensity of expansion. But as a firm grows larger it can maintain a given rate of growth only if the absolute increments to its size become ever larger, and there is little reason to believe that this can be accomplished by an indefinite increase in the size of plant. Consequently on all counts we would expect that the managerial requirements per unit of expansion will begin to rise at some point.

CHANGES IN THE RATE OF GROWTH WITH INCREASING SIZE

The import of the above considerations is clear and can be easily summarized. There is a maximum rate at which each individual firm can grow under given circumstances. If we consider only firms for which these circumstances are extremely favourable, we should expect the rate of growth of the medium-sized and moderately large firms to be higher than that of the very new and

---

[1] Furthermore from the above analysis we cannot as yet say anything about the relative rates of growth of large firms as a group and small firms as a group where the large firms are in a position to block the expansion of small firms. It must be remembered that we have been considering the individual growing firm with an opportunity enabling it eventually to reach the ' large ' category; the other question is dealt with in Chapter XI.

[2] That acquisition is quantitatively less significant for large than for small firms in the United States in recent times has been clearly demonstrated by J. K. Butters, J. Lintner, and W. L. Cary, *The Effect of Taxation on Corporate Mergers* (Boston: Harvard, 1951), Ch. IX.

very small firms and higher also than that of the very large firms. The pattern sketched need fit no individual firm; firms of the same size will not necessarily grow at the same rate, and the point at which the rate of growth starts its real decline will be different for different firms. Furthermore, this point may be extremely hard to locate statistically, for in practice growth takes place in spurts, and periods of relative decline may well be followed by periods of accelerated growth.

The ' Growth Curve '

The testing of the theory set forth here is difficult indeed; all sorts of factors other than those controlling its ' maximum ' rate of growth will affect the actual rate of growth of an individual firm in specific circumstances at a particular time, and the pitfalls of interpreting a ' growth curve ' when the end is not in sight are well known.[1] Indeed, it could be argued that the discussion has been in a sense trivial and the conclusion obvious, for perhaps the central point is that firms, in common with most other things, cannot be expected to grow indefinitely at a compound rate. Nevertheless, what we have set forth is an explanation of the ' typical ' pattern of growth (or ' growth curve ') that is widely believed to characterize the successful business firm, an explanation couched in terms of the mechanism of growth and related to the problems of growing bigger and not merely to the complexities of absolute size.[2]

When a firm reaches a point at which its rate of growth tends to diminish, its absolute size is continuing to increase, and there is no reason to believe that *some* increase in the size of even the largest firms imaginable will ever become impossible. The limit to size, as demonstrated in Chapter II, lies not in the process of growth but rather is set by the administrative criteria that we choose to apply

[1] Furthermore, calculations of the statistical rate of growth of a firm will vary depending on the measure of size adopted, whether total sales, assets of one kind or another, employment, or something else. It should be noted that if total employment is used as a measure of size and growth, the above analysis of the substitution of capital for labour as a means of maintaining the rate of growth will not be applicable.

[2] See, for example, the analysis of the pattern of growth of twelve major steel companies in the United States between 1900 and 1950 in Gertrude C. Schroeder, *The Growth of Major Steel Companies*, 1900–1950 (Baltimore: Johns Hopkins Press, 1952), especially, pp. 206–207. Although average rates of growth from one short period to the next indicate, as would be expected, substantial spurts and lags, the trend or ' growth curve ' is clear enough. It is astonishing how little careful statistical work has been done on the growth pattern of individual firms. This study and an unpublished dissertation by Edgar O. Edwards, *Studies on the Growth of the Individual Firm* (Baltimore: Johns Hopkins Univ. 1951) are the only works of which I know dealing with the rates of growth of a number of industrial firms over a considerable period.

in deciding whether or not a given collection of economic activities constitutes a business firm instead of an investment holding company or financial ' community of interest '.

The decline in the rate of growth of the firm (as we have defined it) may be very slight and may show up primarily in a shift of the investment expenditures of the firm from activities within the firm, which we assume to be the preferred investment, to investment outside the firm, that is to say in other companies; there is nothing in this analysis which would lead to the conclusion that a firm's power to grow financially necessarily declines at any point. Under such circumstances if one firm acquires a controlling stock interest in another, the application of a rule of thumb which automatically lumps the two firms together as one, regardless of the administrative arrangements for actual control, can be very misleading.

This analysis of the expansion of an individual firm can in no sense, I must repeat, be taken as a model of the expansion of a ' typical ' firm, whatever that may mean. We assumed a ' special opportunity ' for the small or new firm which enabled it to grow until it reached the position of a large firm and faced the environment of ' big business ' competition. Thus we evaded what is widely held to be the characteristic position of the small firm in a developed industrial economy—an inability to compete with large firms, an inability which precludes its growth into those areas particularly suitable for the operations of larger firms. If this were the characteristic position of small firms, it would be idle to discuss the prospects for their continued growth with reference to the quality of their entrepreneurs and the nature of their resources. The ' environment ' in the shape of competition from large firms would determine their opportunities and would either confine them to certain activities in which large firms could not effectively operate or abruptly shut off their growth in other fields where large firms could operate. In other words, environmental conditions would limit the growth of small firms regardless of their resources or entrepreneurial ability.

That a particular firm may not possess the productive services which would enable it to take advantage of opportunities in the economy for expansion is evident, and of no consequence for our analysis. But if whole groups of firms are in such a position because of their size alone, then the problem is more general and becomes of considerable significance for the theory of the growth of firms. We must now investigate this possibility and analyse the position of small firms in a growing economy.

CHAPTER X

THE POSITION OF LARGE AND SMALL FIRMS IN A GROWING ECONOMY

The special position of small firms. Competitive handicaps, especially finance. The continued existence of small firms. Opportunities for growth. ' Interstices ' in a growing economy. The principle of comparative advantage.

There is considerable evidence that small firms, because of their size alone, are restricted by their environment to certain types of opportunity where the prospects of continued expansion are extremely limited. Aware of the possibility that the growth of this large group of firms may be more controlled by the environment than by the quality of resources or the enterprise and ingenuity of entrepreneurs, many readers have probably been uncomfortable with the way in which external conditions have so far been handled in this study. The environment has been treated not as an objective ' fact ' but rather as an ' image ' in the entrepreneur's mind; the justification for this procedure is the assumption that it is not the environment ' as such ', but rather the environment as the entrepreneur sees it, that is relevant for his actions. While this assumption may be valid enough, it does not justify us in ignoring the effect of external conditions where there is reason to believe that they are sufficiently general and identifiable to enable us to predict, with reasonable assurance, how they will affect an entrepreneur's actions.

We have found that what an entrepreneur sees in his environment, and his ability to take advantage of what the sees, are conditioned by the types and amounts of productive services existing in the firm and with which it is accustomed to operate. For a general theory of the growth of firms this procedure is legitimate if we can assume that opportunities for expansion do ' exist ' in some sense, and that some firms will always see them reasonably correctly and take advantage of them. In effect, then, we ask the questions what, under such circumstances, are the general conditions required for the continuous growth of an individual firm; what determines the direction and method of growth; and what are the fundamental limits to the rate of growth and the ultimate size of the firm. In other words, assuming that ' real ' opportunities for profitable investment are to be found in the economy, what determines who will see them, who will be able to take advantage of them, and to what extent.

In this way we brought to the centre of the analysis the significance of the types of resources of individual firms and the relationship, not only between the ' inherited ' resources of a firm and the ability of the firm to take advantage of the opportunities perceived by its entrepreneurs, but also between these resources and the perceptions of the entrepreneurs. We thereupon examined the process of expansion, leaving by the wayside those firms lacking at any point the ability to grow. We dealt only with the restrictions on growth and size inherent in the nature of the firm, and only with the nature and characteristics of successful growth under specified conditions. The central analysis has not been concerned with the prospects of growth of particular firms, but only with an exploration of the characteristics of firms that can grow successfully, and of the factors shaping and limiting their growth. For this purpose it is appropriate to take the existence of a spectrum of opportunities as given, and to look to the productive services available to firms for the source of their ability to grow and for the determinants of their pattern of growth.

Nevertheless, it remains true that the maximum possible expansion for all firms taken together is determined by the availability of resources (including labour, current output, existing assets, and new resources) for investment purposes, even though the actual amount of expansion attempted is controlled by the expectations of entrepreneurs about the profitability of using their own resources. The relative scarcity of the different kinds of resources in the economy as a whole affects the individual firm through the prices at which resources and finance can be obtained on the market; the expected profitability of expansion is controlled by the ability of the firm to see opportunities for the use of its own resources, and is a function not only of the cost of other resources with which they must be combined in production but also of the external opportunities themselves.

Now none but the most philosophically sophisticated businessman will accept the proposition that the opportunities for the expansion of his firm are simply his ideas about what his firm can do; he will insist that the opportunities he sees reflect the ' facts ' of the world, facts that may be known only with indifferent accuracy to be sure, but facts none the less—the prices of the factors of production, market conditions as determined by the actions of competitors and by the tastes, or at least the psychology, of consumers, the line of credit his bank will give him, etc. And of course the businessman is correct, for in the last analysis these are the ' facts ' with which he must deal and he is right in insisting that unless he has interpreted his environment correctly he is likely to fail in his efforts.

There can be no question that for any particular firm the environment ' determines ' its opportunities, for it must take its resources as given (in the sense that it must recognize the limitations on what it can acquire with what it has) and must look to the opportunities it can find for using them for the source of its power to grow. Whether or not we should treat the resources of the firm or its ' environment ' as the more important factor explaining growth depends on the question we ask: if we want to explain why different firms see the same environment differently, why some grow and some do not, or, to put it differently, why the environment is different for every firm, we must take the ' resources approach '; if we want to explain why a particular firm or group of firms, with specified resources grows in the way it does we must examine the opportunities for the use of those resources.

Clearly no general theory of growth can take into account all of the particular circumstances of particular firms that will determine their ability to grow; but if there are environmental circumstances which affect in a systematic manner whole groups of firms the resources of which have some significant characteristics in common, then it is appropriate to analyse the prospects of growth for firms in such groups. In doing this we go further than we have gone so far in examining a relationship between certain specific characteristics of the resource-base of a firm and the firm's opportunities for expansion.

THE SPECIAL POSITION OF SMALL FIRMS

There is good reason to believe that the amount of resources administered by a firm has in itself a significant influence on the opportunities for expansion open to the firm, that is, that smaller firms as a group are in a different position *vis-à-vis* the external world from that of large firms as a group. We have already noted this in several places, in particular in the preceding discussion of changes in the rate of growth of firms with increasing size, but there, as well as in other places, we were concerned only with the amount and nature of the productive services required for expansion; we did not consider the possibility that the position of the firm might be such that the opportunities open to it were severely limited, not by the quality of its resources, but by impassable barriers existing in the environment. We ignored this possibility because we wanted to examine the processes of growth of only those firms for which no such barriers existed. Now, however, I want to take up the question of the restrictions on the opportunities for growth that are imposed on small firms by external conditions, in particular, by the superior competitive power of large firms.

Competitive Handicaps, Especially Finance

In point of fact, firms that are both larger and older in any economy or industry do tend to have many competitive advantages over smaller or newer firms, no matter how able the management of the latter may be. Their market connections tend to be more extensive, their standing in the capital market better, their internal funds larger—a successful past record is alone an enormous aid to further advance. They have accumulated valuable experience and, by virtue of their size, they can take advantage of many technological and organizational economies not possible at smaller scales of operation. These are not ' monopolistic ' advantages in a restrictive sense, nor are they easily removable—they are corollaries of size, experience, and a successful past. We have already analysed in some detail the economies of size, and if we add the possibility of ' unfair ' competitive practices stemming from the monopolistic power of large firms, the position of the smaller firms is even more unfavorable; but we need not do so in order to establish the point.

The cause and consequence of most of these competitive disadvantages are evident enough, but a few words should perhaps be said about the problem of access to capital, one of the most serious of the competitive handicaps of the small firm. Here we deal with two questions: the relatively higher rate of interest that small firms must pay, and the absolute limit to the amount of capital they can obtain at any rate, both of which are the result of the inescapable fact that on the average the risk of lending to small firms is greater than to large ones. The former, though leaving the small firms at a cost disadvantage *vis-à-vis* larger firms, does not necessarily restrict the expansion plans of those small firms that believe their opportunities are likely to prove sufficiently profitable to justify the payment of a high rate of interest. For small firms as a group the relatively higher interest rate merely means that they must have more profitable opportunities than larger firms before they can obtain the capital for expansion, and that they may be unable to compete in the same field with the large firms.

Restrictions on the amount of credit a small firm can obtain have a more far-reaching effect. Regardless of how bright may be its prospects, its expansion may be limited by an inability to obtain capital on any terms, and it may never get a chance to put its plans to the test. Its prospects are prejudged by outsiders, and the judgment is not based solely on the brightness of the opportunity but also on the fact that failure of the particular venture may involve the loss of the money advanced—the small firm is itself a greater risk. The larger firm, on the other hand, faced with the same risk of failure of a particular venture may nevertheless be able to raise capital because the total ' security ' for the funds is so much better.

It is, incidentally, because rationing is such an important means of restricting credit that anti-inflationary monetary policies can be expected to work to the disadvantage of small firms. If the monetary authorities raise interest rates and restrict the availability of bank credit during periods of high employment when ' easy money ' would result in an inflationary rise of prices, the position of the small firms in the economy is likely to be more prejudiced by the pressure on the reserves of the banks and by the consequent credit rationing than it would have been by rising prices. In general, rising interest rates and restrictions on bank credit are designed merely to reflect the scarcity of real resources for further investment; if credit were cheap and easy to obtain, prices of resources would be bid up, the cost of expansion would rise and, even apart from any subsequent depression brought on by an inflation, no net gain would be obtained by industry as a whole from the ' artificially ' low cost of finance capital.

But when prices of resources other than capital rise, the relative competitive ability of the small firms to obtain resources is not *necessarily* worsened (though it may be), whereas it is necessarily worsened when credit is tightened and the tightening involves not only rises in interest rates but also increased credit rationing. If only interest rates rise, the small firms may be able to obtain the capital necessary to enable them to put their prospects to the market test whenever they are willing to pay the price; if credit is denied them, they are not permitted to do so, and consequently even firms with opportunities they confidently believe would turn out to be genuinely profitable in spite of rising costs or high interest rates, are precluded from taking advantage of them and are not even given a chance to test them. The special ' capital-raising ' ingenuity of entrepreneurs rises in importance for the small firm in relation to the other productive services available to the firm, but there is no presumption that such ingenuity has much relationship either to the firm's productive efficiency or to its competitive ability in the market for its products. We have noted in earlier chapters that this peculiar type of entrepreneurial service may be an essential ingredient of the collection of productive services required for the successful expansion of the small firm.

The Continued Existence of Small Firms

The competitive disadvantages of small firms are so serious that economists have apparently felt some special explanation of the continued existence of small firms to be required. It would seem that at any given time a fair number of small firms would be in existence simply because they were young, and that at a later date the same firms would have developed into medium-size or large firms. This possibility, however, is rarely included among the explanations advanced for the existence of small firms, the analysis usually being presented in terms of the economies and diseconomies of size, using a kind of ' static ' or cross-section approach.[1] Thus, in effect, the various explanations place small firms in our class of ' firms that do not grow ' or, at least, that do not grow very much.

The explanations can, for the most part, be grouped into four general categories: (1) Some kinds of activity are unsuited to large firms, for example, those requiring quick adaptation to changing conditions, close personal attention to detail, the whims of customers, etc.; or those where small plants are required (transport costs may be high) and the supervision of many small plants uneconomic for large firms. (2) Under some circumstances large firms as a matter

[1] See, for example, P. Sargant Florence, *The Logic of British and American Industry* (London: Routledge and Kegan Paul, 1953), pp. 63–66; J. Steindl, *Small and Big Business* (Oxford: Basil Blackwell, 1945), pp. 59–61; and A. D. H. Kaplan, *Small Business* (New York: McGraw-Hill, 1948).

of public relations permit and protect the existence of small firms, sometimes under a price 'umbrella' held over the industry. (3) In some industries entry is very easy and many hopeful would-be businessmen set up shop every year; this leads to the existence at any time of many small firms which, however, are on their way out. (4) Finally, in the development of some industries some small firms get a start because the bigger firms have not got around to mopping them up; in time such firms will be driven out.

Opportunities for Growth

These general explanations, with their numerous possible variants, do account for the existence of large numbers of small firms (perhaps for the majority) and for the fact that small firms are particularly numerous in certain kinds of activity. Prospective entrepreneurs whose primary asset is a small amount of capital, and whose chief claim to entrepreneurial status is a desire to set themselves up in business, are of necessity confined to those fields where the only requirements for getting some kind of a start are a little capital and perhaps a training or skill which is widespread among the non-professional working population.[1] It is in this type of field where we find the peculiar combination of circumstances characterizing the position of firms that cannot be expected to grow—a high rate of entry, and a high rate of exodus, low profit rates and a low level of technical progress. These are not conditions that would be attractive to enterprising entrepreneurs, and only those whose abilities and resources are both extremely limited would in general be expected to enter such blind alleys—fields of activity in which opportunities for further development are most unpromising.[2]

If the existence of all small firms could be accounted for by the explanations advanced, we should expect a shifting population of small firms and a steady expansion of large firms without any significant increase in the numbers of the latter. In fact, however, we find that as an economy grows the number of firms classed as 'large' also increases, even in an advanced economy. How does this come about if existing older and larger firms have such powerful

[1] Where even such skills are lacking there is still the possibility of starting a small commercial shop. Here we are concerned only with manufacturing firms.

[2] Incidentally, it might be noted that if, in fact, it is the type of entrepreneurial and managerial ability as much as the lack of capital, which causes small firms to cluster in fields where opportunities are relatively poor under any circumstances, measures to ease their task of obtaining capital may not have a significant effect on the mortality of small firms.

competitive advantages over newer and smaller firms that the latter are confined to areas where they cannot grow very much? To a considerable extent the survival and growth of a small and new firm depends on superior entrepreneurial ability, and just as prospective entrepreneurs with considerable financial resources have a wider choice of possible activity than do those without capital, so prospective entrepreneurs with unusual ability, original ideas, and considerable versatility have a wider choice of activity than does the 'average' citizen. The more favoured entrepreneurs might be expected to search for fields where the prospects of return are reasonably commensurate with their notions of what they ought to be able to get. Since their choices are wider they would not be attracted in large numbers to fields where profit rates are low and where there is little chance for even the more able to carve out a special position for himself.

But do such fields exist for the new and small firm? And if they do, is it only in special cases, for example where patent protection can be obtained or where the large firms, for some fortuitous reason, fail to see profitable opportunities for expansion? Or are there more fundamental forces at work?

Let us assume that existing large firms do have a competitive advantage over small and new firms in any field they care to enter, and are under no legal or moral pressure to permit the survival of small firms. Under such extreme circumstances what would be the prospects for small firms? We have seen that even under the most favourable external conditions imaginable the rate of growth of an individual firm is limited, and that no firm can take advantage of all possible profitable opportunities for expansion. It follows from this that the fact that large firms have a competitive advantage over small firms in every type of production is not sufficient to ensure that they will actually be in a position to act on their advantage. If, therefore, the opportunities for expansion in the economy increase at a faster rate than the large firms can take advantage of them and if the large firms cannot prevent the entry of small firms, there will be scope for the continued growth in size and number of favourably endowed small firms, some of whom will themselves enter the ' large ' category in time.

I propose to call these opportunities for small firms the *interstices* in the economy. The productive opportunities of small firms are thus composed of those interstices left open by the large firms which the small firms see and believe they can take advantage of. If enough small firms judge their prospects reasonably correctly and act accordingly, then the rate of growth of the economy will exceed the rate of growth of the large firms. And if the existing small firms are unable or unwilling to fill all the interstices, there will be scope for the successful creation of new firms. Plainly, we have here a variant of the long-familiar principle of comparative advantage: given limited resources, a firm that has an advantage over others in numerous fields of activity will find its most profitable expansion in those fields where its advantage is greatest. Essentially the interstices are created because there is a limit on the rate of expansion of every firm, including the larger ones; the nature of the interstices is determined by the kind of activity in which the larger firms find their most profitable opportunities and in which they specialize, leaving other opportunities open.[1]

' Interstices ' in a Growing Economy

Population growth and technological advance leading to increasing productivity, to the development of new resources and of new industries, and to shifts of consumers' tastes and expansion of their wants are, together with the increased flow of savings and capital accumulation which accompany rising incomes, generally considered to be the most powerful forces stimulating the growth of an economy. Where demand is expanding rapidly for all sorts of products, existing firms may well find their most profitable opportunities for expansion in increasing the output of their existing products. It is under these conditions that the managerial effort required for expansion is, in general, lowest, particularly if there are economies of larger-scale production to be obtained from a more extensive use of capital. In consequence, the growth of existing firms in their existing fields may be very rapid indeed, with the largest firms growing faster than the rest in those fields where entry is most difficult because of capital requirements, patent or other protection of technology, early capture of consumers' preferences by branding or advertising, etc.

If growth is accompanied by the creation of important new industries and new technologies which are not in their inception

---

[1] It may often happen, of course, that a field already developed by a small firm will attract the interest of a larger firm which thereupon enters and destroys the small firm's opportunity, either by driving it out of business or purchasing it outright. See the discussion in the next chapter of the effect on the interstices of acquisition and merger.

under the control of the existing large firms, there will be scope for the entry of new firms, with the more favourably endowed earlier established ones soon obtaining a dominant position in the industry. In the earlier stages of rapid industrial development the interstices may be very wide and numerous simply because the established firms are so few and because many new industries are coming into being. There seems considerable evidence, however, that very quickly each of the major industries tends to become dominated by a few large firms and a high degree of concentration develops early.[1] This is partly the result of the competitive advantages of older and larger firms, partly the result of merger and acquisition, and partly the result of the power of the large firms to set up barriers against the entry of smaller competitors. For the moment I want to ignore merger and restrictions on entry and to analyse the course of events on the assumption that all growth is internal growth, for the significance of merger and restricted entry can best be appraised with reference to their impact on a situation in which they are presumed not to be present.

As the larger firms expand, their very growth opens up new opportunities for investment, both because of the concomitant expansion of incomes and because of the increased demand for various kinds of producers' goods. As technological knowledge grows and becomes increasingly diffused it will inevitably create innumerable and unpredictable opportunities for smaller firms. There is no reason to assume that these opportunities will be found only in fields where entry is extremely easy and competition so intense that profitable growth is difficult to maintain. Each of the larger firms will be guided in its expansion programmes as much by the nature of its own resources as by market demand, for every firm is, as we have seen, a more or less specialized collection of resources and cannot move with equal ease in every direction; indeed, a contraction of the sphere of activity of the larger existing firms often takes place as markets widen.

In those industries where the growth of demand exceeds the growth of the largest firms by an amount sufficient to permit new competitors to establish plants taking advantage of the technological

[1] The bearing of the present discussion on the process of industrial concentration is discussed in the next chapter. I remind the reader, incidentally, that all of the analysis in this book is intended to be applicable only to economies where the industrial corporation is the dominant form of business organization; hence not to industrial development occurring before the last quarter of the last century.

economies of production available to the existing occupants, several smaller firms may grow into the ' large ' class. The ensuing struggle of the leading firms to maintain their competitive position against their compeers tends to induce innovation in the processes of production, in marketing, and in the quality and variety of products. The changing productive services created within firms together with their changing position in relation to the market for their products, is apt to induce diversification, much of which will be directly related to the actual and anticipated actions of competitors.

The Principle of Comparative Advantage

Let us consider now an economy where the rate of growth has been sufficiently high in relation to the rate of growth of the earlier established dominant firms to permit more than one large firm to develop in each of the major industries. We shall examine the nature and development of the interstices, starting at a point in time where the capacity to grow of the larger firms in the economy is more than sufficient to keep up with the rate of growth of opportunities in their existing fields of activity; and since we maintain the assumption that large firms have an absolute competitive advantage over small firms in all respects, direct competition from newcomers is impossible. We assume that the economy continues growing; the nature of the interstices will therefore depend on the kind of opportunities the large firms take advantage of, for it is unlikely that they can take advantage of every opportunity for investment that arises in the economy.

The greatest advantage of the large firms over smaller ones will lie in those areas where large-scale operations are most effective, where large-scale production, marketing and research are easiest to introduce and maintain, and where managerial resources can be most effectively economized. This type of advantage is commonplace and need not be elaborated; it leads to the kind of specialization between small and large firms that was mentioned in connection with the earlier discussion of the persistence of small firms in certain types of activity, a specialization that will exist so long as the large firms continue to find opportunities for extending large-scale operations.

In addition, once a firm has reached a point where ' competition in innovation ' becomes necessary if it is to maintain its position vis-à-vis other large firms, the effect of this competition on the nature of its expenditures will deter the firm from entering fields where it competes with other firms not having to incur the same type of expenditure. For any given product larger firms probably do require a larger margin over direct cost for profitable operations, not because of a larger administrative overhead as is sometimes alleged, but because of the kind of oligopolistc competition in which they become engaged.[1]

This kind of competition forces a firm to undertake extensive research, experimentation, market testing and similar activities the cost of which cannot easily be allocated between requirements to maintain its existing position and requirements to prepare the groundwork for further expansion. To a considerable extent the costs of such activities are properly investment costs, but they are of a hybrid variety which often cannot be separated from current costs and for this reason many of them will be classed as general overhead and allocated to current output even though they are in fact incurred largely for the preparation of future expansion. ' Current ' costs will consequently rise as more and more of this kind of activity is demanded of the firm. In other words, more and more concealed investment, that is, the use of resources for future output, becomes written off as current costs, and the rate of profit on the net worth of the firm will be lower than it would have been if such expenditures had been treated as investment out of current profits.[2] The only expenditures of this sort that one sometimes sees

---

[1] I should perhaps once more repeat that none of this discussion has any bearing on the question whether or not large firms have higher profits or lower costs of production than small firms. No consensus on either has yet emerged from the various attempts to investigate comparative profits and costs, the results being conflicting and to a large extent non-comparable because different investigators use different data, different techniques, applied to different types of firms at different periods of time. I am not prepared to take any position on this controversial subject. Useful recent surveys, evaluations, and citations of the literature dealing with attempts to compare profits or costs statistically will be found in P. Sargant Florence, op. cit.; Richard C. Osborn, ' Efficiency and Profitability in Relation to Size ', *Harvard Business Review*, Vol. 29, No. 2 (March 1951), pp. 82–94; and Hans Staub, *Le Profit des Grandes Entreprises Americaines* (Paris: Colin, 1954).

[2] It should be noted that a firm has no incentive to treat ' investment ' expenditures of the kind referred to above as anything other than costs of current operations unless it wants to adjust its earning figures to show a better profit position for the sake of attracting investors or enhancing its general reputation. We have argued that firms prefer to retain as much of their earnings as possible for reinvestment in the firm. To treat certain types of reinvestment expenditures as costs may permit a higher total retention of earnings (as is well known for depreciation) both because it may reduce the pressure to pay higher dividends and because it reduces taxable income of the firm where corporate income is taxed. So long as profit figures are ' satisfactory ' there is, on the contrary, an incentive to increase expenditures which are in fact for the purpose of increasing profits in the future and to call these expenditures ' current costs '.

separated on the books of firms are those for ' research and development ', but even here it is impossible to disentangle the expenditures
that must be carried on in order to maintain the competitive position
of existing product-lines from those that are exclusively for future
expansion and not directly related to the maintenance of the current
position of the firm.

In these circumstances the large firms would not find it profitable
to compete in the market with small firms producing the same products at low cost and willing to put them on the market at a lower
price. If a given product of a large firm cannot bear its share of the
research, development, and other ' necessary ' investment expenditures, that is to say, cannot be sold at a price that will permit
a substantial margin over direct costs (whether this margin be
hidden in the average cost figure or treated as profit), that product
will be ' unprofitable ' for the firm, whose comparative advantage
lies precisely in its ability to undertake such expenditures. At the
same time the product may be very profitable for a small firm.

The fact that a proportionately greater part of the total expenditures of large firms than of small firms is likely to be of the nature
of investment expenditures, regularly written off as current costs,
is a further consideration leading to a kind of specialization between
large and small firms with respect to the nature of the products
produced. The larger firm will be interested in those areas in which
it has a substantial degree of monopolistic control over price or in
those products which small firms cannot well produce (except
perhaps with the consent or under the price protection of large
firms), and where therefore the chief competitors are similar large
firms with similar concealed investment costs.

The rate at which large firms can take advantage of opportunities
to enter new fields and produce new products will, as we saw in
the analysis of the economics of diversification, be severely restricted
by the continued effort and investment which are required for the
maintenance of their competitive position in the ' areas of specialization ' they choose to make their own. As they grow larger and
larger, their rate of growth will tend to decline for the reasons
analysed above. The decline may be very slight, with growth going
on continuously and in very large jumps from time to time; but
if the rate of growth of the economy remains at a high level, the
proportion of the total opportunities for investment that the large
firms will be able to take advantage of will fall, and the smaller firms

will then find the scope for their own expansion widened in the absence of restrictions on their ability to expand into the interstices.

The assumption we have made that large firms have a competitive advantage over small firms in any field they care to enter is not, of course, wholly valid, although if one includes monopolistic advantages arising from the power and the willingness to use unfair competitive practices of various kinds, it has considerable application. On the other hand, if there are activities in which large firms would be at a positive disadvantage because of their size, the small firms have their own peculiar place. But such activities will not, by definition, permit small firms to grow very large.

The ability of small firms to seize on profitable opportunities in which they can grow will be destroyed if barriers are erected against their entry; their growth in the areas they can enter may be cut short by acquisition. Even if small firms have opportunities in which they can protect themselves against large firms—for example, through the possession of unusual ideas or ability which cannot be imitated, or through patents on technology or on products—it will often pay them, as we have seen, to sell out to large firms who may be able to offer extremely attractive terms.

The development and persistence of industrial concentration in a growing economy depends on the number and type of interstices created, and on the ability of small firms to enter and grow in them. The former depends largely on the nature and extent of competition among the large firms; the latter on barriers to entry and the extent of acquisition. These questions will now be explored.

CHAPTER XI

GROWING FIRMS IN A GROWING ECONOMY: THE PROCESS OF INDUSTRIAL CONCENTRATION AND THE PATTERN OF DOMINANCE

Barriers to entry. *General effect on investment in the economy as a whole. The importance of 'Big Business' competition. Capital requirements and consumer loyalty. Artificial barriers and the interstices.* Merger in a growing economy. *Consolidation of many firms. Merger in relation to indices of business activity. The effect on the interstices of natural limitations on acquisition.* Interstices and the business cycle. The process of industrial concentration. *Measurement of concentration. Concentration and growing firms in a growing economy. Some shaky evidence. Concentration within industries.* Concentration and dominance. *The continued dominance of large firms.* Conclusion.

Even in a highly industrialized private-enterprise economy where productive activity is extensively 'dominated' by large firms, competition in the open market is, in principle at least, still held by large and small businessmen alike to be the most powerful force pushing the economy to higher levels of achievement, increasing efficiency in the use of resources, protecting consumers against exploitation, and ensuring reasonable opportunities for men to make the most of their abilities and assets. At the same time, the possible evils of 'unrestrained competition' are recognized by all, and the provision of 'rules of the game' is an accepted function of government.

I shall not here be concerned with the traditional problems of competition and monopoly as they relate to the price and output decisions of firms; rather I want to examine some aspects of the significance for the economy as a whole of the development of opportunities for the growth of small firms, and of the competitive relationships among large firms. In the light of this examination, I shall analyse the relation between the growth of firms of different sizes and the process of industrial concentration. We shall begin with the restrictions on the ability of small firms to fill the 'interstices'—to take advantage of the opportunities for profitable investment left open by the larger firms.

BARRIERS TO ENTRY

Existing firms, though themselves unwilling or unable at particular times to take advantage of opportunities that would yield a respectable return over cost at current prices and interest rates, are often in a position to prevent others from doing so. They may desire to keep others out, either to protect some existing position of their own, or merely to reserve the opportunities for themselves at some later time when it may become more profitable to take advantage of them. The power to keep others out may rest on legal (or illegal) control over the relevant technology, raw materials, or even essential producers' goods, on the ability to threaten ' price wars ', or on various types of relationships with distributors. This kind of restriction on entry I shall term ' artificial ', to contrast it with the difficulties of entry arising from large-scale capital requirements, from the usual cost and market disadvantages of small firms, from the fact that consumers have developed a strong attachment for certain brands, from the superior performance of existing occupants, and similar conditions. The reason for the distinction will become clear when we consider the effects of such restrictions on the interstices in a growing economy.

General Effect on Investment in the Economy as a Whole

If some firms, unable to take advantage of specific opportunities for expansion, succeed in preventing others from doing so, the obvious and immediate effect is either to reduce the effective opportunities for investment in the economy as a whole or to reduce the productivity of investment actually made. The restricting firms may be expanding as much as they can, but the restricted firms are either expanding less than they might, or expanding in less profitable directions. If the power to restrict entry is largely in the hands of the larger firms, the smaller firms are the ones most severely affected. If such power is great and widespread, it may seriously retard the growth of the economy.[1]

---

[1] The following discussion is not relevant to the situation, originally analysed by E. H. Chamberlin and Joan Robinson, in which ' excessive entry ' may reduce economic efficiency by raising the costs of existing producers. In their models, existing producers were forced to contract their output because of competition from newcomers, and no producer had any competitive advantage. On this subject, see the remarks of Fritz Machlup, op. cit., pp. 312 ff. In our discussion, however, we are concerned only with restrictions on the ability of firms to take advantage of opportunities for expansion which would otherwise be neglected, and we assume that the larger producers have a competitive advantage over smaller ones.

Consider the extreme case. In any given state of technology, the rate of growth of all firms taken together, and therefore of the economy as a whole is, in the last analysis, limited by the availability of resources for expansion. But if the opportunities for profitable investment are artificially restricted, it is conceivable that the amount of investment actually attempted will fall short of using the resources available.

Let us maintain our assumption that the large firms in the economy are not restricted in their investment opportunities by the availability or cost of capital but only by the nature of their internal resources, including the quality and amount of the managerial services available to them. To simplify matters, let us further assume that the availability in the economy as a whole of real resources for investment is reflected in the total supply of funds for investment. It follows that the funds available at current interest rates will exceed the amount the large firms will absorb. If at the same time, the large firms are in a position to restrict severely the opportunities for investment of all other groups of firms, even a sharp fall in the rate of interest will not do much to stimulate investment, and the rate of growth of the economy will not only be lower than it would otherwise have been, but unemployment and even prolonged stagnation could be expected. I do not suggest that this is either an explanation of ' secular stagnation ' or an important cause of depressions; I put it forward to bring out the type of underlying general effect that severe restrictions on entry may have. To produce such serious effects, restrictions on entry would have to be extraordinarily widespread. Although mono-polistic restrictions on new competition do play some role in some of the theories of the business cycle, they are rarely given pride of place, other factors usually being considered more important in the explanation of the periods of depressed activity in an economy.

Nevertheless, even if artificial restrictions on entry are not extensive enough to produce really flagrant results or to prevent the full utilization of the resources available for investment, they tend, if thoroughly effective, to reduce the productivity of investment in the economy as a whole, and the rate at which output in the economy grows may be less than it might have been. If individual firms take the trouble to enforce measures designed to restrict the entry of new competitors into a specific field of activity, it can be presumed not only that entry would be profitable but also that further expansion in the field would be an efficient use of resources from the point of view of the economy as a whole. Barred access means, then, that resources which could have been more profitably employed must be diverted to the next best alternatives, which presumably represent less desirable ways of using the economy's resources. In other words, the productivity of investment is lower than it would have been, even if capital formation does not fall below that required to use fully the resources available for investment.

If the restrictions on entry are primarily enforced by large firms against small firms, then of course the ' interstices ' in the economy which provide the opportunities for the expansion of small firms are significantly reduced, and the industrial domination of existing large firms will not in time be diluted from below. If the restrictions are enforced by each large firm not only against small firms but also against all other large firms, then output in each of the protected areas may be lower than otherwise, but this may have a relatively insignificant effect on the economy when the competitive struggle between the large firms takes the form of innovations designed to get round the restrictions. Restrictions against the entry of small firms may effectively keep them out of extensive areas of production; those against large firms are more likely only to prevent the production of identical products or the use of identical technology, for both of which substitutes may quickly be developed. Thus they will not be completely effective.

The Importance of ' Big Business ' Competition

Great and widespread admiration, which is indeed justified, for the technological achievements of ' big business ' appears to be responsible for a distinct tendency in many quarters not only to play down the notion that restrictions on newcomers' competition are deleterious to the economy, but even to insist that they are, within limits, desirable as a means of permitting the large firms to attain the kind of market position necessary to induce them to engage in extensive and expensive research, larger-scale capital investment, and long-range programmes of industrial development.[1]

[1] ' . . . in the modern industry shared by a few large firms, size and the rewards accruing to market power combine to insure that resources for research and technical development will be available. The power that enables the firm to have some influence on prices insures that the resulting gains will not be passed on to the public by imitators (who have stood none of the costs of development) before the outlay for development can be recouped. In this way market power protects the incentive to technical development '. J. K. Galbraith, *American Capitalism: The Concept of Countervailing Power* (Boston:

'Big Business' competition, though different from the classical competition among small firms, is held to be even more beneficial to the economy and more effective in meeting consumers' wants. The competition between the large firms involves large amounts of investment and undoubtedly results in an increasing quantity and variety of goods and services which become cheaper and cheaper under the pressure of competition.

Those who see in this kind of competition the chief sources of the enormous progress in real income in the more advanced capitalist countries urge, and quite correctly, that the large firms could not afford the competitive innovating race if small firms were immediately able to take the fruits of their research, copy their innovation, and put products on the market at prices which did not reflect the costs of developing them. It follows that the control of output, the control of markets, and the control of price must remain in the hands of those who bear between them the 'development cost' required for constantly increasing output and continually improving products. How then are we to evaluate the restrictions against the competition of small firms, restrictions which, at best, may be an important factor maintaining the profit margins of the large firms that make possible the results achieved, and, at worst, have nothing but a thoroughly insignificant effect on the performance of the economy?

It should be noted that the results so widely deemed beneficial flow from competition, from competition among the few to be sure, but competition so effective and intense that no large firm can afford to act the role of a contented monopolist greedily exploiting the economy.[1] Should the numbers of large firms become so reduced

Houghton Mifflin 2nd ed. 1956), p. 88. For an attempt at a statistical investigation of this argument see Almarin Phillips, 'Concentration, Scale and Technological Change in Selected Manufacturing Industries 1899–1939', *The Journal of Industrial Economics*, Vol. IV, No. 3 (June 1956), pp. 179–193. Using census data this study attempted to test the hypothesis that large firms are in a better position to innovate than are small firms. It was found that the 'hypothesis that industries with large numbers of small firms tend to be technologically more progressive, while not disproved, received no support from the data' (p. 193); in general the conclusion was drawn, though 'with caution', that 'industries in which production is concentrated in a few firms and in which firms are relatively large' do show more signs of technical change than industries in which these conditions do not exist' (p. 192).

[1] This is clear from the most cursory glance at the literature, and is evident in the very phrase 'New Competition' which has been widely adopted to describe the relations between big business units. 'Competition, always the mainspring of our economy and of the dynamics of American life, in mid-twentieth century America has been stimulated and quickened by Big Business. As a consequence competition has taken on a renewed vitality and diversity, a new dimension and a new content.' David

that competition between them were significantly impaired, a new
' case ' for big business would have to be made.[1] How many firms
are sufficient for the purpose is perhaps a question to be settled in
the light of experience, but it seems clear that if there is only one
firm (or perhaps even two or three when they arrange to stay out of
each other's way) effectively dominating each major line of activity,
the process of competition in innovation will be substantially diluted.
Thus in an economy whose market is not large enough to sustain
extensive and vigorous oligopolistic competition, the effect of
barriers against the rise of smaller firms may be serious indeed, and
the lack of interstices for the smaller firms may greatly retard the
economy's growth.

With the possible exception of patent protection of limited scope
for a reasonably short period, the economist can fairly safely insist
that economic advance is impaired by artificial barriers against the
rise of new competitors wherever such barriers are enforced on
behalf of a few firms that are not in competition with each other;
here the incentive to innovate and the pressure of competition,
which are the chief sources of the advantages alleged to flow from
the power of the large firms to protect and stabilize their markets,
are absent. The problem becomes more complicated when we turn
to an evaluation of the effect of barriers to entry against new competitors when competition among the large firms is very active. It
remains true that the opportunities for smaller firms are restricted
and the prospects of the dilution of the dominant positions of the
large firms reduced. But what is the importance of this result?

There are two approaches to this question. One is essentially
political and revolves round the desirable nature of a vigorous and
free society, the political significance of a concentrated structure of
economic power, and the social significance of the absence of
widespread economic opportunities for the ' independent ' man. I
do not intend to discuss this aspect of the matter here. The other

E. Lilienthal, *Big Business: A New Era*. (New York: Harper, 1952), p. 47. See also
Oswald Knauth, *Business Practices, Trade Position, and Competition* (New York: Columbia
Univ. Press, 1956); Peter Drucker, *Concept of the Corporation* (New York: John Day,
1946), pp. 122 ff., 247 ff., Herrymon Maurer, *Great Enterprise: Growth and Behavior of
the Big Corporation* (New York: Macmillan, 1955), pp. 171 ff.; and A. D. H. Kaplan,
Big Enterprise in a Competitive Society (Wash. D.C.: Brookings Institution, 1954) Chs.
VIII, IX, X.
[1] It may be that the seeds of the ' new case ' are already being planted by those who
stress the influence on the decisions of the large firms of a strong sense of responsibility
towards the public, and sometimes go so far as to give the impression that the large
firm operates primarily as a public service.

approach, perhaps more relevant for economic analysis, relates to the effect on output in the economy, and here enters the significance of the difference between the kinds of barrier I have called ' artificial ' and other barriers to the entry of small firms into those areas of production only partly occupied by large firms. Of these latter barriers, two are widely considered to be of primary significance— the capital requirements for large-scale operations, and the difficulty of breaking through an extensive attachment of consumers to well known brands.[1] Both of these are more effective barriers against smaller and little-known firms than against other large and well-known firms.

Capital Requirements and Consumer Loyalty

In some types of activity there are important economies in production or distribution to be obtained from producing on a large scale, and new firms, to produce efficiently, must be able to undertake extensive initial capital investment. This will bar many firms from taking up that type of production so long as the existing large producers put their products on the market at prices which prevent smaller-scale high-cost producers from making profits and which do not encourage other large firms with adequate capital to enter. As demand grows, existing firms must be able to expand output sufficiently to keep prices below these levels, or new firms will come in. The position of existing producers is thus protected only to a limited extent, and they must be willing and able to maintain both quality and output at a level sufficient to leave no profit openings for newcomers. Profits will, of course, be higher than they could have been if the outlays required of newcomers were lower, but as the market grows, the economies of large-scale operation will not alone be sufficient to relieve the firm of extensive pressure to maintain its position against competitors.

The fact that existing large firms are often able to establish relationships with distributors or to capture the preferences of consumers for their own brands will also limit entry of new firms, since any attack on such positions may be very expensive indeed

---

[1] A recent American study of barriers to entry found that economies of scale or ' absolute cost advantages of established firms ' were less significant in most concentrated industries than ' the advantage to established sellers accruing from buyer preferences for their products ', especially when the size of the United States market was considered. See Joe S. Bain, *Barriers to New Competition* (Cambridge: Harvard Univ. Press, 1956), p. 216.

and it may take a very long time to break down long-established preferences. Nevertheless, even this kind of entrenched position is protected only so long as the protected firm's performance is acceptable to the public. The willingness of consumers to pay a premium for 'favourite' brands, or even more, to put up with poor quality or poor service, sets limits to the protection given to the competitive position of firms who have succeeded in establishing market positions of this kind. Such protection against potential competitors may well permit somewhat higher profits in spite of the extensive expenditures required to establish and maintain the protection, and such profits, together with the resultant 'stability' of the firm's market position, may be necessary for the encouragement of large-scale innovation and research, but again, any decline in the performance of the large firms from the point of view of the consumer will weaken their position.

The essential point is the difference between barriers to entry that are weakened by a firm's inability to maintain an 'adequate' level of performance and those that can be maintained regardless of performance. So long as the protected firms are in active competition, and so long as their profits are used to improve old products and introduce new products and technology, one cannot assert categorically that either type of barrier against new competition necessarily reduces total output. Nor can one assert categorically that output is necessarily greater because of 'big business' competition than it would be with a different type of competitive organization. This is the crux of the argument between those who insist on the advantages of 'creative' big-business and those who emphasize the restrictiveness of strong monopoly power. The composition of output is undoubtedly different from what it would have been; the output of some products is lower and prices higher than they might have been, but other products are produced that might not have even been 'created' under different circumstances. There is no easy way of resolving this issue on economic grounds alone, especially if we take account of the 'irrational' satisfactions of consumers. An unweighted list of sins and virtues, with the attackers listing innumerable examples of exploitation and clear-cut abuse of power, and the defenders listing innumerable examples of creativeness and public spirit, helps but little; a weighted list might be relevant, but we do not know what weights to use.

Artificial Barriers and the Interstices

Nevertheless, if we accept the ' case ' for big-business competition as put forth by its proponents, we must note that it rests entirely on the assumption that competitive pressures are intense. Therefore, any barriers to competition that protect a firm regardless of its competitive performance are presumably to be condemned by both sides.

It will be recalled that the significance of barriers to entry derives in part from the fact that there is a limit on the rate of growth of the large firms as a result of which they are unable to take advantage of all opportunities for investment in the economy and thus leave openings for the small firms. The opportunities left open are determined by the rate of growth that the large firms can maintain in relation to the rate of growth of the economy as a whole. If the growth of large firms must eventually level off, as we have argued, the opportunities for the smaller firms may increase, but only if there are few artificial barriers to their entry, that is to say, barriers which do not depend on the performance of the large firms.

The decline that we have analyzed in the rate of growth of the large firm occurs precisely because a continued expansion of operations at the same rate becomes inconsistent with the maintenance of standards of performance imposed on the firm by competitive conditions. When the larger firms in an economy reach the size where this restriction on their rate of expansion becomes significant, it then becomes important for the growth of the economy that these firms are not in a position to prevent smaller firms from taking up those investment opportunities that they themselves cannot take up. Even patent protection may be undesirable if the large firms as a group have developed, and in fact control, a significant proportion of the patentable technology of the economy.[1] It is highly probable

---

[1] It is under these circumstances that the strictures of J. M. Clark might have their greatest significance. He called knowledge the ' . . . industrial instrument with unlimited capacity, which shows increasing economy with increasing utilization, and never reaches the stage of " diminishing return ". To be efficient, the enterprise of extending the frontiers of industrial and economic knowledge must be carried out on a large scale; yet the results must also be made available for the benefit of smaller scale producers, unless we are to submit to a ruinous waste of overhead in this respect. If industrial research becomes the sole perquisite of the concern which can afford an expensive laboratory, there is an end of economic freedom, and as a long-run result, perhaps, an end of economic efficiency, owing to bureaucratic stagnation.' J. M. Clark, *Studies in the Economics of Overhead Costs* (Chicago: Univ. of Chicago Press, 1923), p. 141. See also a discussion of an analogous problem from an international point of view in E. T. Penrose, *The Economics of the International Patent System* (Baltimore: The Johns Hopkins Press, 1951), Ch. VI.

that patents are less effective against other large firms, who often can develop alternative technology, than against small firms who in general cannot; and if an attack is made on artificial barriers to the entry of smaller firms, patents must receive their share of attention, for if small firms are not permitted to take advantage of the leftover opportunities, the rate of growth of the economy will suffer.[1] From the point of view of the growth of firms, the most significant attribute of monopoly power is the power to restrict the entry of new competitors, and especially smaller ones, into promising areas of production.

MERGER IN A GROWING ECONOMY

There can be little question that historically merger and acquisition have been one of the most powerful forces offsetting the tendency of an expanding economy to produce widening opportunities for smaller firms.[2] The maximum rate of growth of firms is, as we have seen, immeasurably increased when acquisition is a possible method of expansion, and firms have not been slow to take advantage of this method. It is generally agreed that much of the dominant position of the large firms in the United States economy to-day can still be traced to the 'waves' of merger at the end of the last century[3]; the very early rise to dominance of one or two firms

[1] Another, rather different approach would be to break up the big firms into several smaller firms. This might have temporary disruptive effects but would have no long-run adverse effects on economic progress if economies of growth rather than of size account for their size. The strongest case to be made for the big firms rests on the costs of research, and in this respect the Chairman of the United States Steel Corporation has recently stated that the largest firms in the United States to-day are still too small to achieve the maximum rate of progress. But see the discussion of dominance later in this chapter.

[2] G. W. Nutter, I think, was quite correct in his observation that it is ' . . . not unreasonable to view mergers as a force counteracting expansion of markets, and hence as leading to less change in the structure of dominance than is usually believed. . . . The ea rly merger movement is important in the history of industrial concentration because it made concentration, taken in a relevant sense, greater than it otherwise would have been, irrespective of whether it actually increased concentration or not'. G. Warren Nutter, 'Growth by Merger', *Journal of the American Statistical Association*, Vol. 49, No. 267 (Sept. 1954), p. 456.

[3] For example, Butters, Lintner and Cary, speaking of merger activity between 1879 and 1903 state, ' Even though many of these early mergers subsequently proved to be un successful, the evidence is clear that this wave of merger activity in itself largely cre ated the characteristic twentieth-century pattern of corporate concentration '. J. K. Butters, J. Lintner, and W. Cary, *Effects of Taxation on Corporate Mergers* (Harvard: 1951), p. 289. And Jesse Markham states, ' The conversion of approximately 71 important oligopolistic or near-competitive industries into near monopolies by merger between 1890 and 1904 left an imprint on the structure of the American economy that fifty years have not yet erased '. ' Survey of the Evidence and Findings on Mergers ', *Business Concentration and Price Policy* (Princeton: Princeton Univ. Press for the National Bureau of Economic Research, 1955), p. 180.

in so many industries in Australia, still relatively young as an
industrial economy, can undoubtedly be traced to merger[1]; and in
Canada merger has been important 'in many of the industries in
which concentration is high '.[2]

Although in a rapidly expanding economy, early acquisition and
merger may quickly enable the larger firms to achieve near-monopoly
positions in many industries, it is a game that two can play, and if
the market is expanding rapidly enough, the merger of smaller
firms or later arrivals may enable them quickly to overcome the
handicaps of small size, and through merger to challenge the
dominant position of the larger earlier-established firms. If merger
is a ' cause ' of early dominance, it is sometimes equally a ' cause '
of a subsequent weakening of that dominance.[3] But the mere fact
that merger raises the maximum rate of growth of the individual
firms means that some firms will be larger than they would have
been in the absence of merger, and in all probability larger also in
relation to the economy as a whole.

The occasion for profitable acquisition exists under numerous
and varied circumstances and it therefore is not surprising that
extensive acquisition should mark industrial history. When the rate
of expansion is straining the productive services available to the

[1] The ' holding company ' device is very widely used in Australia to consolidate
ownership interests, although some of the largest companies scarcely meet our definition
of an industrial firm. See the paper by L. Goldberg and D. M. Hocking, ' Holding
Companies in Australia ' delivered before the 1949 meeting of the Australian and New
Zealand Association for the Advancement of Science. Some of the companies originally
only holding companies have subsequently converted themselves into operating firms
with much closer administrative structure, for example, Felt and Textiles, Ltd., of
Melbourne. (See the *Annual Report* of this firm for 1954).

[2] Gideon Rosenbluth, *Concentration in Canadian Manufacturing Industries* (Princeton:
Princeton Univ. Press for the National Bureau of Economic Research, 1957), p. 102.

[3] George Stigler has maintained that since the 1900s in the United States merger has
been a significant force in a shift from monopoly to oligopoly in significant industries:
' The change has been most striking in the industries which were merged for monopoly
at the beginning of the century. The merger firm has declined continuously and substantially relative to ʌhe industry in almost every case. The dominant firm did not
embark on a new program of merger to regain its monopolistic position, however;
the new mergers were undertaked by firms of the second class. The industry was
transformed from near-monopoly to oligopoly'. ' Monopoly and Oligopoly by
Merger ', *American Economic Review*, Vol. XL, No. 2 (May 1950), p. 31, J. F. Weston
challenges Stigler's conclusions on the ground that other forces, notably antitrust
dissolutions and internal expansion of rivals, were more important in the emergence of
oligopoly than was merger. J. Fred Weston, *The Role of Mergers in the Growth of Large
Firms* (Berkeley: Univ. of California Press, 1953), pp. 35–37. (See, however, G. Warren
Nutter's review of Weston's argument with Stigler in the *Journal of the American
Statistical Association*, loc. cit.). We are not here concerned with the motives for merger
(whether ' for ' monopoly or ' for ' oligopoly) as were Stigler and Weston, but rather
with its effects, and as to the latter, there seems little question that the later merger movements in the United States did increase oligopoly. Cf. Jesse Markham, loc. cit. p. 179.

large firms, while at the same time extensive opportunities for profitable expansion are to be seen on all sides by the enterprising entrepreneur, acquisition and merger will appear particularly attractive; and not only attractive but at times ' necessary ' to a particular firm as a safeguard for its long-run position whenever other firms are observed to be taking advantage of opportunities so closely related to that firm's own activities that they appear as a competitive threat.   In addition, acquisition will be attractive if continued expansion appears likely to be hindered by bottlenecks in the flow of supplies, and integration by merger the most appropriate safeguard. Acquisition will also tend to be unusually prevalent when economic growth is stimulated by important innovations or discoveries that are not in their inception substantially within the preserve of the larger firms.   Under these circumstances there may be a scramble of old and new firms to gain a footing in the new fields of activity. If entry is easy there will be many failures, the environment will be favourable to merger, and the few who survive the initial struggle will often gain their advantage in this way.

Merger in Relation to Indices of Business Activity
     Economists have not been particularly satisfied with a heterogeneous list of ' causes ' to explain the occurrence of merger and acquisition, and have tried to discover whether there are not more persuasive considerations giving rise to ' waves ' of mergers. Interest has centred particularly on the business cycle and on the levels of security prices, but the results of attempts to correlate the number of mergers with other indices of business behaviour have not been very successful, for the differences between ' merger movements ' seem to be more significant than the similarities.[1] The same factors seem to have different effects under different conditions. For example, high security prices are said to have encouraged merger in the 1920s because they made outside capital relatively cheap, while low security prices are supposed to have done so in recent years because the assets of many existing firms were undervalued at ruling prices.[2]

     [1] Whereas some of the earlier students of the subject held that there was a close correlation between mergers and the business cycle (for example, Willard Thorp, 'The Persistence of the Merger Movement', *American Economic Review* (Vol. XXI, No. 1), p. 85), more recent research has cast much doubt on the existence of any correlation. See Jesse Markham's excellent summary of the research on this subject, loc. cit., pp. 146–154.
     [2] 'Whereas the high security prices of the 1920s, for instance, encouraged merger

The failure of the attempts to correlate the number of mergers with other indices of economic change is not surprising, partly because of the variety of more or less independent economic and institutional factors influencing merger, many of which were discussed in Chapter VIII, and partly because the usual indices of merger activity do not necessarily reflect changes in the strength of the inducement to expand through acquisition. Merger is one of two possible methods of expansion, and whether or not it is the method chosen will depend on its relative profitability. The number of mergers in a given period, or even the ratio of the number of mergers to the number of existing firms, will tell us nothing about the ratio of expansion through merger to expansion through new capital formation; yet this is the information we require if the purpose of comparing merger activity to other indices of business behaviour is to discover the conditions under which merger is promoted.

If the number of mergers rises in a period, for example, but expansion through new investment rises even faster, presumably the existing constellation of circumstances, while favourable for expansion of capital investment, is not particularly conducive to the choice of merger as the method of expansion. And whether high or low security prices are conducive to merger can only be tested by finding out whether the proportion of merger to total expansion varies with the level of security prices.

It has been objected that although merger and internal expansion may be alternative uses of funds from the point of view of the individual firm, merger does not, from the point of view of the economy as a whole, absorb real savings. Hence in prosperity real investment must be high by definition. Only in depression could acquisition be the dominant form of expansion in the economy as a whole.[1] While it is true that the condition of prosperity is a large amount of real investment, and depression, by definition, is a deficiency of real investment, the relevant question is whether or not acquisition forms a larger *percentage* of total expansion at times when real investment is high than it does when investment is low.

---

activity by making outside capital relatively cheap, the low security prices of recent years (in relation to asset values) have also made the merger route of expansion attractive to many companies by providing an attractive outlet for the accumulated financial resources of the acquiring companies '. J. K. Butters, J. Lintner, and W. Cary, op. cit., p. 312.

[1] I am indebted to Donald Whitehead for raising this point.

The answer to this is not *a priori* clear; yet to know whether prosperity or depression is relatively more favourable to expansion by acquisition than to internal expansion, we would have to examine this percentage in the two conditions. The difficulties of constructing an index of the importance of merger that takes account of its role in total capital expansion would be considerable and the results might not justify the effort. But in the absence of such a measure, it is hard to see what purpose is served by correlating merger activity with security prices, business activity, or other measures of cyclical or secular change.

The Effect on the Interstices of 'Natural' Limitations on Acquisition

In general the inducements to merger are so numerous and so pervasive that the appropriate question perhaps is not, why so much merger? but rather, why not more merger? Except where owners are stubbornly independent in the face of attractive offers for their firms, why should not small firms with bright prospects always have opportunities to sell out on especially favourable terms? Why should they ever grow large in the interstices of the economy?

We have already touched on one type of explanation—the limits on the ability of any one firm to absorb others in a given period of time. In periods of very rapid growth of the economy, therefore, many smaller firms may find no other firm actively seeking to buy them. But there is another, perhaps even more relevant, explanation that is also implied by our previous analysis. It is obvious that for acquisition to be the preferred method of expansion there must be ' suitable ' firms available, that is to say, firms that fit the expansion plans of the acquiring firms. Yet there are many types of expansion for which suitable firms are unlikely to exist; for example, the type which is stimulated by the prospects of introducing new products or of using new technology developed by the expanding firm. Or when the internal inducement to expand arises partly from special skill in the organization and operation of particular processes in production, internal development may have overwhelming advantages over acquisition. Large firms maintaining their own research and development laboratories may be expected to develop new processes and products the best use of which can often be made only if the firm itself undertakes both the creation of new factories and the promotion of its products. So far as the large firms are themselves the source of much of the new technology introduced into the economy, this alone will decrease their desire to expand through acquisition. Similarly the introduction of new industries into new geographical areas may require the building of new plants.

For these and allied reasons, internal expansion may often be more profitable than acquisition for individual firms, and this 'natural' restriction on the advantages of expanding through acquisition, together with the general limit on the rate of expansion of the firm may, if the large firms are very large, reduce the extent to which the small firms growing into the interstices are absorbed by larger firms. It is true that in the United States economy at the present time, large firms make more acquisitions than do smaller firms,[1] but at the same time acquisition is a less important source of growth for large firms than for small firms.[2] This means that acquisition promotes the growth of those small firms that make acquisitions more than it does the growth of large firms making acquisitions, and thus promotes an increase in the number of medium-size and larger firms, which may improve the competitive position of these firms *vis-à-vis* the older large firms. On the other hand, there can be no question that acquisition facilitates the diversification of the larger firms and in this respect it may partly offset the tendency of an expanding, changing economy to create opportunities for smaller firms.

INTERSTICES AND THE BUSINESS CYCLE

Before pulling together the analysis of this and the two previous chapters into a general theory of the process of industrial concentration, we should briefly examine some of the more important effects of cyclical fluctuations in industrial activity on the relative positions of small and large firms. Severe downswings in industrial activity obviously reduce the interstices in the economy chiefly because they

---

[1] The available information on the contribution of merger to the growth of small and large firms in the several merger 'movements' in the United States is well discussed by Butters, Lintner, and Cary, op. cit., Ch. X. No purpose would be served by summarizing it here.

[2] The finding by Butters, Lintner, and Cary that merger was a more important source of growth for small firms as a group than for large firms (ibid., p. 267) has been challenged by John Blair and M. F. Houghton in the *Review of Economics and Statistics*, Vol. XXXIII, No. 1 (Feb. 1951), pp. 63–67 and by John Blair in Vol. XXXIV, No. 4 (Nov. 1952), pp. 343–364. The central issue of the controversy turns on the amount of unreported mergers undertaken by small firms. Lintner and Butters effectively sustained their position in a rejoinder to Blair's second reply, ibid., pp. 364–367.

reduce the opportunities for expansion of all firms; the question is whether small firms are relatively worse off in comparison with large firms.

One of the significant characteristics of cyclical fluctuations is the interaction between actual and expected changes in economic activity: a change in one direction tends to cause anticipations of further change in the same direction which may themselves actually induce the change anticipated. Thus, in spite of idle resources during a depression, and in spite of the fact that widespread efforts to use these resources would, within limits, create the income which itself would justify the effort, firms in general do not make it because of unfavourable expectations on the part of each individual firm. The cumulative effect is to reduce both anticipated and actual opportunities for profitable investment.

If the larger firms have competitive advantages over smaller firms, one would expect that the impact of depression on them would be lighter even if their competitive advantage showed up only in relatively fewer failures. As a group they have greater financial strength; individual large firms may have more control over prices, and if the income elasticity of demand for their products is low enough, they may be able to maintain earnings at a level higher than would have been possible under more competitive conditions. In addition, large firms often plan further ahead than do smaller firms, partly because their greater financial strength enables them to afford it, and partly because the nature of their operations more or less forces them to. For this reason, depression is sometimes looked on as a good time to expand: costs are low, plant can be constructed and equipment bought cheaply. All that is necessary to justify such action is the ability to finance the project and an anticipation that demand will pick up in the not-too-distant future. Needed improvements in organization and productive processes may be undertaken which were not profitable at peak levels of activity. Depressed economic conditions unquestionably favour large firms as a group in comparison with small firms, and often permit individual large firms to consolidate their position and further improve their competitive strength.

However, all of the advantages of the larger firms are equally available to medium-sized firms with adequate finances, and although there are probably more outright failures among the smaller firms, individual medium-sized and small firms may well come out of the depression in equally good shape.[1] To the extent that these smaller firms have lower overheads and are more able to reduce costs as ouput is reduced, they may even incur proportionately lower losses than many of the larger firms. Consequently, although the depression may permit larger firms as a group to improve their position, and may eliminate many small firms, there will, when the upswing comes, still be numerous smaller and medium-sized firms in a position to expand as the interstices widen.

The upswing, especially if sustained for a considerable period, is particularly favourable for the medium-sized and smaller firms; in some respects they may be in a better position to expand rapidly than the largest firms, for, as we have suggested above, the moderately large firms are likely to have some advantages in expansion over the largest ones. The interstices may increase appreciably and a long period of sustained activity may then see an improvement in the relative positions of smaller and medium-sized firms. When monetary policy becomes exceedingly stringent, however, severe credit rationing may reduce the expansion of small firms.[2]

THE PROCESS OF INDUSTRIAL CONCENTRATION

An analysis of the process of industrial concentration is an analysis of the forces determining changes in the relative importance of firms of different sizes in an economy or an industry. Firms may be looked on as employers of labour, owners of assets, or producers of goods, and a measure of their relative importance in each of these respects can be used as an index of the state of concentration at any given time. Plainly, the significance of any index of concentration depends upon the measure used, and a brief discussion of this problem is in order.

Measurement of Concentration

There are several ways of going about the measurement of concentation, and there is no general agreement on the best measure, or even the most useful concept. One may be concerned with inequality in the size distribution of firms (sometimes called ' relative concentration '), or with the extent to which the quantity being

---

[1] In one study it was found, for example, that the younger and newer of the major firms in the United States steel industry did not expand less and sometimes expanded more in depression than did the largest firms. Gertrude Schroeder, *The Growth of Major Steel Companies*, 1900–1950 (Baltimore: The Johns Hopkins Press, 1952), pp. 207–208.

[2] See Ch. X.

measured is concentrated in the hands of a few firms (sometimes called 'absolute' concentration). Though changes in one may affect the other, inequality and absolute concentration are distinct concepts with a different significance and different uses in analysis.

Absolute concentration may be high, for example, and inequality very low, for an index of absolute concentration indicates nothing about the size distribution of firms within the group of largest firms nor within the remaining group of smaller firms. If an entire industry contained two firms only, the industry would be highly concentrated in the former sense, but if the two firms were of equal size an index of relative concentration (e.g., a Lorenz curve) would show perfect equality. Conversely inequality is not indicative of absolute concentration. Inequality may decrease while absolute concentration increases when the smaller firms leave an industry; extensive merger may reduce inequality but cannot reduce absolute concentration.[1] I am not here concerned with inequality, but only with 'absolute' concentration, which I shall call simply 'concentration', for our analysis of the growth of firms is most directly relevant to the question how and to what extent economic activity becomes and will remain concentrated in the hands of a few large firms.

The usual indexes of concentration relate either to some measure of assets or output, or to employment, and are most generally expressed in terms of an index of the percentage of total activity in the hands of a stated (few) number of firms or of the number of firms required to account for some stated (large) percentage of total activity.[2] The basic purpose of attempts to estimate concentration is to discover whether a 'few' firms control a 'large' percentage of output, employment, or assets, presumably because this information is considered relevant for an appraisal of economic performance in some significant sense.

Each of the various economic quantities with respect to which concentration can be measured will yield results with a different significance, and the type of measure adopted will depend partly

[1] See the excellent discussion of the subject in Gideon Rosenbluth, 'Measures of Concentration', *Business Concentration and Price Policy*, op. cit., pp. 57 ff.

[2] The United States Federal Trade Commission for the most part presents its estimates of concentration in terms of the per cent of the value of total shipments in given industries which can be attributed to the four largest companies, but it also uses alternative measures, in one of which concentration is expressed in terms of the number of firms controlling 60 per cent of output. Rosenbluth's study of concentration in Canada related primarily to the number of firms required to account for 80 per cent of output. Gideon Rosenbluth, *Concentration in Canadian Manufacturing Industries*, op. cit.

on the kind of problem one is interested in and partly on the type of data available. In any attempt to measure concentration a number of judgments have to be made, but we shall not be concerned with these here, for an analysis of the process of concentration does not require that we decide what level of concentration is significant for different purposes or even what economic quantities are relevant for the measurement of concentration. Nor is it practicable to attempt to take account of all of the qualifications required to adapt the analysis to each of the possible ways of measuring concentration. These questions have been the subject of much debate;[1] I mention them only in order to indicate some of the simplifications of the following brief discussion, and I shall not deal further with any of the statistical or conceptual problems involved in measuring concentration or interpreting the results. Fortunately, over broad areas the various measures seem to be reasonably consistent, at least with regard to the direction of change, though not always with regard to the 'level' of concentration—concentration measured with respect to assets, for example, runs significantly higher than concentration measured with respect to employment or output,[2] which, as we shall see, is not surprising.

Concentration and Growing Firms in a Growing Economy

The emergence, extent, and persistence of industrial concentration, whether in the economy as a whole or in individual industries, is clearly a function of the relative rates of growth of the small and large firms, for the amount of growth that takes place in an economy (or industry) in a given period of time must be equal to the growth of all firms (including new firms) in the economy (or industry) in the period. With any given rate of growth of the

[1] For an excellent discussion of the statistical and conceptual problems relating to the measurement and meaning of concentration, see the papers by Conklin and Goldstein, Rosenbluth, and Scitovsky, and the comments thereon in *Business Concentration and Price Policy*, op. cit.

See also the discussion of the possible uses of the logarithmic normal curve for measuring concentration (in this case inequality or relative concentration) in P. E. Hart and S. J. Prais, 'The Analysis of Business Concentration: A Statistical Approach', *Journal of the Royal Statistical Society*, Series A. Vol. 119, Part 2 (1956); also reprinted by the National Institute of Economic and Social Research, London, Reprint Series No. 8.

[2] In a valuable survey both of the methods of measuring concentration and of the empirical evidence regarding concentration, Adelman concluded that concentration in terms of total assetswas about 60 per cent higher for the largest 200 firms in the United States in 1948 than concentration when measured in terms of employment. M. A. Adelman, 'The Measurement of Industrial Concentration', *Review of Economics and Statistics*, Vol. XXXIII, No. 4 (Nov. 1951), p. 278.

economy (no matter how measured), a point will be reached at which a higher rate of growth of some firms will be inconsistent with the continued growth of some other firms, and finally with their continued existence. The total possible amount of expansion of an economy is not unlimited at any one time, and when the absolute growth of a few firms becomes greater than the absolute growth of the economy as a whole there must be a decline and eventual elimination of some other firms.

It follows that if concentration increases as an economy grows, the absolute expansion of the given number of larger firms (however selected) must have been greater than the expansion of all other firms. Therefore, if an economy (or industry) is growing at a constant rate, the larger firms must be growing at a faster rate. If concentration remains unchanged or declines, on the other hand, the large firms must be growing at the same or a slower rate relative to the rate of growth of the economy as a whole.

If we maintain the assumption that the older and larger firms have a competitive advantage over newer and smaller firms, it is clear that concentration will continue to increase so long as the limits on the rate of expansion of the larger firms do not prevent them from taking advantage of the opportunities for expansion in the economy at a greater rate than these opportunities develop. All circumstances that lift the maximum rate of growth of the larger firms relative to the economy (or industry) will increase the rate at which concentration can develop, raise the ' level ' of concentration, and encourage its persistence. Thus merger, economies of large-scale production, extensive diversification as opportunities for expansion in existing fields become reduced, restriction on entry, and fluctuations in the rate of growth of the economy, are all conducive to the rapid emergence or prolonged persistence of concentration.

These are, of course, the considerations usually put forward to explain the emergence of concentration, but if our analysis of the factors determining the rate of growth of individual firms is valid, we should expect a tendency for concentration to decline in a steadily growing economy once the larger firms have reached a point where their rate of growth slackens. This decline would show up in an increase in the number of large firms, a reduction in their overall importance and a reshuffling in the relative positions of the firms at the very top, but not necessarily, nor even probably, in any decline in the size of the largest firms, exclusive of their purely financial size.[1]

On the other hand, no economy can be expected to grow indefinitely at a steady compound rate. Not only will there be secular fluctuations in the rate of growth, but some tendency for the rate of growth to decline is apparently already evident in many older industrial countries.[2] In these circumstances, the course of concentration will depend, first upon the length of the periods of rapid expansion relative to the periods of decline, and secondly, on the size of the largest firms. It seems highly probable that the rate of growth of many of the large firms in the United States economy today has already started to decline, although the statistical investigations are too few to permit generalization. The depressed period of the 1930s has still such an important effect on statistical measurements of average rates of growth both of the economy and of individual firms that interpretation is hazardous. Consequently it is difficult to say whether or not we should expect concentration to be declining as yet. But it is interesting to note that in spite of all of the developments which have raised the rate of growth of large firms, and in spite of the powerful position of these firms in the economy, there is so little evidence of any substantial increase in concentration that economists can debate with vigour and conviction the question whether it is in fact increasing or declining.

If there has been a levelling off or an actual decrease in concentration, however, it is not because there are no new fields to conquer; on the contrary, as the economy grows, the total opportunities for the expansion of firms also grow. Concentration slackens because it becomes more difficult for large firms as a group to take advantage of the same percentage of total opportunities as they did when they could sustain a more rapid rate of growth. The unreliability of the

[1] As we have shown earlier, the fact that there is a limit on the rate at which a firm can expand its productive operations may be responsible for an increase in its financial investments in other firms. Thus if we measure the expansion of large firms in terms of their total assets we may very much overstate their expansion as producing units, for the decline in the rate of growth of large firms as producing units may be marked by an increase in their financial size. Consequently, concentration of the kind we are discussing here—neglecting purely financial as contrasted to organizational relationships—is not a measure of total economic and financial power.

[2] See Simon Kuznets, ' Quantitative Aspects of the Economic Growth of Nations: Levels and Variability of Rates of Growth ', *Economic Development and Cultural Change*, Vol. 5, No. 1 (Oct. 1956) Table 9, pp. 38–40, where calculations of changes in the average rates of growth of a number of countries are presented for three different periods since around the last quarter of the 19th century.

statistics and the difficulties of interpreting them are very great, but the evidence is worth looking at.

Some Shaky Evidence

Such studies as are available of the course of concentration over time, dangerous as they are to interpret because of the nature of the data, lend support to the hypothesis that concentration tends to develop rapidly to a high point, increase fairly slowly thereafter, and eventually, when existing large firms become very large, to decline. Each of the various studies of the question measures concentration in a different way, some being concerned with inequality, rather than concentration in the sense used here, and some relating concentration to assets, some to output, and some to employment. Consequently, none of them can directly and unequivocally be used to support the present analysis. All we can say is that in general, their results are not inconsistent with the results we should expect from the line of reasoning presented here.

In the United States the weight of the evidence seems to point to a slow decline in concentration in the last forty to fifty years, with the exception of the period surrounding the 1930s, although a recent Federal Trade Commission report shows a slight increase in concentration between 1935 and 1950 measured in terms of the total value of product accounted for by the 200 largest companies.[1]

---

[1] Federal Trade Commission, *Report on Changes in Concentration in Manufacturing, 1935 to 1947 and 1950* (Wash. D.C.: 1954). Between 1935 and 1950 the Commission, using Census data, found that the percentage of total value of product accounted for by the five largest companies rose from 10.6 to 11.4; by the 50 largest, from 26.2 to 26.6; by the 100 largest, from 32.4 to 33.3; and by the first 200 companies, from 37.7 to 40.5 (p. 17). See also page 19 of this report for a discussion of other attempts to measure concentration in the same period.

One of the more comprehensive surveys of the data concerning concentration in the United States since the turn of the century is to be found in M. A. Adelman, ' The Measurement of Industrial Concentration ', loc. cit. After examining the various measures and various studies of concentration, he concluded that since 1901 ' The odds are better than even that there has actually been *some* decline in concentration. It is a good bet that there has at least been no actual increase; and the odds do seem high against any substantial increase '. Professor Adelman's methods and conclusions were criticized by Corwin Edwards, George Stocking, Edwin George, and A. A. Berle, Jr., but none of the discussion seriously upset his basic contention regarding the long-run trend. See ' Four Comments on " The Measurement of Industrial Concentration "; With a Rejoinder by Professor Adelman ', *Review of Economics and Statistics*, Vol. XXXIV No. 2 (May 1952), pp. 156–178. Adelman's conclusions were also attacked by John Blair ' The Measurement of Industrial Concentration: A Reply ', *Review of Economics and Statistics*, Vol. XXXIV, No. 4 (Nov. 1952), pp. 343 ff. The controversy became rather heated and confusing, but by and large the evidence offered does not seem to be sufficient to challenge the conclusion as stated by Lintner and Butters that ' Even though imperfections and gaps in the data counsel caution, the best available evidence establishes a rather strong presumption that there has been no increase in over-all concentration

Thus the interpretation of the trend of concentration in the United States is still a subject of great controversy, and this fact alone is sufficient to support the presumption that the fears commonly expressed twenty or thirty years ago that concentration would continue to increase at a rapid rate were unfounded.[1]

With respect to Great Britain, an older industrialized country with some very large firms, many of which, however, produce for international markets even more than for the national market, I have found no studies of changes over time of the type of concentration discussed here. The only extensive analysis I know of that is at all relevant to the problem, attempted to measure changes in 'relative concentration' (or inequality) from 1885 to 1950 using the log-normal distribution and dealing with firms quoted on the stock exchanges.[2] The authors concluded that, in general, inequality among surviving firms has tended to increase in the last fifty years, but that the rise of new industries and new firms, together with a substantial decline in inequality in the period 1939–1950, offset this tendency to such an extent that ' changes in business concentration in the economy as a whole over the past half century may not be very great '.[3] The decline in the period 1939–1950 is attributed to the ' exceptionally profitable record ' of smaller firms, which means,

over the last fifty-year period and indicates that there probably has been some decrease in concentration over this period, at least so far as manufacturing is concerned '. John Lintner, and J. Keith Butters, ' Effects of Taxation on Concentration ', *Business Concentration and Price Policy*, op. cit., p. 239.

Adelman's analysis was based largely on total assets and he gave strong reasons for rejecting net capital assets. For his purposes his reasons are good, but in the framework of this study, total assets would be an inappropriate measure. However, there is no reason to presume that the trend of concentration would be towards substantially higher levels over the long haul if measured in terms of capital assets; rather I should expect long-run concentration to show even more of a decline.

[1] For example, the fears of Berle and Means: ' The corporate system has done more than evolve a norm by which business is carried on. Within it there exists a centripetal attraction which draws wealth together into aggregations of constantly increasing size, at the same time throwing control into the hands of fewer and fewer men. The trend is apparent; and no limit is as yet in sight. Were it possible to say that circumstances had established the concentration, but that there was no basis to form an opinion as to whether the process would continue, the whole problem might be simplified. But this is not the case. So far as can be seen, every element which favoured concentration still exists, and the only apparent factor which may end the tendency is the limit on the ability of a few human beings effectively to handle the aggregates of property brought under their control '. A. A. Berle Jr. and Gardiner C. Means, *The Modern Corporation and Private Property* (New York: Macmillan, 1932), p. 18. It is the contention of our analysis that the process cannot be expected to continue, at least in the form of the expansion of the industrial firm, which, to be sure, Berle and Means were not specifically concerned with, but not for the reasons they advanced. We have found no evidence that the limit to concentration lies in the inability of men to administer large units.

[2] P. E. Hart and S. J. Prais, 'An Analysis of Business Concentration ', loc. cit.

[3] Ibid., p. 175.

of course, that in this period small firms were able to improve their relative position, a state of affairs which we should expect on the basis of our general analysis. Unfortunately, however, this study tells us little about changes in absolute concentration.

Comparisons between countries are especially hazardous because of differences in industrial structure, rates of growth, the importance of international trade in total activity, and similar matters, but a recent careful study of concentration in Canada is worth noting. In some ways Canada can be looked upon as an economy similar to the United States, though in an earlier stage of industrial development, where the rate of growth of the economy in relation to the size of firms is still such that concentration may be expected to be increasing. On the average, Canadian firms are not much smaller than are United States firms, but Canadian industries are smaller.[1] Thus concentration was found to be higher in Canada than in the United States, that is, in general a smaller *number* of firms in Canada controlled the same or a greater percentage of the output of industry; on the other hand, inequality was higher in the United States, that is, in general, a higher *percentage* of the industry was accounted for by an equal or lower *percentage* of the firms.[2] In other words, there are more big firms in the United States than in Canada, but there are also more smaller firms and the big firms control a smaller percentage of total output. As the Canadian economy grows, if it follows the pattern of the United States, more firms will grow into the large category, more new firms will appear, and concentration will cease increasing and probably decrease.[3]

[1] Gideon Rosenbluth, *Concentration in Canadian Manufacturing Industries*, op. cit. pp. 80 ff.

[2] Rosenbluth's comparison was between concentration of employment in Canada and of output in the United States because these were the figures available. Concentration when measured by output tends to be higher than when measured by employment, and consequently his figures probably overstate concentration in the United States relative to that of Canada. Ibid., p. 76. Furthermore, his study dealt only with concentration in specific industries and his general statements about concentration in the economy as a whole are based on a comparison of industry concentration in the two economies.

[3] 'Growth of the market is therefore revealed as an important factor, which a theory of concentration cannot afford to neglect. Further growth of the Canadian economy can be expected to exercise a continued moderating influence on the level of concentration. Should concentration nevertheless increase, the theory that such increase is necessary for technological efficiency should be treated with distrust'. Ibid., p. 108. This statement was made with specific reference to plant concentration, but it is equally valid for firm concentration.

Concentration Within Industries

The above remarks refer primarily to concentration in industry as a whole, specifically in manufacturing. This type of concentration is often held to be a useful measure of concentration of control over industrial assets, but from the point of view of the market behaviour of firms, it is of less significance than concentration of output in individual industries. There is, of course, a relation between industry concentration and concentration in the economy as a whole, although I think estimates of the latter from a weighted average of the former are of little value, for the significance of concentration in particular industries is fundamentally different from that of concentration in the economy as a whole.[1] If ' concentration is itself highly concentrated ',[2] for example, if a few large but concentrated industries account for the bulk of it, surely the significance of a high concentration index is very different from the significance of an index that is high because a large number of small industries are heavily concentrated while no firm or industry is very large.

Nevertheless, if industrial concentration is very high in industries which are themselves quantitatively very large in the economy, not only will the large firms in these industries be large, but concentration in the economy as a whole will be high; for the most part this is the characteristic of high over-all concentration, since many industries (though by no means all) that tend to be large in any industrialized economy tend also to have characteristics which are conducive to concentration. Unless diversification of the largest firms in the economy is so extensive that few of them bulk large in any single industry, it is to the processes of concentration in individual industries that we must look in order to explain concentration in the economy as a whole.

The interstices in the economy which provide the opportunities for the growth of smaller firms appear as opportunities to expand the production of specific products or to enter specific industries. Since under our assumptions these are, by definition, the opportunities the large firms ignore, their significance for smaller firms depends upon the type of difficulty which must be overcome in taking advantage of them—upon barriers to entry. The competitive

[1] Furthermore, concentration in particular industries and concentration in the economy as a whole can move in different directions, the one increasing and the other remaining constant or even decreasing. See Federal Trade Commission, op. cit., p. 19.

[2] In the United States in 1947, for example, 'Among manufacturing industries, four industries—steel, automobiles, chemicals, and oil—account for nearly two-thirds of the assets of the over-$100 million group ', Adelman, loc. cit., p. 276.

advantages of the older and larger firms in an industry may or may not be of a kind which make it difficult for newcomers to enter the interstices, but the most common type of advantage seems, as we have seen, to be associated either with the amount of capital required or with the possibilities of attaching consumers' loyalty through branding and advertising. Although there may not be significant technological advantages associated with large multiplant operations, the mere fact that individual plants are fairly large militates against the easy entry of new firms and facilitates the rapid expansion of existing large firms. And branding and advertising give competitive advantages very largely because they impede easy entry of new-comers. Thus we should expect concentration to develop most rapidly in industries where this type of advantage is greatest or where the size and growth of the market are such that large firms can expand sufficiently rapidly to leave no interstices.

The rate at which the large firms can expand in an industry is itself closely related to the rate of growth of demand in the industry in relation to the growth of total capacity.[1] In industries where the advantage of the larger firms is not overwhelming (for example certain branches of the textile and apparel industry) and where entry is fairly easy, the constant competition of newcomers may prevent the larger established firms from expanding rapidly, even though they have a sufficient advantage to maintain themselves and perhaps grow slowly in conditions where the rate of failure among new and small firms is very high. Of all the factors that we have considered which keep down the rate of growth of firms, those related to the necessity of meeting competition are of the greatest significance with respect to their effect both on the managerial services required for existing operations and on those required per dollar of expansion. Thus if newcomers seriously compete with existing firms, even though they are eventually eliminated, the necessity of meeting constant new competition will keep down the rate of growth of the established firms and result in low or only slowly growing concentration. A decline in the profitability of the industry reducing the rate of entry of newcomers may lay the groundwork for the

[1] I am making no attempt here to distinguish ' industry ' from ' product '. We can treat the interstices as opportunities to produce new products within or outside existing industries, or as opportunities to enter old or establish new industries, whichever seems most appropriate. The amorphous boundary lines between ' industries ' and ' products ' provide one of the reasons why it may be misleading to estimate concentration in the economy as a whole from a weighted average of ' industry ' concentration. The narrower the definition of industry or product, the higher is concentration likely to be.

development of a semblance of concentration, perhaps through the consolidation by merger of some of the surviving firms.

On the other hand, even where there are substantial advantages of large-scale production to be obtained, the rate of expansion of the larger firms may not be sufficient to prevent the rapid entry of smaller. high-cost producers if the level and growth of demand is very high. But in this case the expansion of the larger firms need not be inhibited by the smaller producers since they present no serious competition and will be quickly eliminated as the large firms expand, especially when the initially high rate of growth of the industry tends to decline.[1]

The growth of an economy is marked by substantial shifts in the relative importance of different industries, which implies that industries grow at different rates. Since rapid growth has often promoted concentration in a new industry, while a decline in the rate of growth promotes concentration in old industries, industrial shifts will offset to some extent the tendency of concentration to decline with continued growth of an economy, and may result in industry concentration moving in a direction opposite to that of concentration in the economy as a whole, where the latter is defined as the percentage of total non-financial assets held by a given number of firms.[2] The growth of the leading firms in the

---

[1] Cf. the following comment: ' In the early stages of the development of a new industry, entry very often is easy, not only (or even mainly) because the design of the product and the technique of production are primitive by the standards of later developments, but because as the product " takes on " the aggregate demand expands rapidly of its own momentum, so that custom is easily acquired. Hence the " mushroom " of small-scale, high-cost producers is characteristic of the early development of a new industry. In time, however, as the rate of expansion slackens and the process of production is consolidated in order to realize the full potentialities of the production function, a price equal to the cost of production in the most efficient manner—the " right " price—is possible. It is at this stage (" settled " conditions), and if such a price prevails, that new entry is very difficult '. H. R. Edwards, ' Price Formation in Manufacturing Industry and Excess Capacity ', *Oxford Economic Papers* (New Series), Vol. 7, No. 1 (Feb. 1955), p. 101.

[2] Our analysis of the growth of firms has been primarily concerned with the growth and size of the total organization of a firm measured in terms of capital assets. Consequently it is not entirely adapted to the analysis of concentration measured in terms of output or employment. Increases in productivity, for example, may permit increases in output (and of concentration of output) without corresponding increases in capital investment and hence of size in terms of capital assets; a change in the capital-labour ratio may cause a decrease in the size of a firm measured in terms of employment and an increase measured in terms of capital assets. Asset concentration tends to run higher than output concentration largely because a high capital-output ratio facilitates concentration; output concentration tends to run higher than employment concentration for much the same reason—a higher capital-labour ratio usually implies higher labour productivity. See, for example, the discussion of mechanization in particular industries in Federal Trade Commission, op. cit., p. 29.

newer industries, even though sufficient to produce great concentration in these industries, need not affect the position of the dominant firms in the older industries. Thus, if the older industries, though losing in relative importance, are still the largest industries in the economy, the leading firms in these industries may remain the largest firms in the economy, but they will be controlling a smaller percentage of the economy's total assets. On the other hand, a growing concentration in the newer industries and no reduction in concentration in the older industries implies an increase in industry concentration.

`Since firms are not confined to particular industries, however, industry concentration cannot effectively be analysed with reference to the factors controlling the rate of growth of the firm as a whole. Rather one must look to competitive relationships and to the conditions of supply and demand for particular products, an examination of which would lead us far from the central problem of this study. However, some of the questions we have discussed in relation to the diversification of firms are relevant for the process of industry concentration.

Diversification and Industry Concentration

We have already analysed in some detail the factors determining the nature of diversification, the limitations on the rate of diversification, and the kinds of new fields that the large firms will in general find the more profitable. Large firms can move into industries where entry is difficult for smaller firms and will tend to avoid products where margins over direct cost are too low to support the long-range investment, research and development programmes, advertising, and other types of ' overhead ' that characterize their operations. For these and similar reasons, many of the profitable opportunities for diversification will bring the large firms into competition with each other; to the extent that oil firms move into chemicals, automobile firms into locomotives and airplane engines, steel firms into shipbuilding, soap producers into cosmetics, etc., industry or product concentration may be reduced without any reduction in the concentration of the economy as a whole.[1]

---

[1] Compare the following suggestion: ' Since established firms operating *in other industries* frequently have the least disadvantage of all potential entrants to a given industry in acquiring the requisite capital, we should perhaps go slow in frowning officially on expansion of large firms via diversification to enter new fields. To discourage or prohibit this sort of diversification may well tend to raise the barriers to entry to

The diversification of large firms into new industries may in the early stages keep down industry concentration, but the course of competition between the large firms will tend to involve a 'shaking down' process analogous to that which occurs in any new industry where large numbers of producers enter in the beginning and are weeded out as competition becomes more intense. Where the bulk of the new 'entrants' are large firms diversifying into a new and growing industry, the weeding out process may occur more rapidly than it would if the entrants were small, because it is not necessary that prices and profits sink low enough to cause 'failures' of whole firms; as we have seen, larger firms finding themselves at a competitive disadvantage in any field can often sell their new 'business' without loss, sometimes at a profit, long before they actually start losing money on it.[1]

CONCENTRATION AND DOMINANCE

One of the outstanding characteristics of an industrialized economy is the dominant position in the economy as a whole occupied by a relatively small number of large firms. We have enquired how this comes about, relating our enquiry to the processes of growth of individual firms in a growing economy. So far as I am aware no theory of the emergence of dominance or the development of concentration has so far been attempted from this point of view, with the possible exception of what might be called a 'theory of the headstart', which states simply that the earlier established and larger firms have a headstart over younger and smaller firms that gives them certain advantages enabling them to maintain their position and to grow at the expense of the younger firms and of firms not yet established.[2] Clearly this has much in common with

industries generally, with adverse effects on competition. This disadvantage of an anti-diversification policy *vis-à-vis* large firms must be weighed carefully against the alleged dangers of the growth of gigantic firms *per se*. Joe S. Bain, op. cit., p. 215.

[1] Incidentally it should be noted that concentration of assets is not the appropriate measure for the analysis of the effect of diversification. Not only is it extremely difficult to allocate in any satisfactory manner the total capital assets of a large diversified firm among specific products, or to analyse the increase in the output of particular products with reference to the factors limiting the expansion of the firm as a whole, but it does not make much sense to do so from any of the points of view from which we might be interested in concentration. Only a measure of output is appropriate for this purpose.

[2] The Marxian analysis of capitalism implies, of course, a theory of increasing concentration; the Marshallian theory of the rise and fall of firms implies a theory of a constant degree of concentration with a continual change of the individual population of firms; and the theoretical analysis of the question of increasing returns to scale is

the analysis we have developed, but it has never been examined in in any detail nor have the logical consequences been at all worked out. We have gone further and, in the light of the possibilities for growth open to individual firms, have enquired how far the advantages derived from a favourable start will lead to an increase in concentration. We have concluded that in a steadily growing economy, or in an economy where expansion is more prevalent than stagnation, the process of concentration will come to an end and eventually reverse itself.

In general the empirical evidence available, weak and uncertain as it is, at least does not contradict either the main propositions of our analysis or our conclusions. The analysis of the growth of firms that we have developed is fully applicable only to corporations in an industrial economy, and consequently the historical period to which it can be applied reaches no further back than the last quarter of the 19th century. Although corporations were widely prevalent in certain fields, notably railroads and public utilities, they did not become the dominant form of business enterprise until the 1870s and '80s in the United States or England; for many other countries, for example, Canada and Australia, it has been only since just before the Second World War that industrial activity, let alone industrial corporations, began to play a dominant role in the economy as a whole. Consequently, we can look at a period not longer than 80 years, and in this period have occurred two major wars, numerous minor ones, and one of the most severe depressions in history, bringing in their train after-effects which persisted longer than the disturbances themselves. Furthermore, there are extremely meagre data available before 1900 and no really reliable data until at least the end of the first quarter of the century. An adequate 'testing' of the theory advanced is, in the present state of our knowledge, virtually out of the question, but the approach is, I think, a useful one for the theoretical analysis of the subject and one which has the advantage of relating the process of concentration (or 'deconcentration') to the economic characteristics of a growing economy.

The Continued Dominance of Large Firms

In spite of the weakness of the data, there can be little doubt

also an analysis of one aspect of the problem of increasing concentration of industry. What I have called the ' theory of the headstart ' has been floating around in a nebulous form for a long time, its most recent statement, perhaps, being that of J. K. Galbraith, op. cit., esp. pp. 33–35.

that the place of the large firms over the last fifty years has been remarkably secure and seems in many ways to become more secure as they grow bigger. Even a slow decrease in concentration need not substantially undermine their importance, and, potentially at least, they are in a powerful position to impose serious restrictions on the entry of smaller firms into the interstices. In a recent study the identity of the 100 largest industrial firms (measured in terms of total assets) were compared for every decade from 1909 to 1948.[1] If the list of firms in 1909 is taken as it is presented (unfortunately it includes a number of large merger-created ' firms ' which were primarily financial structures and not at any time fully established as industrial firms, and which disappeared very soon after their creation) and if allowance is made for merger and acquisition within the group of largest firms, it appears that some 48 per cent of the largest firms in 1909 can be found among the 250 largest manufacturing firms as listed by the Federal Trade Commission 30 years later, and 60 per cent among the first 500.[2] Again making allowance for merger, only five of the first 50 in 1919 were not listed among the 100 largest in 1948, and of the 100 largest in 1919, 80 per cent were among the 200 largest as listed by the F.T.C. in 1948.[3]

The process of deconcentration, if it has set in in the United States, is clearly very slow, although it might be greater than appears

[1] A. D. H. Kaplan, *Big Enterprise in a Competitive System* (Wash. D.C.: Brookings Institution, 1945), pp. 145 ff.
[2] United States Federal Trade Commission, *A List of 1,000 Large Manufacturing Companies, Their Subsidiaries and Affiliates,* 1948 (Washington, D. C., 1951).
[3] Kaplan draws the conclusion from his tables that ' industrial leadership at the big business level is precarious' (p. 141) and that the turnover among the leaders is great. But the data, if examined carefully, do not support this conclusion. The way in which merger among the group of large firms is handled by Kaplan is inaccurate, and, as Carl Kaysen has shown in a review (*Explorations in Entrepreneurial History,* Vol. 7, No. 4, April 1955, pp 237–239) the data as presented show a substantial *decline* in the turnover of the identity of the firms among the 100 largest in the 30-year period, the number of firms dropping out of the list in each decade declining steadily and significantly from 1909 to 1935. It rises from 1935 to 1948, but even apart from the fact that several mergers were neglected by Kaplan, five of the firms that he had ranked among the 100 largest at some time and which do not appear in his list of the 100 largest in 1948, are listed among the 100 largest in 1948 by the Federal Trade Commission. Both lists relate to total assets, Kaplan's referring to ' industrials ' and the Commission's to ' manufacturing firms '. There are apparently differences between the two universes, but it is hard to account for the extent of the variation, which at least throws doubt on the ' precarious ' nature of leadership as deduced from the shifting position of firms in Kaplan's tables. Furthermore, if one makes allowance for the growth in the total number of large firms in the period (and Kaplan admits that to confine the analysis to 100 is arbitrary), one will find that remarkably few firms really suffered a significant loss of ' leadership ' position. Kaplan's fundamental point—that there is a good deal of competition ' at the top ' and that the relative rank of firms constantly shifts—is sound enough, but to deduce ' precarious ' leadership from this is going too far.

if one measured it excluding the purely financial assets of firms. Fluctuations in economic activity may retard it in the future and may even reverse it for significant periods of time. But the more important consideration governing the course of concentration is likely to be found in the extent to which large firms will be able to set up ' artificial ' barriers against expansion of smaller firms into the interstices. As we have seen, some of the competitive disadvantages of the smaller firms are part and parcel of the very conditions which account for the superior ability of the larger firms, in particular their apparent superiority in research, their easier access to capital, and their ability to attract and hold the confidence of consumers. These advantages of large firms will not necessarily promote further increases in concentration in a growing economy; for if the large firms are to maintain their position in the various fields in which they operate, their performance must be acceptable to consumers. This, together with ' big business ' competition, will restrict their ability to take advantage of all the opportunities for profitable investment that open up in a changing and growing economy. In the absence of artificial barriers to their expansion, the smaller firms have a chance to grow until they too achieve positions in which their growth is no longer handicapped by their size.

CONCLUSION

A strong case can be made for the big firm and for ' big business ' competition, especially with respect to the rate of development of new technology and new and improved products, and it may be that economists have been slow to recognize some of its advantages.[1] Part of the reason for this, I think, can be traced to the influence on economic analysis of the so-called ' theory of the firm ', which has tended to confine the theoretical approach to the firm within the

[1] One economist, at least, has wholeheartedly endorsed the case: ' There can be little doubt that oligopoly, both in theory and in fact, is strongly oriented toward change. There can be no serious doubt at all that the setting for innovation, which is so favorable in this market structure, disappears almost entirely as one approaches the competition of the competitive model '. J. K. Galbraith, op. cit., p. 90. Galbraith has stressed the importance of what he called ' countervailing power ', as a means of preventing the exploitation of the weaker groups in the economy by the stronger. The power of big buyers can offset that of big sellers, the power of organized business can be matched by organized labour, etc. In some areas, e.g., agriculture, the government may have to support the less powerful in order to achieve a balance. Even if ' countervailing power ' is effective in preventing exploitation, however, it is not a means for insuring that the interstices are kept open for the smaller firms.

frame of reference provided by the traditional categories of monopoly and competiton and by the problems of price and output determination. In consequence, this part of economic theory has attained a high state of refinement, but, as we saw in Chapter II, it does not provide suitable tools for the analysis of the growth and, in particular, of the innovating activities of firms treated as administrative organizations free to produce any kind of product they find profitable.

We have been concerned in this study with questions that the traditional 'theory of the firm' was not designed to answer, and from our analysis, in particular from the distinction between the economies of size and the economies of growth, have come a number of propositions which are relevant for the appraisal of the place of large and growing firms in the modern world. Let us briefly review some of the conclusions we have reached.

1. There is no evidence to support the proposition often advanced that 'diseconomies of size' will arise at some point in a firm's growth and that the large firms will eventually become inefficient. They may reach a stage where their structure and behaviour become more akin to those of financial holding companies than of industrial firms, thus raising the question whether the two types of firm should be examined with the same type of analysis, but the efficiency of their productive activities need not suffer because of the change in organizational form.

2. Equally there is no evidence, and indeed there is a presumption to the contrary, that the largest firms enjoy economies in the production and distribution of their existing products that would disappear if these operations were carried on in a smaller administrative framework. Economies of large-scale operation are indeed important up to a point, and the minimum size of firm which can take full advantage of them in particular types of economic activity may be fairly large, but it is likely that this minimum is far below the size of the largest firms in the United States, as well as in many other industrial economies to-day.

3. On the other hand, no matter how large a firm becomes, economies of growth are still available to it. Up to a point economies of growth may be of a kind that give large firms an advantage in expansion over smaller firms; these are properly treated as economies of size, as well as economies of growth; but they differ greatly from the traditional economies of large-scale production and opera-

tion. They often make it possible for large firms to expand more efficiently than smaller firms, but by their very nature, particular economies of growth disappear once an expansion based on them has been completed; they facilitate expansion, but they do not endure throughout the subsequent operations. Any continuing advantages the large firm may have in subsequent operating activities will not rest on the economies of growth that gave it the initial advantage but, unless other economies of size are present, merely on the advantages normally possessed by any established producer with the appropriate type of resources.[1] The great prestige of the large firm rests on its ability to explore, to experiment, and to innovate; it is this ability, together with the market position (carefully cultivated by advertising) that its reputation, and the reputation of its products, can command, which give rise to many of its economies in expansion.[2] Again, however, there is no evidence that the *largest* firms have appreciably greater economies of growth, even of this kind, than do the smaller of the large firms.

4. Economies of growth exist for all sizes of firm, and therefore growth for any size of firm may be an efficient use of resources both from the point of view of the firm and from the point of view of the economy as a whole.

5. To the extent that the economies of size available to the large firms are primarily economies of growth, no loss in efficiency would result if those activities that are already established and run more or less as separate ' businesses ', were divorced from the parent firm and permitted to operate as independent businesses. There is every reason to presume that the ' new ' firms thus created

---

[1] I am making no attempt to explain here the difference between the economies of size alone, the economies of size that are also economies of growth, and the economies of growth that are not economies of size. I would ask the all-too-common busy reader who attempts to grasp the nature and import of this book from the few conclusions re-stated here to turn to Chapter VI, a short chapter dealing specifically with these distinctions, and of fundamental importance for the understanding of our entire argument.

[2] As we have noted, the innovating competition of the big firms can degenerate into almost senseless competition to be first to introduce the ' new ', exciting, or the ' original ', of which the chief contribution to consumers' ' satisfaction ' seems to lie in its ability to satisfy a restless desire for the ' latest '—whatever that may be. If this is a senseless procedure, it is made possible only by the folly of consumers, which it is difficult for the economist to appraise, even though he may be unhappy over what he feels is the ' waste ' of resources involved, and may condemn it in the light of criteria of ' welfare ' other than those traditionally accepted in economics. It should be clear that the mere fact that consumers' market demand appears to be ' satisfied ' is insufficient so elicit ' approval ' from the social scientist, particularly since the very desires of contumers are powerfully influenced by the actions of producers and by the competitive processes described.

would continue growing, taking advantage of their own economies of growth, without any reduction in the efficiency of production or distribution of either the original firm or the new ones created. The decentralized type of organization that is becoming increasingly characteristic of the large firm facilitates the severance of a particular business from the rest; this is shown in the growing numbers of such ' businesses ' that are bought and sold by the large firms.

To be sure, attempts of the government to force large firms to divest themselves of any of their operations would meet political, legal, and psychological objections—in particular, the incentive of the large firms to create and to take advantage of opportunities for growth would probably be impaired if the procedure were frequent and widespread. To restrict the innovating, competitive expansion of the big firms could possibly reduce the rate of technological advance both in the process of production and in the kind and quality of end products produced. The diversification of these firms is itself a response to changing economic opportunities and is made possible by extensive innovations in administrative organization. In both respects big firms have led the way in experimentation.[1]

6. There is a limit to the rate at which any firm can grow, a limit provided by the capacities of its existing management. Although the large firms may continue to undertake very large amounts of expansion, their rate of growth will, after a point, begin to fall, especially under the impact of big business competiton. In a progressive and expanding economy, the reduction in the rate of growth of the largest firms will retard the process of industrial concentration, and may eventually lead to a decline in concentration—provided that the interstices in the economy are not artificially closed against the smaller firms.

---

[1] It was largely for this reason that John G. McLean and Robert W. Haigh concluded from their studies of the growth of corporations that '. . . as a matter of national policy we should proceed with the utmost caution in placing restraints on the avenues of growth and development open to industrial corporations. By imposing such restraint we may interfere with the processes of business evolution and thereby preclude the development of new corporate structures that would be ideally suited and perhaps essential to conditions of the future which none of us can now foresee. Moreover, management's experiments with different types of corporation structures *are in themselves an important aspect of competition.* If, therefore, we limit the types of growth corporations may undertake, we may modify in significant degree the vigor of competition in our industrial society.' John G. McLean, and Robert W. Haigh, ' How Business Corporations Grow ', *Harvard Business Review*, Vol. 32, No. 6 (Nov.–Dec. 1954), pp. 92–93.

Compare also the discussion of Corwin D. Edwards, *Maintaining Competition* (New York, McGraw-Hill, 1949), pp. 120 ff.

7. To the extent that small firms are prevented from taking advantage of economies of growth by artificial restrictions on their ability to expand into those areas not occupied by the larger firms (which we have called the 'interstices'), resources in the economy will be inefficiently used.

8. It cannot be too forcefully emphasized that the whole case made by the advocates of big business rests on the insistence that competition in a very real and pressing form is constantly and powerfully in evidence. Hence, the case as presented breaks down if a few big firms get so big or so powerful that they are in a position substantially to restrict competition among themselves. It has recently been suggested that the largest firms in the United States to-day are not yet big enough to take full advantage of the opportunities for continued research and discovery, and that some form of 'super cartel' will be required.[1] At the same time it is argued, and quite reasonably, that the fruits of extensive research and development must be protected from competition, and must accrue to those who make the investments required to produce them.

Here is the basic dilemma: competition is the essence of the struggle among the large firms that induces and almost forces the extensive research and innovation in which they engage and provides the justification for the whole system; at the same time the large firms expect reward for their efforts, but this expectation is held precisely because competition can be restrained.

9. Because there is a limit to the amount of expansion any firm, no matter how large, can undertake in a given period, there is no reason to assume that the large firms as a group can effectively exploit all of the opportunities for profitable investment that they themselves create in the economy. They may be expected to insist

---

[1] '. . . if we look at the facts realistically, we are bound to conclude, I believe, that even some of our biggest corporations are rapidly getting too small to do all of the things that are expected of them . . . it would seem that we are now witnessing another significant step in the evolution of big business. First came the individual entrepreneur; then the partnership in which a number of people pooled their resources and their managerial skills; then the modern corporation where hundreds of thousands of persons provide the necessary capital and share the risks involved; and now we see these great corporations themselves necessarily forming partnerships—for one reason and one reason alone: to do the job that is expected of them in an enterprise system where size and responsibility are companion words.' 'Great Expectations,' speech by Roger M. Blough, Chairman of the Board, United States Steel Corporation published by the Corporation, 1957. On the other hand, Mr. Blough also regards competition as 'the key to America's industrial success', which is not quite the same thing as the spirit of responsibility to the public, and would presumably be somewhat impaired by the suggested 'partnership'.

on retaining the power to protect themselves against competition, but so far as they get such protection by means other than their superior ability to produce, to innovate, and to attract consumers, the interstices in the economy are reduced ' artificially ', and not only will their dominant position be maintained, but the growth of the economy itself may be kept down.

If the case for big firms, and for big-business competition, is a strong one, its strength rests on conditions that are not self-perpetuating, but may themselves be destroyed by collusion, by the extension of financial control, and by the struggle to resolve the contradictions in a system where competition is at once the god and the devil, where the growth of firms may be efficient but where their consequent size, though not in itself inefficient, may create an industrial structure which impedes its own continued growth.

INDEX

DATE DUE
